W9-AOS-311

CICS for the COBOL programmer

Part 2: An advanced course

CICS for the COBOL programmer

Part 2: An advanced course

Doug Lowe

Mike Murach & Associates, Inc.

4697 West Jacquelyn Avenue
Fresno, California 93722
(209) 275-3335

Development Team

Editors:	Steve Eckols
	Judy Taylor
Designer and production director:	Steve Ehlers
Artist:	Lori Davis

Other books from Mike Murach & Associates, Inc.

CICS for the COBOL Programmer, Part 1 by Doug Lowe
The CICS Programmer's Desk Reference by Doug Lowe
VSAM: Access Method Services and Application Programming by Doug Lowe
MVS JCL by Doug Lowe
DOS/VSE JCL by Steve Eckols
MVS TSO by Doug Lowe
DOS/VSE ICCF by Steve Eckols

© 1985, Mike Murach & Associates, Inc.
All rights reserved.
Printed in the United States of America.

20 19 18 17 16 15 14 13 12 11 10 9 8 7 6 5

Library of Congress Catalog Card Number: 83-62724

ISBN: 0-911625-16-X

Contents

Preface   1

Part 1   **Advanced file processing features**   5

Chapter 1   Sequential processing using browse commands   7

Chapter 2   VSAM alternate index processing   39

Chapter 3   DL/I data base processing   63

  Topic 1   DL/I data base concepts and terminology   64
  Topic 2   How to process a DL/I data base   76

Part 2   **Queue management features**   113

Chapter 4   Temporary storage control   115

Chapter 5   Transient data control   141

Part 3   **Advanced terminal processing features**   **161**

Chapter 6   BMS features for logical message building   163

   Topic 1   Logical message building concepts and terminology   164
   Topic 2   Two techniques for building a logical message   173
   Topic 3   Printer output and message routing   202

Chapter 7   How to use color and extended highlighting   221

Chapter 8   Terminal control   237

Part 4   **Other advanced CICS features**   **257**

Chapter 9   Interval control   259

Chapter 10   Error processing   273

   Topic 1   Abend processing   274
   Topic 2   Recovery processing   281
   Topic 3   Journal control   288

Chapter 11   Task control, program control, and storage control   297

Appendix   CICS command summary   309

Index   317

Preface

CICS is a complex system that provides many powerful features. For a given programming problem, there are probably half a dozen different CICS facilities you can chose from to solve that problem in slightly different ways. Because CICS provides so much flexibility, it's crucial that programmers and analysts have a broad understanding of what its facilities are, how they're used, and how they interact.

Too often, though, a programmer's training ends before he or she has mastered all of the important elements of CICS. Consider, for example, the typical CICS programming course: one week of intensive training in which just about every CICS command and facility is presented. As part of this course, the student codes three or four simple programs that use the basic CICS elements. With luck, one or two of them work. But there just isn't enough time to learn anything more than the basics in that short week. As a result, most trainees get just part of a CICS education. They're expected to figure out the rest on the job.

What this book does

This is the second of a two-part series of CICS training. In *Part 1, An introductory course*, I presented a basic subset of CICS command-level programming that included programming for 3270-type display terminals and direct access to VSAM files. This book presents the advanced features of CICS—features like file browsing, transient data control, temporary storage control, message building, and much more.

Although I designed this book to stand on its own, it also works well when used with other training programs. In particular, if you attend a CICS training course, this book will help you both before and after the course. If you read through the book before hand, you'll be that much better prepared for the intensity of the week-long course. And after the course, you can turn to this book to gain a fuller understanding of the CICS facilities there just wasn't time for in that short week of training.

Why this book is effective

I believe this book is effective for three reasons. First, I spent much time selecting the content of this book. It would be easy to go through the IBM manual and cover every available CICS command. I'm sure you've seen, as I have, books that do...almost verbatim, sometimes. Unfortunately, many of those commands just aren't that useful in a command-level environment.

Second, I emphasize a solid understanding of how CICS works so you can use it more effectively. Learning advanced features of CICS means more than learning the syntax of a few commands. It means understanding how those commands work and how they relate to other CICS and operating system elements. So this book goes beyond presenting command syntax: it shows you what happens inside CICS when you issue a command.

Third, I've included extensive illustrations to show you how various CICS elements are used in programs. You'll find 11 complete program listings, plus several shorter program segments. These examples not only illustrate CICS language elements, but also serve as models for similar programs you'll write on the job.

Who this book is for

This book is for CICS programmers who want to learn how to use more than the basic elements of CICS. In particular, this book is meant to follow *CICS for the COBOL programmer, Part 1: An introductory course*. Table 1 shows the essential CICS programming skills *Part 1* teaches. Any course that teaches these minimum skills will serve as a prerequisite to this book.

You should be able to do the following:

1. Design, code, and test simple interactive programs using pseudo-conversational programming techniques.

2. Define mapsets, use the SEND MAP, SEND TEXT, and RECEIVE MAP commands, position the cursor on the screen, and detect the use of PF keys, PA keys, and the clear key.

3. Use the following file control commands:

READ	DELETE
WRITE	UNLOCK
REWRITE	

4. Use the XCTL and LINK commands to manage the execution of programs within a task.

Table 1   What you should be able to do before studying this book

Because CICS is nearly identical under all of IBM's operating systems, you can use this book regardless of the operating system (or systems) installed at your shop. I tested all of the programs in this book using CICS version 1.5 running under DOS/VSE on an IBM 4331. All of the features this book presents are supported by CICS version 1.6 as well.

As you may know, IBM is on the verge of releasing a new compiler, called VS COBOL II. Because VS COBOL II wasn't available as I wrote this book, I wasn't able to test any of the programs using the new compiler. According to the VS COBOL II manuals, the only significant change that affects material in this book is how areas outside your program are addressed: the BLL-cell convention will be replaced by a special register named ADDRESS. That shouldn't have a dramatic effect on the way you code the majority of your CICS programs.

How to use this book

The organization of this book gives you many choices as to the sequence in which you study CICS facilities. Table 2 shows the general plan of this book. With one exception, the chapters are self-contained so you can read them in any order you wish. The exception is chapter 2: it builds on information presented in chapter 1. In a few cases, a chapter will make a minor reference to a

Part	Chapters	Title	Subjects
1	1-3	Advanced file processing features	Browsing, alternate indexes, and DL/I
2	4-5	Queue management features	Temporary storage and transient data
3	6-8	Advanced terminal processing features	Message building, color and extended highlighting, and terminal control
4	9-11	Other advanced CICS features	Interval control, abend processing, recovery, journal control, task control, program control, and storage control

Table 2 How this book is organized

subject presented earlier in the book. So if you read the chapters in order, those references will make perfect sense. But because they are minor references, I don't think they'll cause any problems if you read the chapters out of order. And feel free to skip topics or entire chapters that present CICS facilities your installation doesn't use.

Conclusion

I'm confident that this book will make you a more effective CICS programmer. If I'm wrong, let me know. Return the book and you'll get a full refund, with no questions asked.

As always, I welcome your comments, suggestions, criticism, and questions. I'll even pay the postage: just use the postage-paid comment form at the back of this book. With your help, we'll be able to improve not only this product, but future products as well.

Doug Lowe
Fresno, California
March, 1985

Part 1

Advanced file processing features

In *Part 1: An introductory course*, you learned how to use basic file control commands to process VSAM files randomly. The chapters in this part show you how to use advanced file handling features. In chapter 1, you'll learn how to process a file sequentially using browse commands. In chapter 2, you'll learn how to process VSAM alternate index files. And in chapter 3, you'll learn how to process DL/I data bases in a CICS program.

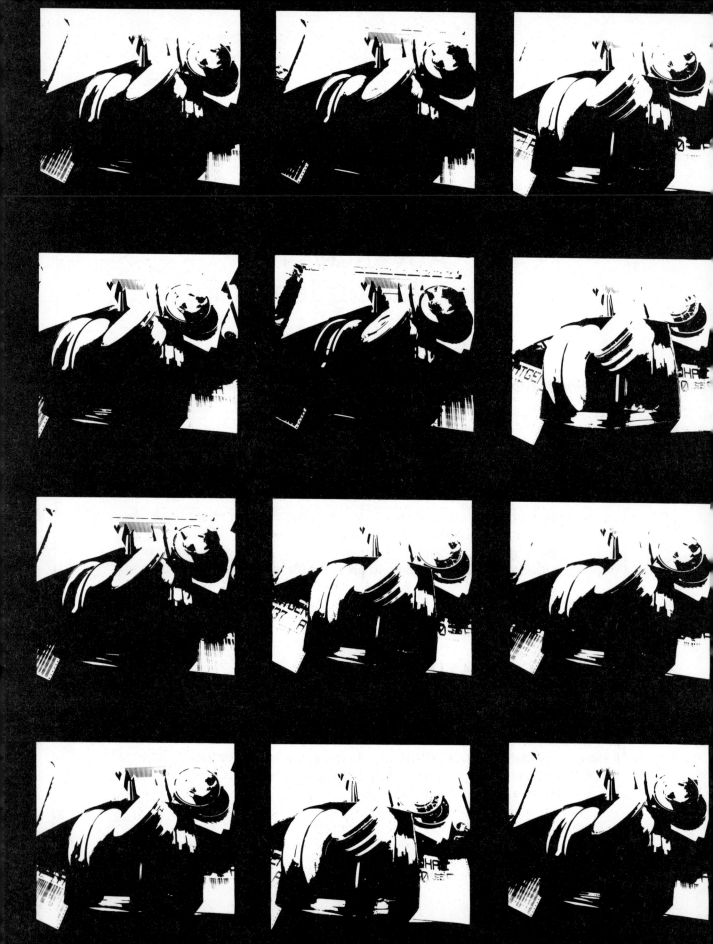

Chapter 1

Sequential processing using browse commands

Most on-line applications process files using the random file processing elements you learned in *Part 1: An introductory course*. Still, some on-line applications need to access files sequentially. Under CICS, accessing a file sequentially is called *browsing*. That's just what you'll learn how to do in this chapter. After I show you the commands you use for sequential processing (called *browse commands*), I'll illustrate how they're used with two program examples.

BROWSE COMMANDS

The two browse commands you'll use most are STARTBR and READNEXT. The STARTBR command initiates a browse operation, and the READNEXT command retrieves records sequentially. Other browse commands are READPREV (read a record in *reverse* order), ENDBR (end a browse operation), and RESETBR (change the current position during a browse operation).

You can issue browse commands for all three types of VSAM data sets: key-sequenced data sets (KSDS), relative-record data sets (RRDS), and entry-sequenced data sets (ESDS). Sequential processing of a typical KSDS is based on the file's key values. For an RRDS, browse operations use relative-record numbers. And for an ESDS, browse operations are based on relative-byte addresses. You can also issue browse commands for non-VSAM files. But since most files in a CICS environment are VSAM files, all of the examples in this chapter are for VSAM files.

The STARTBR command

The STARTBR command, shown in figure 1-1, initiates a browse operation and identifies the location within the data set where the browse begins. The STARTBR command doesn't retrieve a record from the file; it just establishes a position in the file so subsequent READNEXT or READPREV commands can retrieve records.

You can think of a STARTBR command like a standard COBOL START statement—its function is similar. The main difference is that a STARTBR command is *always* required when you want to browse a data set, even if you want to begin with the first record in the file. In contrast, standard batch COBOL requires a START statement only when you want to begin sequential retrieval at a point other than the first record in the file.

In its simplest form, you code the STARTBR command like this:

```
EXEC CICS
    STARTBR DATASET('CUSTMAS')
            RIDFLD(CM-CUSTOMER-NUMBER)
END-EXEC
```

This STARTBR command initiates a browse operation for the KSDS named CUSTMAS. The browse begins at the record identified by the value of CM-CUSTOMER-NUMBER. For example, if CM-CUSTOMER-NUMBER has a value of 10000, the browse begins at the record in CUSTMAS whose key is 10000. If there's no record with that key, processing starts with the first record whose key is greater than 10000. That's because GTEQ is in effect by default for this STARTBR command.

If there's no record in the KSDS whose key is greater than or equal to the value you specify in the RIDFLD field, the NOTFND condition is raised. Because the default action for the NOTFND condition is to abend your program, you should always issue a HANDLE CONDITION command for NOTFND before you issue a STARTBR command. You'll see an example of that in a moment.

The STARTBR command

```
EXEC CICS
      STARTBR DATASET(data-name|literal)
              RIDFLD(data-name)
              [RRN|RBA]
              [GTEQ|EQUAL]
END-EXEC
```

Explanation

DATASET	The file-name from the File Control Table.
RIDFLD	The field identifying the record at which the browse operation will start. For VSAM key-sequenced files (KSDS), the value is the key of the record. For relative-record files (RRDS), the value is the relative-record number. And for entry-sequenced files (ESDS), the value is a relative-byte address (a full-word binary field).
RRN	You must code RRN if the file is a VSAM relative-record file (RRDS).
RBA	You must code RBA if the file is a VSAM entry-sequenced file (ESDS).
GTEQ	The browse operation will start at the first record whose key is greater than or equal to the value in RIDFLD.
EQUAL	The browse operation will start at the record whose key is equal to the value in RIDFLD. If there is no such record, the NOTFND condition is raised.

Figure 1-1   The STARTBR command

So far, I've assumed you're processing a VSAM key-sequenced data set. You can also use the STARTBR command (and any of the other browse commands) to process a relative-record data set or an entry-sequenced data set. For a relative-record data set, the value of the RIDFLD field is a relative-record number within the file, and you must specify the RRN parameter in the STARTBR command. For an entry-sequenced data set, the RIDFLD value is a relative-byte address, and you must code RBA in the STARTBR command. For an ESDS, the RIDFLD field must be a full-word binary field (PIC S9(8) COMP).

How to start a browse at the beginning of a file   You can start processing with the first record in a KSDS by moving LOW-VALUE to the RIDFLD field before you issue the STARTBR command. That way, processing begins at the first record whose key is greater than or equal to hexadecimal zeros—and that's always the first record in the file. If a KSDS has a numeric key, though, you must move ZERO rather than LOW-VALUE to the key field to start a browse at the first record. That's because the COBOL compiler won't let you move LOW-VALUE to a numeric field.

To start a browse at the beginning of an ESDS, move ZERO to the RIDFLD field. That way, the browse starts at the record whose RBA is zero—the first record in the file. And to browse an RRDS from the beginning, move 1 to the RIDFLD field.

How to start a browse at a specific record   You can start a browse at a specific record that *must* exist in the file by coding EQUAL on the STARTBR command, like this:

```
EXEC CICS
    STARTBR DATASET('CUSTMAS')
            RIDFLD(CM-CUSTOMER-NUMBER)
            EQUAL
END-EXEC
```

Suppose CM-CUSTOMER-NUMBER contains 10000. Then, processing will start only with record 10000. If there's no record in the file with the key value you specify, the NOTFND condition is raised.

How to start a browse at the end of a file   In some unusual cases, you might want to start processing with the last record in a file. If you do, move HIGH-VALUE (hexadecimal FFs) to the RIDFLD field. Issuing the STARTBR command when the RIDFLD field contains HIGH-VALUE is a special case—it doesn't cause the NOTFND condition to be raised, as you might expect. Instead, it establishes the position in the file at the last record.

Unfortunately, you can't move all 9's to a numeric RIDFLD field to start processing at the last record. That's because the NOTFND condition will be raised if there isn't a record with that key in the file. Since the compiler won't let you move HIGH-VALUE to a numeric field, you'll have to redefine the RIDFLD as alphanumeric to be able to move HIGH-VALUE to it.

A typical STARTBR module   Figure 1-2 shows the coding for a typical start-browse module. After the HANDLE CONDITION command, I move LOW-VALUE to the file's RIDFLD field. That way,

```
    210-START-ACCOUNT-BROWSE SECTION.
*
        EXEC CICS
            HANDLE CONDITION NOTFND(210-NOTFND)
        END-EXEC.
        MOVE LOW-VALUE TO AR-ACCOUNT-NUMBER.
        EXEC CICS
            STARTBR DATASET('ACCOUNT')
                    RIDFLD(AR-ACCOUNT-NUMBER)
        END-EXEC.
        GO TO 210-EXIT.
*
    210-NOTFND.
*
        MOVE 'Y' TO ACCOUNT-EOF-SW.
*
    210-EXIT.
*
        EXIT.
```

Figure 1-2   Typical coding for a start-browse module

the STARTBR command positions the file at the first record. In the error routine for the NOTFND condition, I set a switch (ACCOUNT-EOF-SW) that indicates the end of the file has been reached. Then, that switch can be tested to determine if the STARTBR command executed normally.

By the way, if you haven't read *Part 1: An introductory course*, the coding in figure 1-2 may seem strange to you. I usually code I/O functions in a single, self-contained section that I invoke using a PERFORM statement (*without* the THRU option). At the beginning of the section, I place any required HANDLE AID or HANDLE CONDITION commands, followed by other CICS commands and COBOL statements required by the module. Then, I use a GO TO statement to branch to a paragraph that contains an EXIT statement. Between that GO TO statement and the EXIT paragraph, I code the paragraphs that process the conditions I specified in the HANDLE AID and HANDLE CONDITION commands. Each of these paragraphs also ends with a GO TO statement that branches to the EXIT paragraph, except the last one before the EXIT paragraph. Control falls through from it to the EXIT paragraph anyway. If you study the coding in figure 1-2, you'll see how I apply this general structure to the start-browse module.

The READNEXT command

```
EXEC CICS
    READNEXT DATASET(data-name|literal)
             INTO(data-name)
             RIDFLD(data-name)
            [RRN|RBA]
END-EXEC
```

Explanation

DATASET   The file-name from the File Control Table.

INTO   The area that will contain the record being read.

RIDFLD   You must specify the same data-name you specified in the
                           STARTBR command. After completion of the READNEXT
                           command, this field is updated to indicate the key, RRN, or
                           RBA of the record read.

RRN   You must code RRN if the file is a VSAM relative-record file
                           (RRDS).

RBA   You must code RBA if the file is a VSAM entry-sequenced file
                           (ESDS).

Figure 1-3   The READNEXT command

The READNEXT command

The READNEXT command, shown in figure 1-3, retrieves records
from a file in sequential order. Each time you issue a READNEXT
command, the next record in the file identified by the DATASET
parameter is retrieved and stored in the INTO field. When there
are no more records in the file, the ENDFILE condition is raised.
So be sure a HANDLE CONDITION command for the ENDFILE
condition is in effect before you issue a READNEXT command.

The data-name you specify in the RIDFLD parameter in a
READNEXT command must be the same as the one you've already
specified in the STARTBR command. Your program shouldn't alter
the contents of this field during the browse. Instead, the
READNEXT command updates it to indicate the key, RRN, or
RBA value of the record it retrieved. That way, subsequent
READNEXT commands continue to retrieve records in sequence.

```
            .
            .
            .
        EXEC CICS
            HANDLE CONDITION ENDFILE(210-ENDFILE)
        END-EXEC.
        PERFORM 200-PROCESS-ACCOUNT-RECORD
            UNTIL ACCOUNT-EOF.
            .
            .
            .

    *
     200-PROCESS-ACCOUNT-RECORD SECTION.
    *
        PERFORM 210-READ-NEXT-ACCOUNT-RECORD.
        IF NOT ACCOUNT-EOF
            .
            .
            .

    *
     210-READ-NEXT-ACCOUNT-RECORD SECTION.
    *
        EXEC CICS
            READNEXT DATASET('ACCOUNT')
                     INTO(ACCOUNT-RECORD)
                     RIDFLD(AR-ACCOUNT-NUMBER)
        END-EXEC.
        GO TO 210-EXIT.
    *
     210-ENDFILE.
    *
        MOVE 'Y' TO ACCOUNT-EOF-SW.
    *
     210-EXIT.
    *
        EXIT.
```

Figure 1-4 Typical coding for a read-next module

To retrieve records sequentially from an RRDS, you code RRN on the READNEXT command. Similarly, to retrieve records sequentially from an ESDS, specify RBA. If you omit both RRN and RBA, CICS assumes you're processing a KSDS.

Figure 1-4 shows the coding for a typical READNEXT module that's executed repeatedly by a PERFORM UNTIL statement. Here, I place the HANDLE CONDITION command just before the PERFORM UNTIL statement that repeatedly invokes a module which in turn invokes a READNEXT module. Had I placed the HANDLE CONDITION command in the READNEXT module itself, it would be executed once for each record accessed during the browse. An inefficiency like that degrades the performance of the program—particularly if the file contains thousands of records.

Following the PERFORM statement in module 200 would be statements that process the record retrieved by module 210. What those statements would be depends on the requirements of the application. For the sake of clarity, I omitted them in figure 1-4.

The READPREV command

The READPREV command, shown in figure 1-5, is similar to the READNEXT command except that it retrieves records in reverse order. In short, the READPREV command lets you read a file backwards, from the current position toward the beginning of the file. When a READPREV command tries to retrieve a record that would be beyond the beginning of the file, the ENDFILE condition is raised. You should handle it just as you do for the READNEXT command.

Frankly, the READPREV command provides a rather unusual function. As a result, you probably won't use it often. But it does come in handy for those few cases where you need it.

The READPREV command has two peculiarities you should know about. First, if you issue a READPREV command following a READNEXT command, the same record is retrieved twice. For example, suppose a file contains three records, with keys 1000, 1001, and 1002. You issue a READNEXT command that retrieves record 1001. If you then issue a READPREV command, it too retrieves record 1001. To retrieve record 1000, you must issue *two* READPREV commands: the first retrieves record 1001, the second record 1000. The opposite is true as well: if you issue a READNEXT command following a READPREV command, the same record is retrieved.

The second peculiarity of READPREV has to do with issuing the command immediately after a STARTBR command. If the STARTBR command establishes positioning for the file at the last record because the RIDFLD field contains HIGH-VALUE, it's safe to issue a READPREV command. But if the RIDFLD field for the STARTBR command doesn't contain HIGH-VALUE, you shouldn't follow it with a READPREV. That's because READPREV raises the NOTFND condition if the STARTBR command refers to a

---

The READPREV command

```
EXEC CICS
     READPREV DATASET(data-name|literal)
              INTO(data-name)
              RIDFLD(data-name)
              [RRN|RBA]
END-EXEC
```

Explanation

DATASET   The file-name from the File Control Table.

INTO   The area that will contain the record being read.

RIDFLD   You must specify the same data-name you specified in the
                   STARTBR command. After completion of the READPREV
                   command, this field is updated to indicate the key, RRN, or
                   RBA of the record read.

RRN   You must code RRN if the file is a VSAM relative-record file
                   (RRDS).

RBA   You must code RBA if the file is a VSAM entry-sequenced file
                   (ESDS).

Figure 1-5   The READPREV command

record that isn't in the file—even if the GTEQ option on the
STARTBR command positions the file to the next record in
sequence. So as a rule, don't code a READPREV command right
after a STARTBR command unless the STARTBR command's
RIDFLD field contains HIGH-VALUE.

How can you achieve the effect of a STARTBR command with
a RIDFLD field that doesn't contain HIGH-VALUE followed by a
READPREV? You must issue four commands: STARTBR,
READNEXT, READPREV, and READPREV. The STARTBR
command positions the file to the record you specify. Then, the
READNEXT command retrieves the record. Next, the READPREV
command changes the direction of the browse. But since it retrieves
the same record as the READNEXT command, another
READPREV command is required to read the previous record.

The ENDBR command

```
EXEC CICS
     ENDBR DATASET(data-name|literal)
END-EXEC
```

Explanation

DATASET   The file-name from the File Control Table.

Figure 1-6   The ENDBR command

You'll see an example of this coding later in this chapter, so don't worry if this seems confusing. I think it will make sense when you see the example. And frankly, it's a function you won't have to code often.

Because the READPREV command is so similar to the READNEXT command, I don't provide an example of a typical READPREV module. If you wish, you can use the coding in figure 1-4 as a model. Just change the READNEXT command to a READPREV command.

The ENDBR command

Figure 1-6 gives the format of the ENDBR command, used to terminate a browse operation. Normally, you don't need to issue an ENDBR command, since your browse is terminated automatically when your task ends. However, if your program does extensive processing after it completes a browse operation, you should issue an ENDBR command for efficiency's sake. As long as your browse is active, VSAM resources are allocated to your task. Releasing those resources by terminating your browse frees them for other users.

The RESETBR command

Figure 1-7 shows the RESETBR command. As you can see, its format is similar to the format of the STARTBR command. You use

The RESETBR command

```
EXEC CICS
    RESETBR DATASET(data-name|literal)
            RIDFLD(data-name)
            [RRN|RBA]
            [GTEQ|EQUAL]
END-EXEC
```

Explanation

DATASET   The file-name from the File Control Table.

RIDFLD   The field identifying the record at which the browse operation
                   will be repositioned. For VSAM key-sequenced files (KSDS),
                   the value is the key of the record. For relative-record files
                   (RRDS), the value is the relative-record number. And for entry-
                   sequenced files (ESDS), the value is a relative-byte address (a
                   full-word binary field).

RRN   You must code RRN if the file is a VSAM relative-record file
                   (RRDS).

RBA   You must code RBA if the file is a VSAM entry-sequenced file
                   (ESDS).

GTEQ   The browse operation will be repositioned at the first record
                   whose key is greater than or equal to the value in RIDFLD.

EQUAL   The browse operation will be repositioned at the record whose
                   key is equal to the value in RIDFLD. If there is no such record,
                   the NOTFND condition is raised.

Figure 1-7   The RESETBR command

the RESETBR command to restart a browse operation at a new
position in a file. It has the same effect as issuing an ENDBR
command followed by a STARTBR command, but it's more
efficient. That's because when you issue an ENDBR command, the
VSAM resources allocated to your task are released and a
subsequent STARTBR command must reallocate them. In contrast,
if you issue a RESETBR command, VSAM resources are not
released, so they don't need to be reallocated.

Condition	Cause
DSIDERR	The data set isn't defined in the FCT.
ENDFILE	A browse operation has reached the end (READNEXT) or beginning (READPREV) of the file.
ILLOGIC	A VSAM error has occurred.
INVREQ	The I/O request is invalid. You didn't issue a STARTBR before a READNEXT or READPREV, or the RIDFLD you specified in a READNEXT or READPREV is different than the one you specified in the STARTBR.
IOERR	An I/O error has occurred.
LENGERR	A length error has occurred.
NOTFND	The record specified in a STARTBR or RESETBR command doesn't exist.
NOTOPEN	The data set isn't open.

Figure 1-8   File-control exceptional conditions that might be raised during browse operations

Browse exceptional conditions

Besides the NOTFND and ENDFILE conditions I've already mentioned, a number of other conditions might be raised during a browse operation. Figure 1-8 summarizes those conditions, including NOTFND and ENDFILE. Most of them are caused by programming errors or CICS problems, so there's usually no need to provide for them in production programs. Still, you should find out your shop's standards for handling these conditions and follow them.

PROGRAM EXAMPLES

Now that I've explained the CICS commands you use for a browse operation, I'll present two programming examples. The first is a simple, non-interactive program that reads through a file of order records and displays information summarized from the file. The

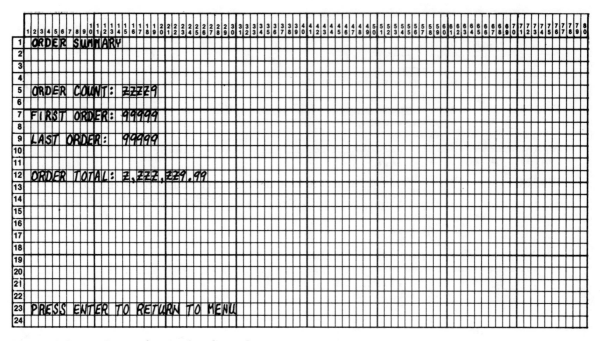

Figure 1-9   Screen layout for the order-summary program

second is a more complex pseudo-conversational inquiry program
that lets an operator retrieve records from a customer master file.

An order-summary program

Figures 1-9 through 1-13 present the order-summary program. The
program accumulates summary information by browsing through
an ESDS that contains order records. You can see from the screen
layout in figure 1-9 that the program displays a summary screen
showing the number of orders in the file, the first and last order
numbers, and the sum of the values in the order total fields of the
records in the file. To accumulate this summary information, the
program browses through the entire file.

Because the order-summary program doesn't interact with a
user, its processing is done at computer system speed rather than
operator speed. As a result, it's not pseudo-conversational—its
structure is more like what you'd expect for a batch COBOL
report-preparation program than for a CICS program. Keep in
mind, however, that the order-summary program is not typical;
most CICS programs have to be pseudo-conversational.

```
          PRINT NOGEN
SUMSET1   DFHMSD TYPE=&SYSPARM,                                           X
                 LANG=COBOL,                                              X
                 MODE=INOUT,                                              X
                 TERM=3270-2,                                             X
                 CTRL=FREEKB,                                             X
                 STORAGE=AUTO,                                            X
                 TIOAPFX=YES
*********************************************************************************
SUMMAP1   DFHMDI SIZE=(24,80),                                           X
                 LINE=1,                                                  X
                 COLUMN=1
*********************************************************************************
          DFHMDF POS=(1,1),                                              X
                 LENGTH=13,                                               X
                 ATTRB=(BRT,PROT),                                        X
                 INITIAL='ORDER SUMMARY'
*********************************************************************************
          DFHMDF POS=(5,1),                                              X
                 LENGTH=12,                                               X
                 ATTRB=(BRT,PROT),                                        X
                 INITIAL='ORDER COUNT:'
COUNT     DFHMDF POS=(5,14),                                             X
                 LENGTH=5,                                                X
                 ATTRB=PROT,                                              X
                 PICOUT='ZZZZ9'
*********************************************************************************
          DFHMDF POS=(7,1),                                              X
                 LENGTH=12,                                               X
                 ATTRB=(BRT,PROT),                                        X
                 INITIAL='FIRST ORDER:'
FIRST     DFHMDF POS=(7,14),                                             X
                 LENGTH=5,                                                X
                 ATTRB=PROT
*********************************************************************************
          DFHMDF POS=(9,1),                                              X
                 LENGTH=11,                                               X
                 ATTRB=(BRT,PROT),                                        X
                 INITIAL='LAST ORDER:'
LAST      DFHMDF POS=(9,14),                                             X
                 LENGTH=5,                                                X
                 ATTRB=PROT
*********************************************************************************
          DFHMDF POS=(12,1),                                             X
                 LENGTH=12,                                               X
                 ATTRB=(BRT,PROT),                                        X
                 INITIAL='ORDER TOTAL:'
TOTAL     DFHMDF POS=(12,14),                                            X
                 LENGTH=12,                                               X
                 ATTRB=PROT,                                              X
                 PICOUT='Z,ZZZ,ZZ9.99'
```

Figure 1-10   Mapset listing for the order-summary program (part 1 of 2)

```
**************************************************************************
          DFHMDF POS=(23,1),                                            X
                 LENGTH=29,                                             X
                 ATTRB=(BRT,PROT),                                      X
                 INITIAL='PRESS ENTER TO RETURN TO MENU'
**************************************************************************
          DFHMSD TYPE=FINAL
          END
```

Figure 1-10   Mapset listing for the order-summary program (part 2 of 2)

```
   01   ORDER-SUMMARY-MAP.
*
        05   FILLER                     PIC X(12).
*
        05   OS-L-ORDER-COUNT           PIC S9(4)      COMP.
        05   OS-A-ORDER-COUNT           PIC X.
        05   OS-D-ORDER-COUNT           PIC ZZZZ9.
*
        05   OS-L-FIRST-ORDER           PIC S9(4)      COMP.
        05   OS-A-FIRST-ORDER           PIC X.
        05   OS-D-FIRST-ORDER           PIC 9(5).
*
        05   OS-L-LAST-ORDER            PIC S9(4)      COMP.
        05   OS-A-LAST-ORDER            PIC X.
        05   OS-D-LAST-ORDER            PIC 9(5).
*
        05   OS-L-ORDER-TOTAL           PIC S9(4)      COMP.
        05   OS-A-ORDER-TOTAL           PIC X.
        05   OS-D-ORDER-TOTAL           PIC Z,ZZZ,ZZ9.99.
```

Figure 1-11   Programmer-generated symbolic map for the order-summary program (SUMSET)

Figure 1-10 gives the mapset listing for the order-summary program, and figure 1-11 gives the symbolic map I created. If you haven't read *Part 1: An introductory course*, you may be wondering about the symbolic map in figure 1-11. Because the symbolic map generated by BMS is difficult to use, I usually discard it and create my own, like the one in figure 1-11. While BMS creates five data names for each map field, I create only three: a length field, an attribute field, and a data field. And while BMS follows assembler-language naming rules to form its data names, I follow COBOL naming rules to create more readable and understandable names. For a detailed explanation of how to create a symbolic map like the one in figure 1-11, read chapter 5 of *Part 1: An introductory course.*

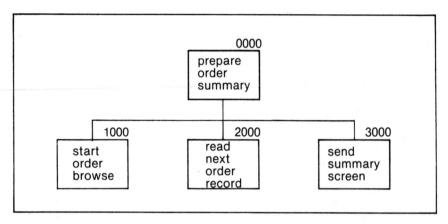

Figure 1-12   Structure chart for the order-summary program

Figure 1-12 shows the structure chart for this program. Here, module 0000 is the main processing module. It performs module 1000 to start the browse. Then, it invokes module 2000 repeatedly to read records sequentially from the order file. When the end of the file has been reached, module 0000 calls module 3000 to send the summary display to the terminal.

Figure 1-13 gives the complete source listing for this program. Module 0000 controls the execution of modules 1000, 2000, and 3000, just as the structure chart shows. Because module 2000 is executed repeatedly, the HANDLE CONDITION command for the ENDFILE condition is in module 0000. That way, it's executed only once for the entire program. After module 3000 sends the summary map to the terminal, a RETURN command terminates the program. So when the operator presses the enter key after looking at the summary display, the MENU transaction is started because of the TRANSID specification on the RETURN command.

Because the file this program processes is an entry-sequenced data set, the STARTBR command specifies RBA and the RIDFLD field (ORDER-RBA) is defined in the Working-Storage Section as a full-word binary item. Because its initial value is ZERO, this STARTBR command establishes the position in the ORDERS file at the first record.

Notice that the NOTFND routine for the STARTBR command (1000-NOTFND) and the ENDFILE routine for the READNEXT command (2000-ENDFILE) both move Y to ORDER-EOF-SW. Since module 2000 is performed until ORDER-EOF, records are read until the end of the file is reached. And since a COBOL PERFORM UNTIL test is done *before* the specified paragraph is performed, module 2000 isn't performed at all if the NOTFND

```
     IDENTIFICATION DIVISION.
*
  PROGRAM-ID. ORDSUM1.
*
  ENVIRONMENT DIVISION.
*
  DATA DIVISION.
*
  WORKING-STORAGE SECTION.
*
  01  SWITCHES.
*
      05  ORDER-EOF-SW           PIC X           VALUE 'N'.
          88  ORDER-EOF                          VALUE 'Y'.
      05  FIRST-RECORD-SW        PIC X           VALUE 'Y'.
          88  FIRST-RECORD                       VALUE 'Y'.
*
  01  WORK-FIELDS.
*
      05  ORDER-COUNT            PIC S9(5)    COMP-3  VALUE ZERO.
      05  ORDER-TOTAL            PIC S9(7)V99 COMP-3  VALUE ZERO.
*
  01  ORDER-RBA                  PIC S9(8)    COMP    VALUE ZERO.
*
  01  ORDER-RECORD.
*
      05  ORD-ORDER-NUMBER       PIC 9(5).
      05  ORD-ORDER-DATE         PIC 9(6).
      05  ORD-CUSTOMER-NUMBER    PIC X(5).
      05  ORD-PO-NUMBER          PIC X(10).
      05  ORD-LINE-ITEM          OCCURS 10.
          10  ORD-ITEM-NUMBER    PIC 9(5).
          10  ORD-QUANTITY       PIC S9(5)    COMP-3.
          10  ORD-UNIT-PRICE     PIC S9(5)V99 COMP-3.
          10  ORD-EXTENSION      PIC S9(5)V99 COMP-3.
      05  ORD-ORDER-TOTAL        PIC S9(5)V99 COMP-3.
*
  COPY SUMSET1.
*
  PROCEDURE DIVISION.
*
  0000-PREPARE-ORDER-SUMMARY SECTION.
*
      MOVE LOW-VALUE TO ORDER-SUMMARY-MAP.
      PERFORM 1000-START-ORDER-BROWSE.
      EXEC CICS
          HANDLE CONDITION ENDFILE(2000-ENDFILE)
      END-EXEC.
      PERFORM 2000-READ-NEXT-ORDER-RECORD
          UNTIL ORDER-EOF.
      PERFORM 3000-SEND-SUMMARY-SCREEN.
      EXEC CICS
          RETURN TRANSID('MENU')
      END-EXEC.
*
```

Figure 1-13   Source listing for the order-summary program (part 1 of 2)

```
    1000-START-ORDER-BROWSE SECTION.
*
        EXEC CICS
            HANDLE CONDITION NOTFND(1000-NOTFND)
        END-EXEC.
        EXEC CICS
            STARTBR DATASET('ORDERS')
                    RIDFLD(ORDER-RBA)
                    RBA
        END-EXEC.
        GO TO 1000-EXIT.
*
    1000-NOTFND.
*
        MOVE 'Y' TO ORDER-EOF-SW.
*
    1000-EXIT.
*
        EXIT.
*
    2000-READ-NEXT-ORDER-RECORD SECTION.
*
        EXEC CICS
            READNEXT DATASET('ORDERS')
                     INTO(ORDER-RECORD)
                     RIDFLD(ORDER-RBA)
                     RBA
        END-EXEC.
        IF FIRST-RECORD
            MOVE ORD-ORDER-NUMBER TO OS-D-FIRST-ORDER
            MOVE 'N' TO FIRST-RECORD-SW.
        MOVE ORD-ORDER-NUMBER TO OS-D-LAST-ORDER.
        ADD 1 TO ORDER-COUNT.
        ADD ORD-ORDER-TOTAL TO ORDER-TOTAL.
        GO TO 2000-EXIT.
*
    2000-ENDFILE.
*
        MOVE 'Y' TO ORDER-EOF-SW.
*
    2000-EXIT.
*
        EXIT.
*
    3000-SEND-SUMMARY-SCREEN SECTION.
*
        MOVE ORDER-COUNT TO OS-D-ORDER-COUNT.
        MOVE ORDER-TOTAL TO OS-D-ORDER-TOTAL.
        EXEC CICS
            SEND MAP('SUMMAP1')
                 MAPSET('SUMSET1')
                 FROM(ORDER-SUMMARY-MAP)
                 ERASE
        END-EXEC.
```

Figure 1-13   Source listing for the order-summary program (part 2 of 2)

condition is raised on the STARTBR command. As a result, this program works properly even if the order file is empty.

A customer-inquiry program

Figures 1-14 through 1-18 present a customer-inquiry program that lets a terminal operator display records from a file of customer records. An operator can choose which record to display by pressing one of these AID keys:

ENTER	Display the customer record indicated by the number entered in the CUSTOMER NUMBER field
PF1	Display the first customer record in the file
PF2	Display the last customer record in the file
PF4	Display the previous customer record
PF5	Display the next customer record

In other words, this program lets an operator display a specific customer record by entering that customer's number. Alternatively, an operator can browse through the customer file, displaying the next customer or the previous customer or going directly to the start or end of the file. The operator can browse forward through the entire customer file by pressing PF5 repeatedly.

Bear in mind, however, that this is a pseudo-conversational program. As a result, even though the entire terminal session might appear to the user to be a single browse session, it isn't. Each pseudo-conversational execution of the program that performs a browse requires one STARTBR command and one or more READNEXT or READPREV commands.

The screen layout for this program, given in figure 1-14, is almost identical to the layout for the customer maintenance program I presented in *Part 1: An introductory course*. So are the mapset listings and programmer-generated symbolic maps in figures 1-15 and 1-16. There are three minor differences. First, only the customer-number field is unprotected; the customer data fields are protected against operator entry. Second, I specified the FSET option for the customer-number field. That way, the customer number displayed at the terminal is always sent back to the program. When the operator presses PF4 or PF5, the program uses this field in a STARTBR command to determine the starting location for the browse. And third, I included the operator instructions as a constant in the mapset rather

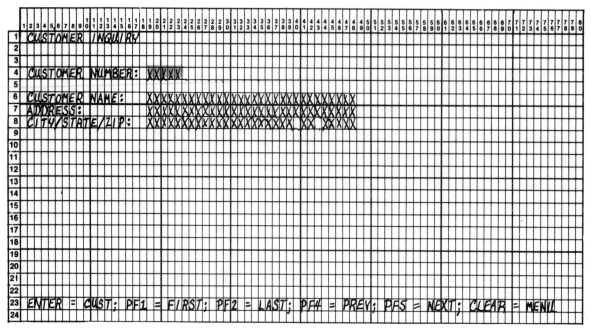

Figure 1-14   Screen layout for the customer-inquiry program

than as a variable field set by the program. That's because the operator instructions don't change during a terminal session.

Figure 1-17 gives the structure chart for this program. Although module 1000 is the main control module, the key to understanding this program's sequential processing lies in module 1200 and its subordinates. It's those modules that are responsible for retrieving the record the operator requests.

Figure 1-18 gives the complete source listing for the customer-inquiry program. Here, module 0000 handles the pseudo-conversational processing requirements much like the programs in *Part 1: An introductory course.* Quite simply, the presence of a communication area indicates whether first-time processing should be done. If there's no communication area, module 8000 is performed to send a fresh map to the terminal. Otherwise, module 1000 is performed to process the customer-inquiry screen. Module 0000 terminates the program with a RETURN command that specifies the TRANSID and COMMAREA options unless the operator signals the end of the session by pressing the clear key. In that case, an XCTL command transfers control directly to a menu program.

Module 1000 invokes three subordinate modules: module 1100 receives the map from the terminal, module 1200 gets the requested customer record, and module 1800 sends the customer data to the

```
        PRINT NOGEN
INQSET1 DFHMSD TYPE=&SYSPARM,                                              X
               LANG=COBOL,                                                 X
               MODE=INOUT,                                                 X
               TERM=3270-2,                                                X
               CTRL=FREEKB,                                                X
               STORAGE=AUTO,                                               X
               TIOAPFX=YES
****************************************************************************
INQMAP1 DFHMDI SIZE=(24,80),                                               X
               LINE=1,                                                     X
               COLUMN=1
****************************************************************************
        DFHMDF POS=(1,1),                                                  X
               LENGTH=16,                                                  X
               ATTRB=(BRT,PROT),                                           X
               INITIAL='CUSTOMER INQUIRY'
****************************************************************************
        DFHMDF POS=(4,1),                                                  X
               LENGTH=16,                                                  X
               ATTRB=(BRT,PROT),                                           X
               INITIAL='CUSTOMER NUMBER:'
NUMBER  DFHMDF POS=(4,18),                                                 X
               LENGTH=5,                                                   X
               ATTRB=(IC,UNPROT,FSET)
        DFHMDF POS=(4,24),                                                 X
               LENGTH=1,                                                   X
               ATTRB=ASKIP
****************************************************************************
        DFHMDF POS=(6,1),                                                  X
               LENGTH=16,                                                  X
               ATTRB=(BRT,PROT),                                           X
               INITIAL='CUSTOMER NAME:'
NAME    DFHMDF POS=(6,18),                                                 X
               LENGTH=30,                                                  X
               ATTRB=PROT
****************************************************************************
        DFHMDF POS=(7,1),                                                  X
               LENGTH=8,                                                   X
               ATTRB=(BRT,PROT),                                           X
               INITIAL='ADDRESS:'
ADDRESS DFHMDF POS=(7,18),                                                 X
               LENGTH=30,                                                  X
               ATTRB=PROT
```

Figure 1-15   Mapset listing for the customer-inquiry program (part 1 of 2)

terminal. In addition, module 1000 formats the display by moving values from fields in the retrieved customer record to fields in the symbolic map.

Module 1100 issues a RECEIVE MAP command to get the operator's inquiry request. It uses a HANDLE CONDITION command

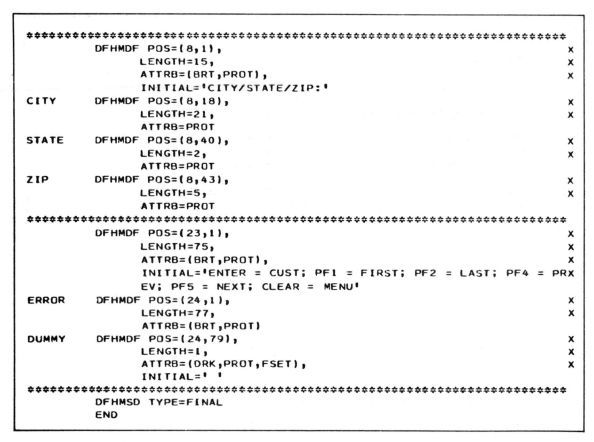

```
**************************************************************************
          DFHMDF POS=(8,1),                                              X
                 LENGTH=15,                                              X
                 ATTRB=(BRT,PROT),                                       X
                 INITIAL='CITY/STATE/ZIP:'
CITY      DFHMDF POS=(8,18),                                             X
                 LENGTH=21,                                              X
                 ATTRB=PROT
STATE     DFHMDF POS=(8,40),                                             X
                 LENGTH=2,                                               X
                 ATTRB=PROT
ZIP       DFHMDF POS=(8,43),                                             X
                 LENGTH=5,                                               X
                 ATTRB=PROT
**************************************************************************
          DFHMDF POS=(23,1),                                            X
                 LENGTH=75,                                              X
                 ATTRB=(BRT,PROT),                                       X
                 INITIAL='ENTER = CUST; PF1 = FIRST; PF2 = LAST; PF4 = PRX
                 EV; PF5 = NEXT; CLEAR = MENU'
ERROR     DFHMDF POS=(24,1),                                            X
                 LENGTH=77,                                              X
                 ATTRB=(BRT,PROT)
DUMMY     DFHMDF POS=(24,79),                                           X
                 LENGTH=1,                                               X
                 ATTRB=(DRK,PROT,FSET),                                  X
                 INITIAL=' '
**************************************************************************
          DFHMSD TYPE=FINAL
          END
```

Figure 1-15   Mapset listing for the customer-inquiry program (part 2 of 2)

to set a flag (PF-KEY-FLAG) to indicate which PF key (if any) the operator uses. Notice that if the operator presses the enter key, PF-KEY-FLAG isn't changed. As a result, it retains its initial value of zero.

Module 1200 performs one of five subordinate modules to retrieve the correct customer record based on the value of PF-KEY-FLAG. The first of those modules (1300) uses a standard READ command to retrieve a specific record from the customer file. It's invoked when the operator presses the enter key. The other four modules (1400, 1500, 1600, and 1700) use browse commands to read forward or backward through the file.

Module 1400 is invoked when the operator presses PF1. It performs module 1410 to start a browse operation. Because module 1400 moves LOW-VALUE to CM-CUSTOMER-NUMBER, the browse will start at the beginning of the file. As a result, the READNEXT command in module 1420 retrieves the first record in the file.

```
    01   INQUIRY-MAP.
*
         05   FILLER                    PIC X(12).
*
         05   IM-L-CUSTOMER-NUMBER      PIC S9(4)    COMP.
         05   IM-A-CUSTOMER-NUMBER      PIC X.
         05   IM-D-CUSTOMER-NUMBER      PIC X(5).
*
         05   IM-L-NAME                 PIC S9(4)    COMP.
         05   IM-A-NAME                 PIC X.
         05   IM-D-NAME                 PIC X(30).
*
         05   IM-L-ADDRESS              PIC S9(4)    COMP.
         05   IM-A-ADDRESS              PIC X.
         05   IM-D-ADDRESS              PIC X(30).
*
         05   IM-L-CITY                 PIC S9(4)    COMP.
         05   IM-A-CITY                 PIC X.
         05   IM-D-CITY                 PIC X(21).
*
         05   IM-L-STATE                PIC S9(4)    COMP.
         05   IM-A-STATE                PIC X.
         05   IM-D-STATE                PIC XX.
*
         05   IM-L-ZIP-CODE             PIC S9(4)    COMP.
         05   IM-A-ZIP-CODE             PIC X.
         05   IM-D-ZIP-CODE             PIC X(5).
*
         05   IM-L-ERROR-MESSAGE        PIC S9(4)    COMP.
         05   IM-A-ERROR-MESSAGE        PIC X.
         05   IM-D-ERROR-MESSAGE        PIC X(77).
*
         05   IM-L-DUMMY                PIC S9(4)    COMP.
         05   IM-A-DUMMY                PIC X.
         05   IM-D-DUMMY                PIC X.
```

Figure 1-16   Programmer-generated symbolic map for the customer-inquiry program (INQSET1)

When the operator presses PF2, module 1500 is invoked. It retrieves the last record in the file by moving HIGH-VALUE to CM-CUSTOMER-NUMBER, performing module 1410 to start a browse operation, then performing module 1510, which in turn issues a READPREV command.

Module 1600, performed when the operator presses PF4, retrieves the previous record in sequence by calling modules to (1) issue a STARTBR command, (2) issue a READNEXT command, (3) issue a READPREV command to retrieve the same record retrieved in step 2, and (4) issue another READPREV command to retrieve the previous record.

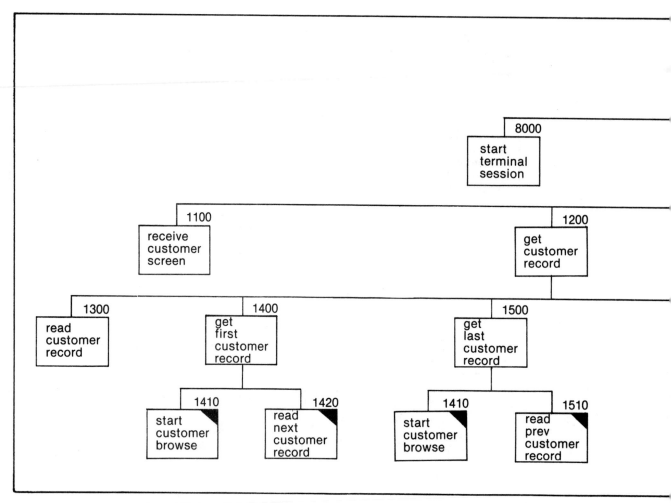

Figure 1-17 Structure chart for the customer-inquiry program

If the operator uses the PF5 key, module 1700 is invoked. This routine moves the customer number from the symbolic map to CM-CUSTOMER-NUMBER and performs module 1410 to start a browse operation. Then, module 1420 is called to read that record. Next, an IF statement checks to see if the READNEXT command in module 1420 retrieved the customer record that's already displayed. If so—and in most cases it is—module 1420 is invoked again to retrieve the next customer record.

There's one case where the customer number fields in the customer record and the symbolic map won't match after the first execution of module 1420. That's when the operator presses PF5

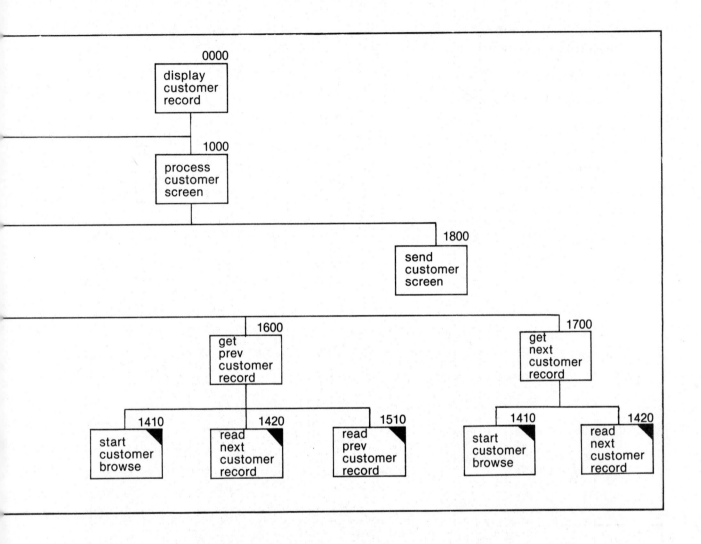

after entering a customer number that does *not* exist in the file. For example, suppose the file contains records with these customer numbers: 10002, 10005, and 10006. If the operator enters 10003 and presses PF5, the STARTBR command sets up the READNEXT command to retrieve customer 10005, because 10003 doesn't exist. If module 1420 were invoked twice, though, customer 10006 would be displayed instead of customer 10005.

Terminology

browse
browse command

```
     IDENTIFICATION DIVISION.
*
     PROGRAM-ID. CUSTINQ1.
*
     ENVIRONMENT DIVISION.
*
     DATA DIVISION.
*
     WORKING-STORAGE SECTION.
*
     01   SWITCHES.
*
          05   END-SESSION-SW        PIC X          VALUE 'N'.
               88   END-SESSION                     VALUE 'Y'.
          05   CUSTOMER-FOUND-SW     PIC X          VALUE 'Y'.
               88   CUSTOMER-FOUND                  VALUE 'Y'.
*
     01   FLAGS.
*
          05   PF-KEY-FLAG           PIC X          VALUE '0'.
               88   ENTER-KEY                       VALUE '0'.
               88   PF-KEY-1                        VALUE '1'.
               88   PF-KEY-2                        VALUE '2'.
               88   PF-KEY-4                        VALUE '4'.
               88   PF-KEY-5                        VALUE '5'.
               88   INVALID-KEY                     VALUE SPACE.
*
     01   COMMUNICATION-AREA         PIC X          VALUE SPACE.
*
     01   CUSTOMER-MASTER-RECORD.
*
          05   CM-CUSTOMER-NUMBER    PIC X(5).
          05   CM-NAME               PIC X(30).
          05   CM-ADDRESS            PIC X(30).
          05   CM-CITY               PIC X(21).
          05   CM-STATE              PIC XX.
          05   CM-ZIP-CODE           PIC X(5).
*
     COPY INQSET1.
*
     LINKAGE SECTION.
*
     01   DFHCOMMAREA                PIC X.
```

Figure 1-18   Source listing for the customer-inquiry program (part 1 of 6)

Objective

Given specifications for a CICS program that retrieves records from a file sequentially, code an acceptable program using the browse commands this chapter presents.

```
*
 PROCEDURE DIVISION.
*
 0000-DISPLAY-CUSTOMER-RECORD SECTION.
*
     MOVE LOW-VALUE TO INQUIRY-MAP.
     IF EIBCALEN = ZERO
         PERFORM 8000-START-TERMINAL-SESSION
     ELSE
         PERFORM 1000-PROCESS-CUSTOMER-SCREEN.
     IF END-SESSION
         EXEC CICS
             XCTL PROGRAM('INVMENU')
         END-EXEC
     ELSE
         EXEC CICS
             RETURN TRANSID('INQ1')
                    COMMAREA(COMMUNICATION-AREA)
                    LENGTH(1)
         END-EXEC.
*
 1000-PROCESS-CUSTOMER-SCREEN SECTION.
*
     PERFORM 1100-RECEIVE-CUSTOMER-SCREEN.
     IF NOT END-SESSION
         PERFORM 1200-GET-CUSTOMER-RECORD
         MOVE CM-CUSTOMER-NUMBER TO IM-D-CUSTOMER-NUMBER
         MOVE CM-NAME            TO IM-D-NAME
         MOVE CM-ADDRESS         TO IM-D-ADDRESS
         MOVE CM-CITY            TO IM-D-CITY
         MOVE CM-STATE           TO IM-D-STATE
         MOVE CM-ZIP-CODE        TO IM-D-ZIP-CODE
         PERFORM 1800-SEND-CUSTOMER-SCREEN.
*
 1100-RECEIVE-CUSTOMER-SCREEN SECTION.
*
     EXEC CICS
         HANDLE AID CLEAR(1100-CLEAR-KEY)
                    PF1(1100-PF1-KEY)
                    PF2(1100-PF2-KEY)
                    PF4(1100-PF4-KEY)
                    PF5(1100-PF5-KEY)
                    ANYKEY(1100-ANYKEY)
     END-EXEC.
     EXEC CICS
         RECEIVE MAP('INQMAP1')
                 MAPSET('INQSET1')
                 INTO(INQUIRY-MAP)
     END-EXEC.
     GO TO 1100-EXIT.
```

Figure 1-18   Source listing for the customer-inquiry program (part 2 of 6)

```
 *
 1100-CLEAR-KEY.
 *

     MOVE 'Y' TO END-SESSION-SW.
     GO TO 1100-EXIT.
 *
 1100-PF1-KEY.
 *

     MOVE '1' TO PF-KEY-FLAG.
     GO TO 1100-EXIT.
 *
 1100-PF2-KEY.
 *

     MOVE '2' TO PF-KEY-FLAG.
     GO TO 1100-EXIT.
 *
 1100-PF4-KEY.
 *

     MOVE '4' TO PF-KEY-FLAG.
     GO TO 1100-EXIT.
 *
 1100-PF5-KEY.
 *

     MOVE '5' TO PF-KEY-FLAG.
     GO TO 1100-EXIT.
 *
 1100-ANYKEY.
 *

     MOVE SPACE TO PF-KEY-FLAG.
     MOVE 'INVALID KEY PRESSED' TO IM-D-ERROR-MESSAGE.
 *
 1100-EXIT.
 *

     EXIT.
 *
 1200-GET-CUSTOMER-RECORD SECTION.
 *
     MOVE SPACE TO CM-NAME
                   CM-ADDRESS
                   CM-CITY
                   CM-STATE
                   CM-ZIP-CODE.
     IF ENTER-KEY
         MOVE IM-D-CUSTOMER-NUMBER TO CM-CUSTOMER-NUMBER
         PERFORM 1300-READ-CUSTOMER-RECORD
     ELSE IF PF-KEY-1
         PERFORM 1400-GET-FIRST-CUSTOMER-RECORD
     ELSE IF PF-KEY-2
         PERFORM 1500-GET-LAST-CUSTOMER-RECORD
     ELSE IF PF-KEY-4
         PERFORM 1600-GET-PREV-CUSTOMER-RECORD
     ELSE IF PF-KEY-5
         PERFORM 1700-GET-NEXT-CUSTOMER-RECORD.
```

Figure 1-18   Source listing for the customer-inquiry program (part 3 of 6)

```
 *
  1300-READ-CUSTOMER-RECORD SECTION.
 *
      EXEC CICS
          HANDLE CONDITION NOTFND(1300-NOTFND)
      END-EXEC.
      EXEC CICS
          READ DATASET('CUSTMAS')
               INTO(CUSTOMER-MASTER-RECORD)
               RIDFLD(CM-CUSTOMER-NUMBER)
      END-EXEC.
      GO TO 1300-EXIT.
 *
  1300-NOTFND.
 *
      MOVE 'CUSTOMER RECORD NOT FOUND' TO IM-D-ERROR-MESSAGE.
 *
  1300-EXIT.
 *
      EXIT.
 *
  1400-GET-FIRST-CUSTOMER-RECORD SECTION.
 *
      MOVE LOW-VALUE TO CM-CUSTOMER-NUMBER.
      PERFORM 1410-START-CUSTOMER-BROWSE.
      IF CUSTOMER-FOUND
          PERFORM 1420-READ-NEXT-CUSTOMER-RECORD.
 *
  1410-START-CUSTOMER-BROWSE SECTION.
 *
      EXEC CICS
          HANDLE CONDITION NOTFND(1410-NOTFND)
      END-EXEC.
      EXEC CICS
          STARTBR DATASET('CUSTMAS')
                  RIDFLD(CM-CUSTOMER-NUMBER)
      END-EXEC.
      GO TO 1410-EXIT.
 *
  1410-NOTFND.
 *
      MOVE 'N' TO CUSTOMER-FOUND-SW.
      MOVE 'CUSTOMER RECORD NOT FOUND' TO IM-D-ERROR-MESSAGE.
 *
  1410-EXIT.
 *
      EXIT.
```

Figure 1-18   Source listing for the customer-inquiry program (part 4 of 6)

```
 *
  1420-READ-NEXT-CUSTOMER-RECORD SECTION.
 *
      EXEC CICS
          HANDLE CONDITION ENDFILE(1420-ENDFILE)
      END-EXEC.
      EXEC CICS
          READNEXT DATASET('CUSTMAS')
                   INTO(CUSTOMER-MASTER-RECORD)
                   RIDFLD(CM-CUSTOMER-NUMBER)
      END-EXEC.
      GO TO 1420-EXIT.
 *
  1420-ENDFILE.
 *
      MOVE 'THERE ARE NO MORE RECORDS IN THE FILE'
          TO IM-D-ERROR-MESSAGE.
 *
  1420-EXIT.
 *
      EXIT.
 *
  1500-GET-LAST-CUSTOMER-RECORD SECTION.
 *
      MOVE HIGH-VALUE TO CM-CUSTOMER-NUMBER.
      PERFORM 1410-START-CUSTOMER-BROWSE.
      IF CUSTOMER-FOUND
          PERFORM 1510-READ-PREV-CUSTOMER-RECORD.
 *
  1510-READ-PREV-CUSTOMER-RECORD SECTION.
 *
      EXEC CICS
          HANDLE CONDITION ENDFILE(1510-ENDFILE)
      END-EXEC.
      EXEC CICS
          READPREV DATASET('CUSTMAS')
                   INTO(CUSTOMER-MASTER-RECORD)
                   RIDFLD(CM-CUSTOMER-NUMBER)
      END-EXEC.
      GO TO 1510-EXIT.
 *
  1510-ENDFILE.
 *
      MOVE 'THERE ARE NO MORE RECORDS IN THE FILE'
          TO IM-D-ERROR-MESSAGE.
 *
  1510-EXIT.
 *
      EXIT.
```

Figure 1-18   Source listing for the customer-inquiry program (part 5 of 6)

```
*
 1600-GET-PREV-CUSTOMER-RECORD SECTION.
*
     MOVE IM-D-CUSTOMER-NUMBER TO CM-CUSTOMER-NUMBER.
     PERFORM 1410-START-CUSTOMER-BROWSE.
     IF CUSTOMER-FOUND
         PERFORM 1420-READ-NEXT-CUSTOMER-RECORD
         PERFORM 1510-READ-PREV-CUSTOMER-RECORD
         PERFORM 1510-READ-PREV-CUSTOMER-RECORD.
*
 1700-GET-NEXT-CUSTOMER-RECORD SECTION.
*
     MOVE IM-D-CUSTOMER-NUMBER TO CM-CUSTOMER-NUMBER.
     PERFORM 1410-START-CUSTOMER-BROWSE.
     IF CUSTOMER-FOUND
         PERFORM 1420-READ-NEXT-CUSTOMER-RECORD
         IF IM-D-CUSTOMER-NUMBER = CM-CUSTOMER-NUMBER
             PERFORM 1420-READ-NEXT-CUSTOMER-RECORD.
*
 1800-SEND-CUSTOMER-SCREEN SECTION.
*
     EXEC CICS
         SEND MAP('INQMAP1')
             MAPSET('INQSET1')
             FROM(INQUIRY-MAP)
             ERASE
     END-EXEC.
*
 8000-START-TERMINAL-SESSION SECTION.
*
     EXEC CICS
         SEND MAP('INQMAP1')
             MAPSET('INQSET1')
             FROM(INQUIRY-MAP)
             ERASE
     END-EXEC.
```

Figure 1-18   Source listing for the customer-inquiry program (part 6 of 6)

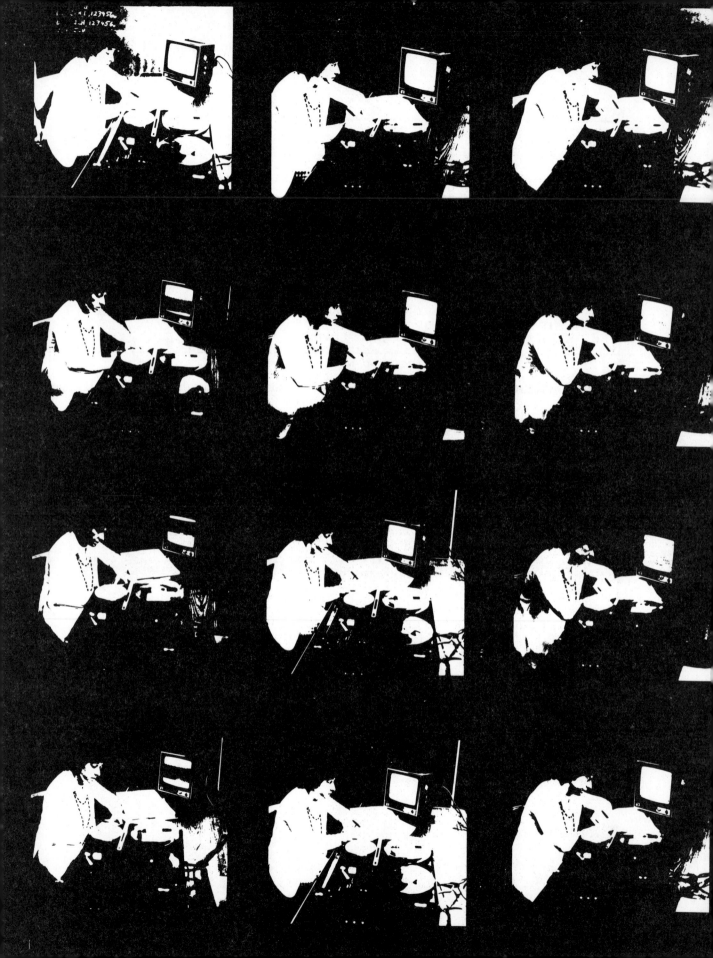

Chapter 2

VSAM
alternate index processing

When you use a simple VSAM key-sequenced file, you can retrieve records directly using basic file-control commands or sequentially using browse commands. In either case, each record in the file is identified by a key value that's maintained in the file's index. Many on-line applications, however, require that you access the records of a key-sequenced file in other sequences as well. When you use key-sequenced files with alternate indexes, you can do just that.

In this chapter, you'll learn how to write CICS programs that process VSAM files with alternate indexes. First, you'll learn some important concepts about alternate indexing. Then, you'll see a sample program that processes a file with an alternate index.

Before I go on, I should point out that this chapter shows you how to process an existing alternate index in a CICS program. To create an alternate index, you use the VSAM Access Method Services (AMS) program. However, AMS is outside the scope of this book, so you'll have to refer to other training materials for a detailed explanation of how to use it.

Alternate indexes

A VSAM *alternate index* lets you access the records of a key-sequenced data set in an order other than that provided by the data

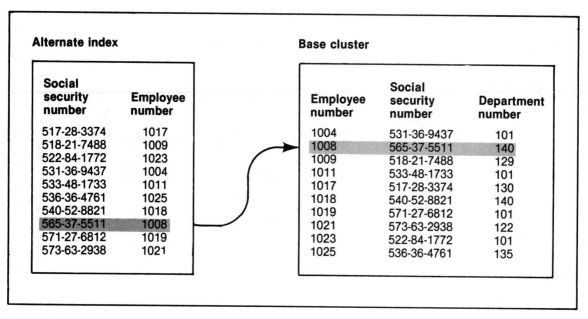

Figure 2-1   An alternate index with unique keys

set's *primary key* (or *base key*). The data set over which an alternate index exists is called a *base cluster*.

To understand the concept of an alternate index, consider figure 2-1. Here, the base cluster is a KSDS containing employee records. Each record of the base cluster contains three fields: employee number, social security number, and department number. The primary key for the base cluster is employee number. As a result, you can access the base cluster sequentially by employee number using the browse commands you learned in chapter 1. Or, you can read any record directly if you know the record's employee number.

The alternate index in figure 2-1 lets you process the base cluster in social security number sequence by relating each *alternate key* value to a primary key value. So, as the shading indicates, when you tell VSAM to retrieve the record for the employee whose social security number is 565-37-5511, VSAM searches the alternate index, retrieves the primary key (1008), and uses that value to locate the correct record in the base cluster.

An alternate index is itself a key-sequenced data set. Its index component contains alternate keys, while the records in its data component contain primary key values for the corresponding records in the base cluster. To simplify the example in figure 2-1, I don't show the index and data components or the control areas and control intervals for the alternate index file or the base cluster.

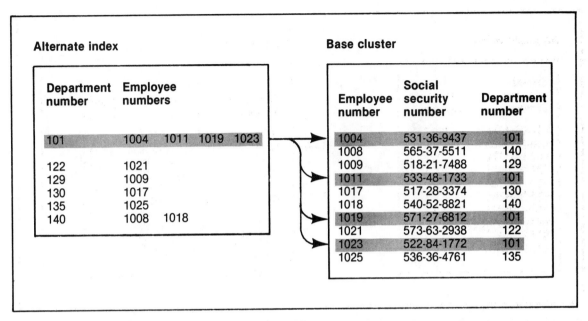

Figure 2-2   An alternate index with duplicate keys

In figure 2-1, each alternate key is associated with one primary key. This type of alternate key is called a *unique key*. In contrast, figure 2-2 illustrates an alternate index with *nonunique*, or *duplicate*, *keys*. Here, the alternate key is department number.

To understand non-unique keys, consider the alternate index record for department number 101. Here, four employee numbers are specified: 1004, 1011, 1019, and 1023. When you use browse commands to process this alternate index sequentially, all four of these employee records are retrieved in turn. However, when an alternate index file with duplicate keys is processed directly, only the *first* base cluster record for each alternate key value is available.

Path

Before you can process a base cluster using an alternate index, you must define a VSAM catalog entry called a *path* to establish a relationship between an alternate index and its base cluster. Figure 2-3 illustrates this relationship for the alternate indexes in figures 2-1 and 2-2. Here, two alternate indexes (SSNAIX and DEPAIX) are defined for a single base cluster (EMPMAST). Each alternate index is related to the base cluster through a path (SSNPATH and DEPPATH).

To process a base cluster through an alternate index, you actually process the path. So, as you'll see in the program example later in this

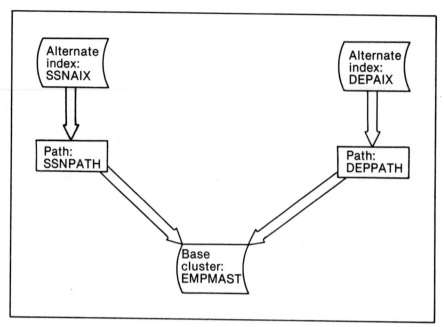

Figure 2-3   The relationships among alternate indexes, paths, and a base cluster

chapter, you specify a path name rather than a file name in the DATASET parameter of file-control commands you issue for alternate index files. Otherwise, the CICS commands you code to process an alternate index file are the same as those you'd code to process a non-alternate index file.

Upgrade set

You would expect that any change you make to the data component of a base cluster would be reflected not only in the base cluster's index component but also in any associated alternate indexes. For example, consider figure 2-4. Here, a record for employee 1013 is added to the base cluster. As the shading indicates, both alternate indexes are updated as well: a new entry is made in the social security number alternate index, and the entry for department 101 in the department number alternate index is extended.

In VSAM, the process of updating an alternate index is called *upgrading*. VSAM doesn't require that an alternate index be upgraded each time its base cluster is changed. An alternate index is an *upgradable index* if you specify (via AMS) that it should be automatically upgraded by VSAM whenever changes are made to the

Base cluster

Employee number	Social security number	Department number
1004	531-36-9437	101
1008	565-37-5511	140
1009	518-21-7488	129
1011	533-48-1733	101
1013	552-57-2735	101
1017	517-28-3374	130
1018	540-52-8821	140
1019	571-27-6812	101
1021	573-63-2938	122
1023	522-84-1772	101
1025	536-36-4761	135

Alternate index (social security number)

Social security number	Employee number
517-28-3374	1017
518-21-7488	1009
522-84-1772	1023
531-36-9437	1004
533-48-1733	1011
536-36-4761	1025
540-52-8821	1018
552-57-2735	1013
565-37-5511	1008
571-27-6812	1019
573-63-2938	1021

Alternate index (department number)

Department number	Employee numbers				
101	1004	1011	1019	1023	1013
122	1021				
129	1009				
130	1017				
135	1025				
140	1008	1018			

Figure 2-4   Base cluster and alternate indexes after insertion of employee number 1013

base cluster. The collection of upgradable alternate indexes for a base cluster is called the base cluster's *upgrade set*. Every time a change is made to the base cluster that affects the alternate indexes, each affected alternate index in the upgrade set is automatically upgraded by VSAM.

Whether an alternate index is upgradable has no effect on how you code your CICS programs. But you should realize that if an alternate index is not upgradable, some changes made to the base cluster won't be reflected in the alternate index until the alternate index is recreated. Normally, alternate indexes—both upgradable and nonupgradable—are recreated on a regular basis, perhaps nightly.

One other point you should realize has to do with the way upgradable alternate indexes are maintained. Notice in figure 2-4 where the entry for employee 1013 was made in the department-number alternate index. Initially, entries for alternate keys with multiple prime key values are made in prime-key sequence. So the entries for department 101 were stored in this sequence: 1004, 1011, 1019, and 1023. Unfortunately, VSAM maintains upgrades in the order in which they're made, not in prime-key sequence. As a result, employee 1013 is at the end of the entries for department 101, rather than between the entries for employees 1011 and 1019. So if you try to process the employee master file sequentially using the department number alternate index, you will *not* receive records in employee-number within department-number sequence.

To return the alternate index entries to prime-key sequence, alternate indexes are generally rebuilt during off hours, even if they are upgradable. Since making an index upgradable doesn't always save additional processing, alternate indexes are generally *not* upgradable unless they really need to be.

An enhanced customer-inquiry program

Now that you understand what an alternate index is, you're ready to learn how to write programs that process alternate index files. Figures 2-5 through 2-10 present a customer-inquiry program that lets an operator display customer information retrieved from two files: a customer master file and an invoice file. This program is an enhancement of the inquiry program presented in chapter 1, which retrieved data from the customer master file only. The program in this chapter displays not just customer information, but related invoices for each displayed customer as well. To do this, it uses an alternate index that's based on the customer number field contained in the invoice records.

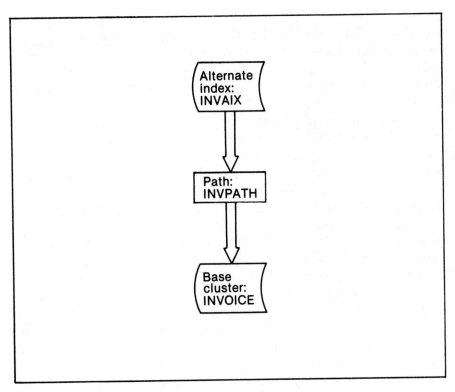

Figure 2-5   The invoice file and its alternate index and path

Figure 2-5 shows the relationship of the invoice file's base cluster to its alternate index and path. To access the invoice file via its alternate index, you specify the path name (INVPATH) in the DATASET parameter of any file-control commands for the file.

Figure 2-6 is the screen layout for this program. As you can see, it's similar to the screen layout for the inquiry program presented in chapter 1. However, it provides an area for displaying information for up to ten invoices for each customer. Figure 2-7 presents the BMS mapset for this program, and figure 2-8 gives the symbolic map I created. Because the repeated invoice line is defined with an OCCURS clause, the program must use a subscript to access each individual invoice line.

Before I go on, I want to point out that an actual production program like this would provide for displaying more invoices than will fit on one screen. Although that's a reasonable requirement for a production program, it makes the program's logic more complicated without illustrating any additional CICS elements related to alternate indexing. So, to help you focus more on the coding requirements for alternate indexes, this program displays a maximum of ten invoices for each customer—that's just enough to fit on one screen.

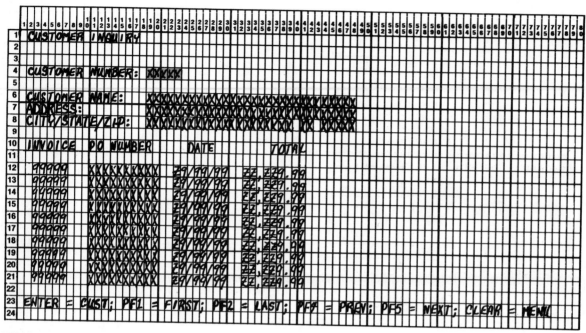

Figure 2-6   Screen layout for the enhanced customer-inquiry program

Figure 2-9 presents the structure chart for this program. Again, it's similar to the structure chart for the inquiry program in chapter 1. In fact, the only difference is that I've added three modules (1800, 1810, and 1820) and I've renumbered module 1900 to allow for the new modules. Module 1800 is invoked to retrieve the invoices for the specified customer. It invokes module 1810 to start a browse operation, then invokes module 1820 to read the invoice records.

Figure 2-10 is the complete source listing for this program. If you need a refresher on the basic operation of this program, refer to chapter 1. I want to concentrate here on the elements required to access the invoice file via its path. In other words, I'm going to focus on module 1800 and its subordinates.

Module 1800 begins by invoking module 1810, which initiates a browse operation with this command:

```
EXEC CICS
    STARTBR DATASET('INVPATH')
            RIDFLD(CM-CUSTOMER-NUMBER)
            EQUAL
END-EXEC.
```

```
          PRINT NOGEN
INQSET2   DFHMSD TYPE=&SYSPARM,                                             X
                 LANG=COBOL,                                                X
                 MODE=INOUT,                                                X
                 TERM=3270-2,                                               X
                 CTRL=FREEKB,                                               X
                 STORAGE=AUTO,                                              X
                 TIOAPFX=YES
*********************************************************************************
INQMAP1   DFHMDI SIZE=(24,80),                                             X
                 LINE=1,                                                    X
                 COLUMN=1
*********************************************************************************
          DFHMDF POS=(1,1),                                                X
                 LENGTH=16,                                                 X
                 ATTRB=(BRT,PROT),                                          X
                 INITIAL='CUSTOMER INQUIRY'
*********************************************************************************
          DFHMDF POS=(4,1),                                                X
                 LENGTH=16,                                                 X
                 ATTRB=(BRT,PROT),                                          X
                 INITIAL='CUSTOMER NUMBER:'
NUMBER    DFHMDF POS=(4,18),                                               X
                 LENGTH=5,                                                  X
                 ATTRB=(IC,UNPROT,FSET)
          DFHMDF POS=(4,24),                                               X
                 LENGTH=1,                                                  X
                 ATTRB=ASKIP
*********************************************************************************
          DFHMDF POS=(6,1),                                                X
                 LENGTH=16,                                                 X
                 ATTRB=(BRT,PROT),                                          X
                 INITIAL='CUSTOMER NAME:'
NAME      DFHMDF POS=(6,18),                                               X
                 LENGTH=30,                                                 X
                 ATTRB=PROT
*********************************************************************************
          DFHMDF POS=(7,1),                                                X
                 LENGTH=8,                                                  X
                 ATTRB=(BRT,PROT),                                          X
                 INITIAL='ADDRESS:'
ADDRESS   DFHMDF POS=(7,18),                                               X
                 LENGTH=30,                                                 X
                 ATTRB=PROT
*********************************************************************************
          DFHMDF POS=(8,1),                                                X
                 LENGTH=15,                                                 X
                 ATTRB=(BRT,PROT),                                          X
                 INITIAL='CITY/STATE/ZIP:'
CITY      DFHMDF POS=(8,18),                                               X
                 LENGTH=21,                                                 X
                 ATTRB=PROT
```

Figure 2-7   Mapset listing for the enhanced customer-inquiry program (part 1 of 2)

```
STATE       DFHMDF POS=(8,40),                                            X
                   LENGTH=2,                                              X
                   ATTRB=PROT
ZIP         DFHMDF POS=(8,43),                                            X
                   LENGTH=5,                                              X
                   ATTRB=PROT
************************************************************************************
            DFHMDF POS=(10,1),                                           X
                   LENGTH=40,                                            X
                   ATTRB=(BRT,PROT),                                     X
                   INITIAL='INVOICE   PO NUMBER      DATE      TOTAL'
************************************************************************************
*           LINE 1
************************************************************************************
INVNO1      DFHMDF POS=(12,2),                                           X
                   LENGTH=5,                                             X
                   ATTRB=PROT
PO1         DFHMDF POS=(12,10),                                          X
                   LENGTH=10,                                            X
                   ATTRB=PROT
DATE1       DFHMDF POS=(12,22),                                          X
                   LENGTH=8,                                             X
                   ATTRB=PROT,                                           X
                   PICOUT='Z9/99/99'
TOT1        DFHMDF POS=(12,32),                                          X
                   LENGTH=9,                                             X
                   ATTRB=PROT,                                           X
                   PICOUT='ZZ,ZZ9.99'


            The BMS macro instructions that define
            invoice lines 2 through 10 are similar
            to those that define line 1.


************************************************************************************
************************************************************************************
            DFHMDF POS=(23,1),                                           X
                   LENGTH=75,                                            X
                   ATTRB=(BRT,PROT),                                     X
                   INITIAL='ENTER = CUST; PF1 = FIRST; PF2 = LAST; PF4 = PRX
            EV; PF5 = NEXT; CLEAR = MENU'
ERROR       DFHMDF POS=(24,1),                                           X
                   LENGTH=77,                                            X
                   ATTRB=(BRT,PROT)
DUMMY       DFHMDF POS=(24,79),                                          X
                   LENGTH=1,                                             X
                   ATTRB=(DRK,PROT,FSET),                                X
                   INITIAL=' '
************************************************************************************
            DFHMSD TYPE=FINAL
            END
```

Figure 2-7   Mapset listing for the enhanced customer-inquiry program (part 2 of 2)

```
01    INQUIRY-MAP.
*
      05    FILLER                    PIC X(12).
*
      05    IM-L-CUSTOMER-NUMBER      PIC S9(4)      COMP.
      05    IM-A-CUSTOMER-NUMBER      PIC X.
      05    IM-D-CUSTOMER-NUMBER      PIC X(5).
*
      05    IM-L-NAME                 PIC S9(4)      COMP.
      05    IM-A-NAME                 PIC X.
      05    IM-D-NAME                 PIC X(30).
*
      05    IM-L-ADDRESS              PIC S9(4)      COMP.
      05    IM-A-ADDRESS              PIC X.
      05    IM-D-ADDRESS              PIC X(30).
*
      05    IM-L-CITY                 PIC S9(4)      COMP.
      05    IM-A-CITY                 PIC X.
      05    IM-D-CITY                 PIC X(21).
*
      05    IM-L-STATE                PIC S9(4)      COMP.
      05    IM-A-STATE                PIC X.
      05    IM-D-STATE                PIC XX.
*
      05    IM-L-ZIP-CODE             PIC S9(4)      COMP.
      05    IM-A-ZIP-CODE             PIC X.
      05    IM-D-ZIP-CODE             PIC X(5).
*
      05    IM-INVOICE-GROUP          OCCURS 10.
*
      10    IM-L-INVOICE-NUMBER PIC S9(4)      COMP.
      10    IM-A-INVOICE-NUMBER PIC X.
      10    IM-D-INVOICE-NUMBER PIC 9(5).
*
      10    IM-L-PO-NUMBER      PIC S9(4)      COMP.
      10    IM-A-PO-NUMBER      PIC X.
      10    IM-D-PO-NUMBER      PIC X(10).
*
      10    IM-L-INVOICE-DATE   PIC S9(4)      COMP.
      10    IM-A-INVOICE-DATE   PIC X.
      10    IM-D-INVOICE-DATE   PIC Z9/99/99.
*
      10    IM-L-INVOICE-TOTAL  PIC S9(4)      COMP.
      10    IM-A-INVOICE-TOTAL  PIC X.
      10    IM-D-INVOICE-TOTAL  PIC ZZ,ZZ9.99.
*
      05    IM-L-ERROR-MESSAGE        PIC S9(4)      COMP.
      05    IM-A-ERROR-MESSAGE        PIC X.
      05    IM-D-ERROR-MESSAGE        PIC X(77).
*
      05    IM-L-DUMMY                PIC S9(4)      COMP.
      05    IM-A-DUMMY                PIC X.
      05    IM-D-DUMMY                PIC X.
```

Figure 2-8   Programmer-generated symbolic map for the enhanced customer-inquiry program (INQSET2)

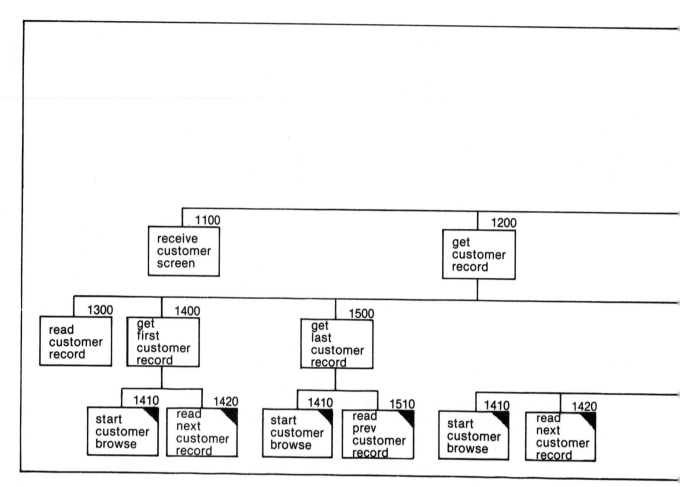

Figure 2-9   Structure chart for the enhanced customer-inquiry program

Here, the DATASET parameter specifies INVPATH, not INVOICE, as the input file. As a result, this command begins a browse operation using the file's alternate key, not its primary key. The RIDFLD parameter specifies CM-CUSTOMER-NUMBER, which contains the primary key of the customer record to be displayed. Notice that CM-CUSTOMER-NUMBER is a field within the customer record, not the invoice record. That makes good sense: the program is retrieving all of the invoice records that relate to a particular customer record.

Because I specify EQUAL on the STARTBR command, the NOTFND condition is raised if there are no records in the invoice file for the specified customer. In the NOTFND routine, I move 'N' to a switch named MORE-INVOICES-SW. As you'll see in a moment, I use this switch to control how many invoice records should be read. If you'll check in the Working-Storage Section, you'll see that the initial value of this switch is Y. And since this is a pseudo-conversational

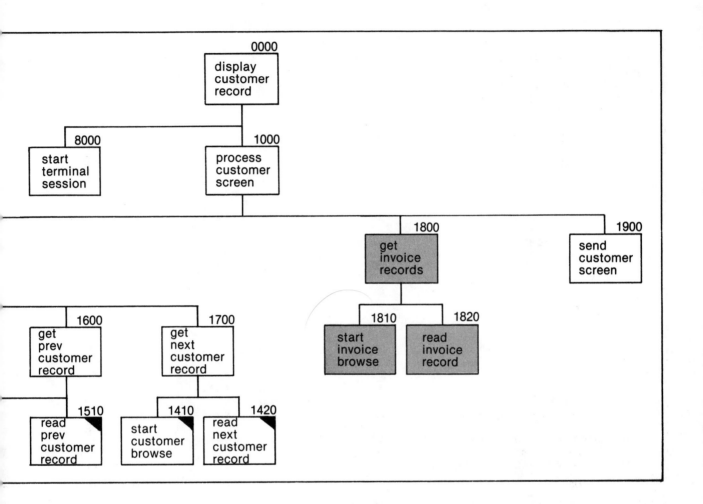

program, the switch value is restored to Y each time the program is invoked. Module 1810 changes the switch to N only if the STARTBR command doesn't find a record.

If the STARTBR command in module 1810 finds an invoice record for the customer, module 1800 invokes module 1820 with this statement:

```
PERFORM 1820-READ-INVOICE-RECORD
    VARYING INVOICE-SUB FROM 1 BY 1
    UNTIL    INVOICE-SUB > 10
         OR NOT MORE-INVOICES.
```

As a result, module 1820 is performed up to ten times to retrieve invoice records. If there are fewer than 10 invoice records for the specified customer, module 1820 turns MORE-INVOICES-SW off, and the PERFORM loop ends.

```
IDENTIFICATION DIVISION.
*
PROGRAM-ID. CUSTINQ2.
*
ENVIRONMENT DIVISION.
*
DATA DIVISION.
*
WORKING-STORAGE SECTION.
*
01  SWITCHES.
*
    05  END-SESSION-SW          PIC X           VALUE 'N'.
        88  END-SESSION                         VALUE 'Y'.
    05  CUSTOMER-FOUND-SW        PIC X           VALUE 'Y'.
        88  CUSTOMER-FOUND                      VALUE 'Y'.
    05  MORE-INVOICES-SW        PIC X           VALUE 'Y'.
        88  MORE-INVOICES                       VALUE 'Y'.
*
01  FLAGS.
*
    05  PF-KEY-FLAG             PIC X           VALUE '0'.
        88  ENTER-KEY                           VALUE '0'.
        88  PF-KEY-1                            VALUE '1'.
        88  PF-KEY-2                            VALUE '2'.
        88  PF-KEY-4                            VALUE '4'.
        88  PF-KEY-5                            VALUE '5'.
        88  INVALID-KEY                         VALUE SPACE.
*
01  COMMUNICATION-AREA         PIC X           VALUE SPACE.
*
01  CUSTOMER-MASTER-RECORD.
*
    05  CM-CUSTOMER-NUMBER      PIC X(5).
    05  CM-NAME                 PIC X(30).
    05  CM-ADDRESS              PIC X(30).
    05  CM-CITY                 PIC X(21).
    05  CM-STATE                PIC XX.
    05  CM-ZIP-CODE             PIC X(5).
*
01  INVOICE-RECORD.
*
    05  INV-INVOICE-NUMBER      PIC 9(5).
    05  INV-INVOICE-DATE        PIC 9(6).
    05  INV-CUSTOMER-NUMBER     PIC X(5).
    05  INV-PO-NUMBER           PIC X(10).
    05  INV-LINE-ITEM           OCCURS 10.
        10  INV-ITEM-NUMBER     PIC 9(5).
        10  INV-QUANTITY        PIC S9(5)       COMP-3.
        10  INV-UNIT-PRICE      PIC S9(5)V99    COMP-3.
        10  INV-EXTENSION       PIC S9(5)V99    COMP-3.
    05  INV-INVOICE-TOTAL       PIC S9(5)V99    COMP-3.
```

Figure 2-10   Source listing for the enhanced customer-inquiry program (part 1 of 7)

```
*
 01    INVOICE-SUB                        PIC S9(4)          COMP.
*
 COPY INQSET2.
*
 LINKAGE SECTION.
*
 01    DFHCOMMAREA                        PIC X.
*
 PROCEDURE DIVISION.
*
 0000-DISPLAY-CUSTOMER-RECORD SECTION.
*
      MOVE LOW-VALUE TO INQUIRY-MAP.
      IF EIBCALEN = ZERO
          PERFORM 8000-START-TERMINAL-SESSION
      ELSE
          PERFORM 1000-PROCESS-CUSTOMER-SCREEN.
      IF END-SESSION
          EXEC CICS
              XCTL PROGRAM('INVMENU')
          END-EXEC
      ELSE
          EXEC CICS
              RETURN TRANSID('INQ2')
                     COMMAREA(COMMUNICATION-AREA)
                     LENGTH(1)
          END-EXEC.
*
 1000-PROCESS-CUSTOMER-SCREEN SECTION.
*
      PERFORM 1100-RECEIVE-CUSTOMER-SCREEN.
      IF NOT END-SESSION
          PERFORM 1200-GET-CUSTOMER-RECORD
          PERFORM 1800-GET-INVOICE-RECORDS
          MOVE CM-CUSTOMER-NUMBER  TO IM-D-CUSTOMER-NUMBER
          MOVE CM-NAME             TO IM-D-NAME
          MOVE CM-ADDRESS          TO IM-D-ADDRESS
          MOVE CM-CITY             TO IM-D-CITY
          MOVE CM-STATE            TO IM-D-STATE
          MOVE CM-ZIP-CODE         TO IM-D-ZIP-CODE
          PERFORM 1900-SEND-CUSTOMER-SCREEN.
*
 1100-RECEIVE-CUSTOMER-SCREEN SECTION.
*
      EXEC CICS
          HANDLE AID CLEAR(1100-CLEAR-KEY)
                     PF1(1100-PF1-KEY)
                     PF2(1100-PF2-KEY)
                     PF4(1100-PF4-KEY)
                     PF5(1100-PF5-KEY)
                     ANYKEY(1100-ANYKEY)
      END-EXEC.
```

Figure 2-10   Source listing for the enhanced customer-inquiry program (part 2 of 7)

```
        EXEC CICS
            RECEIVE MAP('INQMAP1')
                    MAPSET('INQSET2')
                    INTO(INQUIRY-MAP)
        END-EXEC.
        GO TO 1100-EXIT.
*
    1100-CLEAR-KEY.
*
        MOVE 'Y' TO END-SESSION-SW.
        GO TO 1100-EXIT.
*
    1100-PF1-KEY.
*
        MOVE '1' TO PF-KEY-FLAG.
        GO TO 1100-EXIT.
*
    1100-PF2-KEY.
*
        MOVE '2' TO PF-KEY-FLAG.
        GO TO 1100-EXIT.
*
    1100-PF4-KEY.
*
        MOVE '4' TO PF-KEY-FLAG.
        GO TO 1100-EXIT.
*
    1100-PF5-KEY.
*
        MOVE '5' TO PF-KEY-FLAG.
        GO TO 1100-EXIT.
*
    1100-ANYKEY.
*
        MOVE SPACE TO PF-KEY-FLAG.
        MOVE 'INVALID KEY PRESSED' TO IM-D-ERROR-MESSAGE.
*
    1100-EXIT.
*
        EXIT.
*
    1200-GET-CUSTOMER-RECORD SECTION.
*
        MOVE SPACE TO CM-NAME
                      CM-ADDRESS
                      CM-CITY
                      CM-STATE
                      CM-ZIP-CODE.
```

Figure 2-10   Source listing for the enhanced customer-inquiry program (part 3 of 7)

```
        IF ENTER-KEY
            MOVE IM-D-CUSTOMER-NUMBER TO CM-CUSTOMER-NUMBER
            PERFORM 1300-READ-CUSTOMER-RECORD
        ELSE IF PF-KEY-1
            PERFORM 1400-GET-FIRST-CUSTOMER-RECORD
        ELSE IF PF-KEY-2
            PERFORM 1500-GET-LAST-CUSTOMER-RECORD
        ELSE IF PF-KEY-4
            PERFORM 1600-GET-PREV-CUSTOMER-RECORD
        ELSE IF PF-KEY-5
            PERFORM 1700-GET-NEXT-CUSTOMER-RECORD.
*
 1300-READ-CUSTOMER-RECORD SECTION.
*
     EXEC CICS
         HANDLE CONDITION NOTFND(1300-NOTFND)
     END-EXEC.
     EXEC CICS
         READ DATASET('CUSTMAS')
             INTO(CUSTOMER-MASTER-RECORD)
             RIDFLD(CM-CUSTOMER-NUMBER)
     END-EXEC.
     GO TO 1300-EXIT.
*
 1300-NOTFND.
*
     MOVE 'CUSTOMER RECORD NOT FOUND' TO IM-D-ERROR-MESSAGE.
*
 1300-EXIT.
*
     EXIT.
*
 1400-GET-FIRST-CUSTOMER-RECORD SECTION.
*
     MOVE LOW-VALUE TO CM-CUSTOMER-NUMBER.
     PERFORM 1410-START-CUSTOMER-BROWSE.
     IF CUSTOMER-FOUND
         PERFORM 1420-READ-NEXT-CUSTOMER-RECORD.
*
 1410-START-CUSTOMER-BROWSE SECTION.
*
     EXEC CICS
         HANDLE CONDITION NOTFND(1410-NOTFND)
     END-EXEC.
     EXEC CICS
         STARTBR DATASET('CUSTMAS')
                 RIDFLD(CM-CUSTOMER-NUMBER)
     END-EXEC.
     GO TO 1410-EXIT.
```

Figure 2-10   Source listing for the enhanced customer-inquiry program (part 4 of 7)

```
*
 1410-NOTFND.
*
     MOVE 'N' TO CUSTOMER-FOUND-SW.
     MOVE 'CUSTOMER RECORD NOT FOUND' TO IM-D-ERROR-MESSAGE.
*
 1410-EXIT.
*
     EXIT.
*
 1420-READ-NEXT-CUSTOMER-RECORD SECTION.
*
     EXEC CICS
         HANDLE CONDITION ENDFILE(1420-ENDFILE)
     END-EXEC.
     EXEC CICS
         READNEXT DATASET('CUSTMAS')
                  INTO(CUSTOMER-MASTER-RECORD)
                  RIDFLD(CM-CUSTOMER-NUMBER)
     END-EXEC.
     GO TO 1420-EXIT.
*
 1420-ENDFILE.
*
     MOVE 'THERE ARE NO MORE RECORDS IN THE FILE'
          TO IM-D-ERROR-MESSAGE.
*
 1420-EXIT.
*
     EXIT.
*
 1500-GET-LAST-CUSTOMER-RECORD SECTION.
*
     MOVE HIGH-VALUE TO CM-CUSTOMER-NUMBER.
     PERFORM 1410-START-CUSTOMER-BROWSE.
     IF CUSTOMER-FOUND
         PERFORM 1510-READ-PREV-CUSTOMER-RECORD.
*
 1510-READ-PREV-CUSTOMER-RECORD SECTION.
*
     EXEC CICS
         HANDLE CONDITION ENDFILE(1510-ENDFILE)
     END-EXEC.
     EXEC CICS
         READPREV DATASET('CUSTMAS')
                  INTO(CUSTOMER-MASTER-RECORD)
                  RIDFLD(CM-CUSTOMER-NUMBER)
     END-EXEC.
     GO TO 1510-EXIT.
*
 1510-ENDFILE.
*
     MOVE 'THERE ARE NO MORE RECORDS IN THE FILE'
          TO IM-D-ERROR-MESSAGE.
```

Figure 2-10   Source listing for the enhanced customer-inquiry program (part 5 of 7)

```
*
 1510-EXIT.
*
     EXIT.
*
 1600-GET-PREV-CUSTOMER-RECORD SECTION.
*
     MOVE IM-D-CUSTOMER-NUMBER TO CM-CUSTOMER-NUMBER.
     PERFORM 1410-START-CUSTOMER-BROWSE.
     IF CUSTOMER-FOUND
         PERFORM 1420-READ-NEXT-CUSTOMER-RECORD
         PERFORM 1510-READ-PREV-CUSTOMER-RECORD
         PERFORM 1510-READ-PREV-CUSTOMER-RECORD.
*
 1700-GET-NEXT-CUSTOMER-RECORD SECTION.
*
     MOVE IM-D-CUSTOMER-NUMBER TO CM-CUSTOMER-NUMBER.
     PERFORM 1410-START-CUSTOMER-BROWSE.
     IF CUSTOMER-FOUND
         PERFORM 1420-READ-NEXT-CUSTOMER-RECORD
     IF IM-D-CUSTOMER-NUMBER = CM-CUSTOMER-NUMBER
             PERFORM 1420-READ-NEXT-CUSTOMER-RECORD.
*
 1800-GET-INVOICE-RECORDS SECTION.
*
     PERFORM 1810-START-INVOICE-BROWSE.
     EXEC CICS
         HANDLE CONDITION DUPKEY(1820-DUPKEY)
     END-EXEC.
     PERFORM 1820-READ-INVOICE-RECORD
         VARYING INVOICE-SUB FROM 1 BY 1
         UNTIL    INVOICE-SUB > 10
             OR NOT MORE-INVOICES.
*
 1810-START-INVOICE-BROWSE SECTION.
*
     EXEC CICS
         HANDLE CONDITION NOTFND(1810-NOTFND)
     END-EXEC.
     EXEC CICS
         STARTBR DATASET('INVPATH')
                 RIDFLD(CM-CUSTOMER-NUMBER)
                 EQUAL
     END-EXEC.
     GO TO 1810-EXIT.
*
 1810-NOTFND.
*
     MOVE 'N' TO MORE-INVOICES-SW.
*
 1810-EXIT.
*
     EXIT.
```

Figure 2-10   Source listing for the enhanced customer-inquiry program (part 6 of 7)

```
✿
  1820-READ-INVOICE-RECORD SECTION.
✿
      EXEC CICS
          READNEXT DATASET('INVPATH')
                   INTO(INVOICE-RECORD)
                   RIDFLD(CM-CUSTOMER-NUMBER)
      END-EXEC.
      MOVE 'N' TO MORE-INVOICES-SW.
✿
  1820-DUPKEY.
✿
      MOVE INV-INVOICE-NUMBER TO IM-D-INVOICE-NUMBER(INVOICE-SUB).
      MOVE INV-PO-NUMBER      TO IM-D-PO-NUMBER(INVOICE-SUB).
      MOVE INV-INVOICE-DATE   TO IM-D-INVOICE-DATE(INVOICE-SUB).
      MOVE INV-INVOICE-TOTAL  TO IM-D-INVOICE-TOTAL(INVOICE-SUB).
✿
  1820-EXIT.
✿
      EXIT.
✿
  1900-SEND-CUSTOMER-SCREEN SECTION.
✿
      EXEC CICS
          SEND MAP('INQMAP1')
               MAPSET('INQSET2')
               FROM(INQUIRY-MAP)
               ERASE
      END-EXEC.
✿
  8000-START-TERMINAL-SESSION SECTION.
✿
      MOVE LOW-VALUE TO INQUIRY-MAP.
      EXEC CICS
          SEND MAP('INQMAP1')
               MAPSET('INQSET2')
               FROM(INQUIRY-MAP)
               ERASE
      END-EXEC.
```

Figure 2-10   Source listing for the enhanced customer-inquiry program (part 7 of 7)

In module 1820, you can see the one significant CICS variation for processing alternate index files: the DUPKEY condition. The DUPKEY condition is raised whenever you issue a READ, READNEXT, or READPREV command and at least one *more* record—*not* counting the one currently being read—exists with the same key.

To illustrate, suppose the program is reading invoice records for customer 10000. If there's just one invoice record for customer 10000, the DUPKEY condition is never raised, because when the program reads the first invoice record, there aren't any additional invoice records with the same alternate key. If there are two invoices for customer 10000, DUPKEY is raised when the program reads the first record. But when the program reads the second and last record, DUPKEY isn't raised. If there are three invoices for the customer, DUPKEY is raised for the first two but not for the third, and so on. In short, the DUPKEY condition is not raised when you read the last record with a given alternate key.

Although it may seem a bit odd, you must provide for the DUPKEY condition. If you don't, your program will abend. Even though DUPKEY doesn't really represent an error condition, you must handle it.

Look now to see how I handled the DUPKEY condition. First, I coded the HANDLE CONDITION command for DUPKEY in module 1800. Then, in module 1820, immediately after the READNEXT command, I coded:

```
MOVE 'N' TO MORE-INVOICES-SW.
```

Because the DUPKEY condition transfers control to the DUPKEY routine (1820-DUPKEY), this MOVE statement isn't executed if the DUPKEY condition occurs. So MORE-INVOICES-SW is turned off only when the DUPKEY condition doesn't occur—that is, when the last invoice for a given customer is read. After the MOVE statement, control falls through to 1820-DUPKEY, where a series of MOVE statements move fields from the invoice record to the correct invoice line in the symbolic map. The statements in the DUPKEY routine are executed every time module 1820 is invoked, whether the DUPKEY condition occurs or not.

One interesting point about module 1820 is that the READNEXT command never "fails." In other words, it always returns an invoice record for the correct customer. That's because the DUPKEY condition, when it's raised, means the next READNEXT command will retrieve a record with the same alternate key value. When the DUPKEY condition is not raised, the next READNEXT command will not retrieve a record with the same alternate key value. So when module 1820 sets MORE-INVOICES-SW to N, module 1800 knows not to invoke module 1820 again because there are no more invoice records to retrieve for the specified customer.

In contrast, consider how you detect an end-of-file condition during a standard browse operation using a primary key. When the READNEXT command fails, the ENDFILE condition is raised. Because no record is available in the input area when that happens, your program must provide special processing at end-of-file. Although it takes some getting used to, I think it's easier to program for the DUPKEY condition than for the ENDFILE condition.

The program in this chapter uses the DUPKEY condition to end its browse operation because it needs to retrieve only those invoices that have a particular alternate key value. In some applications, however, you need to browse an entire file along a path. In that case, you must handle not only the DUPKEY condition, but the ENDFILE condition as well. When you read the last record in the file, the DUPKEY condition isn't raised because there isn't another record with the same key value. Then, on the next READNEXT command, the ENDFILE condition is raised because there are no more records in the file.

Discussion

As you probably realize, alternate indexes introduce considerable overhead into the processing of VSAM files. Depending on factors such as how many alternate indexes are associated with the file, how many of those alternate indexes are upgradable, and how much free space is available within the file's control intervals, a single WRITE command for an alternate index file can cause dozens of physical I/O operations. And that can result in considerable performance degradation, especially if many users are updating the same alternate index file at once. As a result, alternate indexes—particularly upgradable alternate indexes—are used only when their advantages outweigh their disadvantages.

Terminology

alternate index
primary key
base key
base cluster
alternate key
unique key
nonunique key
duplicate key
path
upgrading
upgradable index
upgrade set

Objectives

1. Briefly explain the meaning of the following terms:

    alternate index
    path
    upgrade set

2. Given a programming problem involving an alternate
    index file, code an acceptable program for its solution.

Chapter 3

DL/I data base processing

So far in this book (and in *Part 1: An introductory course*), all of the file handling examples have used VSAM files. That's certainly not unreasonable because most CICS file processing uses VSAM files. Even so, for some applications, you need to be able to represent more complex relationships than VSAM, even with its alternate indexing capabilities, allows. For those applications, data base packages are often used. In this chapter, you'll learn how to write CICS programs that use one of IBM's most popular data base packages: DL/I.

If you're already familiar with DL/I, this chapter will show you all you need to know to develop CICS programs to process DL/I data bases. If you don't know DL/I, this chapter won't show you all you need to know about DL/I. How DL/I works in a variety of situations is beyond the scope of this book. However, this chapter will give you a basic understanding of DL/I that you can expand by studying other DL/I training materials.

This chapter has two topics. The first introduces you to DL/I data base organization and programming concepts. If you've worked with DL/I before, feel free to skip topic 1. Topic 2 shows you the special programming requirements for processing a DL/I data base under CICS and presents a sample CICS DL/I program.

Topic 1   DL/I data base concepts and terminology

This topic presents a basic introduction to one of IBM's most popular data base management systems: *DL/I (Data Language/I)*. First, I present the basics of how a DL/I data base is organized. Then, I describe in general terms the DL/I considerations for batch COBOL programs that process DL/I data bases.

The DL/I concepts in this topic apply to both OS and DOS systems. However, the software products that let you implement DL/I data bases differ under the two groups of operating systems. On OS systems, DL/I is part of a larger product called *IMS/VS (Information Management System/Virtual Storage)*. IMS provides not only data base management services through DL/I, but data communications services as well. In that respect, it's similar to CICS. In this chapter, I cover just the DL/I facilities of IMS.

IMS isn't available on VSE systems. Even so, you can use IMS-compatible DL/I data bases on VSE systems through a product called *DL/I DOS/VS*. From a practical point of view, the DL/I components of IMS and DL/I DOS/VS are the same.

HOW A DL/I DATA BASE IS ORGANIZED

Hierarchical data relationships

DL/I data bases are organized hierarchically. Simply put, that means the entire data base is organized as a structure of related data elements, some of which are subordinate to others. By using this form of organization, DL/I maintains a high degree of control over the relationships among data elements in a data base.

The idea of hierarchical data organization isn't unique to DL/I. In fact, many applications use ordinary VSAM files with hierarchical relationships. For example, the program in the last chapter used a simple hierarchical data structure, shown in figure 3-1. Here, one customer record can have many invoice records subordinate to it. This structure was implemented using two separate VSAM data sets (CUSTMAS and INVOICE) related to one another by an alternate index. The alternate index's key was the customer number field in the invoice record.

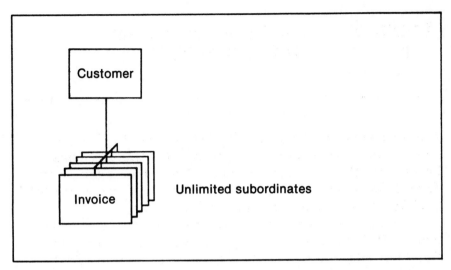

Figure 3-1   The hierarchical data relationship between the customer and invoice files

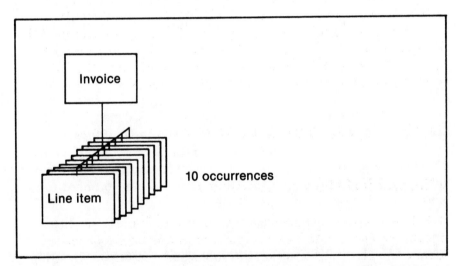

Figure 3-2   The hierarchical data relationship between invoice data and line-item data within the invoice file

Although figure 3-1 doesn't show it, there's another hierarchical relationship in the CUSTMAS/INVOICE pair of files. Each record in INVOICE has ten line items (not all of which have to be used), as figure 3-2 shows. They're stored in a ten-element table within the invoice record.

The physical implementations of the hierarchical relationships illustrated in figures 3-1 and 3-2 differ. One is implemented by

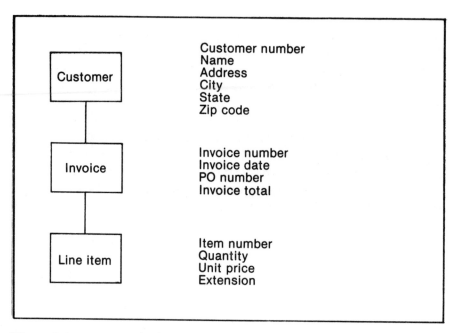

Figure 3-3   How the hierarchical relationships among the data elements in the customer and invoice files can be represented in a DL/I data base

alternate indexing, the other by a table within a record. But each still represents a hierarchical organization of data. It's just such hierarchical organizations of data that DL/I is designed to support. Figure 3-3 shows how the data elements from the customer and invoice files might be combined in one DL/I hierarchy. Of course, DL/I can support data groupings much more complex than the one in figure 3-3. But figure 3-3 illustrates the concepts you need to understand before you can use DL/I.

How DL/I implements hierarchical data structures

The data elements in the hierarchy in figure 3-3 would probably be implemented under DL/I as a single *data base*. Don't confuse this DL/I term with the more general use of "data base" to mean an organization's complete "base of data." A DL/I data base is a set of related data elements stored together to meet the requirements of one or more applications. If you'd like, you can think of a DL/I data base as a single complex file. An organization's complete base of data might consist of dozens of DL/I data bases, as well as VSAM and other files.

Segments   Within a DL/I data base, data is organized in *segments*. A segment is the unit of data DL/I can access for you. The different kinds of segments that make up a data base are called *segment types*. The three segment types in the structure in figure 3-3 are customer, invoice, and line item. Each segment type contains one or more fields, much like a record in a standard file.

I want you to distinguish between the terms segment type and *segment occurrence*. Within a data base, there may be many occurrences of one segment type. For example, the data base structure in figure 3-3 has only one customer segment type. However, the actual data base may contain thousands of customer segment occurrences.

The customer segment in figure 3-3 is at the top of the hierarchy—it's called the *root segment*. A single occurrence of one root segment plus all of the occurrences of all segments subordinate to it comprise one *data base record*. Figure 3-4 illustrates what might be a data base record for one customer segment occurrence in the data base in figure 3-3. As you can see, three occurrences of the invoice segment are subordinate to the customer segment in this record. And each invoice segment occurrence can have a variable number of line item occurrences subordinate to it. Obviously, a data base record isn't of fixed length. It can be as long as necessary to accommodate all the segment occurrences subordinate to a particular occurrence of the root segment.

Don't let the term data base record confuse you. In standard file processing, you retrieve and process records. Not so in data base processing. The closest thing to a file record in DL/I is a segment—that's the unit of information you receive and process in a DL/I program. The idea of data base records just helps you understand the hierarchical nature of a DL/I data base.

Segment dependence and parentage   Some of the terminology you're likely to come across as you work with DL/I has to do with *segment dependence*. Within a DL/I data base, a particular segment is dependent on the segments that are above it. In figure 3-3, the invoice segment type is dependent on the customer segment type, and the line item segment type is dependent on both invoice and customer. The relationships among dependent segments can be described in terms of *parentage*. For example, invoice is dependent on customer. Therefore, invoice is the *child segment* of the *parent segment* customer. A segment that is a child can also be a parent. For example, invoice is the parent segment of line item. The segments at the bottom of the hierarchy cannot be parents. And the

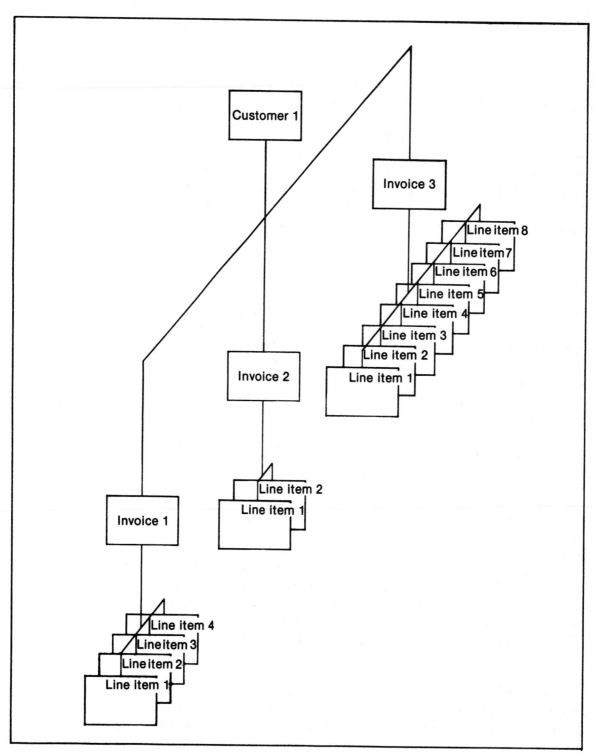

Figure 3-4   One data base record

segment at the top of the hierarchy (the root segment) cannot be a child.

How applications view a DL/I data base

One of the advantages of using DL/I is that each application program that accesses a data base can have a unique *view* of it. Simply put, a *view* (sometimes called an *application data structure*) is a subset of the segments and fields that make up a complete data base. The particular segments and fields that make up a view depend on the requirements of the application program.

Even a simple data base like the one in figure 3-3 can have different views for different application programs. For example, imagine the requirements of two programs: an inquiry program that displays a customer's name and address and an order-entry program that adds invoices and line items to the data base. The inquiry program needs to access only the data in the customer segment. What's in the invoice and line item segments subordinate to a given occurrence of the customer segment doesn't matter to the inquiry program. As a result, the inquiry program's view of the data base includes only the customer segment. In contrast, the order-entry program needs to access segments of all three types. Accordingly, its view of the data base must be complete.

Besides restricting a program's access to specific segments and fields, a view also specifies the type of processing a program can do for each segment or field. For example, the inquiry program is allowed to retrieve customer segments but not to modify or delete them. The order-entry program can not only retrieve customer segments, but it can also create new invoice and line item segments.

These two examples are simple because the data base in figure 3-3 is simple. However, consider a DL/I data base with dozens of segment types at several levels. When the physical data structure is that complex, the chances are slim that any application program will need to view the entire structure. Then, it's useful to be able to specify different views.

Program specification block   The way the data base administrator specifies an application program's view of a data base is by coding and assembling a *Program Specification Block* (or *PSB*) for it. Each application program has its own PSB. For each different data base a program accesses, the program's PSB contains one *Program Communication Block* (or *PCB*). So if a program accesses three different data bases, its PSB contains three PCBs.

Within the PCB, the data base administrator specifies which segments in the data base are in the program's view. These are called *sensitive segments*. And within the sensitive segments, the data base administrator may specify the fields that are in the program's view, called *sensitive fields*. As you can tell, the data base administrator has much control over what application programs can and cannot do with DL/I data bases.

DL/I PROGRAMMING: THE CALL INTERFACE

Now that you have a general idea of how a DL/I data base is organized, I want you to learn a little of how a batch COBOL program processes a DL/I data base. Because a CICS program uses many of the same techniques as a batch program, this material will help you understand what's in topic 2. Note, however, that this section won't teach you everything you need to know to write a DL/I program. Instead, it just introduces you to the most important concepts.

COBOL itself doesn't provide for processing DL/I data bases. To process a DL/I data base in COBOL, you use the *CALL interface*. Basically, that means you code CALL statements to invoke DL/I functions. With the CALL interface, you invoke an interface routine named *CBLTDLI* to process DL/I requests. The relationship of CBLTDLI with your COBOL program is complex, but it's useful from a coding perspective to think of CBLTDLI as a simple subprogram.

Although there are a number of ways you can code a DL/I call, the example in figure 3-5 is typical. Here, I specify four parameters on the CALL statement. They identify (1) the DL/I function to be performed, (2) the PCB of the data base that's to be processed, (3) the segment I/O area, and (4) any required segment search arguments. In some cases, you can specify additional parameters. But most DL/I calls use just these four.

DL/I function

The *DL/I function* parameter is a four-byte alphanumeric field whose value indicates which DL/I function is to be performed. Figure 3-6 lists nine commonly used DL/I functions. I'm not going

```
CALL 'CBLTDLI' USING DLI-GET-UNIQUE
                     CUSTOMER-PCB
                     CUSTOMER-SEGMENT
                     CUSTOMER-SSA.
```

Figure 3-5   A typical DL/I call

Code	Function
GU	Get a unique segment.
GHU	Get a unique segment and hold it for subsequent update.
GN	Get the next segment in sequence.
GHN	Get the next segment in sequence and hold it for update.
GNP	Get the next segment in sequence within the established parent.
GHNP	Get the next segment in sequence within the established parent and hold it for subsequent update.
ISRT	Insert a segment.
REPL	Replace a segment.
DLET	Delete a segment.

Figure 3-6   Nine commonly used DL/I functions

to describe them in detail here, but the information in figure 3-6
should give you a general idea of what each function does.

PCB mask

As you know, each PCB within your program's PSB identifies a
data base your program can process. To tell DL/I which data base
to process, you must specify a PCB name in a DL/I call, just as you
must specify a file-name in each standard file-control command.

```
LINKAGE SECTION.
     .
     .
     .
01  CUSTOMER-PCB.
*
    05  DBD-NAME                    PIC X(8).
    05  SEGMENT-LEVEL               PIC XX.
    05  STATUS-CODE                 PIC XX.
    05  PROCESSING-OPTIONS          PIC X(4).
    05  RESERVE-DLI                 PIC S9(5)     COMP.
    05  SEGMENT-NAME-FEEDBACK       PIC X(8).
    05  KEY-LENGTH                  PIC S9(5)     COMP.
    05  NUMB-SENS-SEGMENTS          PIC S9(5)     COMP.
    05  KEY-FEEDBACK-AREA           PIC X(10).
```

Figure 3-7   A typical PCB mask description

Actually, you don't specify a PCB name directly in a DL/I call. Instead, you specify a Linkage Section field called a *PCB mask*. Figure 3-7 shows the coding for a typical PCB mask. The contents of the first field, DBD-NAME, identifies the data base being processed. For each data base your program processes, your Linkage Section contains one PCB mask group item like the one in figure 3-7.

The other field in the PCB mask you need to know about is the status-code field (STATUS-CODE in figure 3-7). After each DL/I operation on a particular data base has completed, the status code field in that data base's PCB mask contains an indication of any errors that may have occurred during the operation. Because most DL/I error conditions don't cause application programs to abend, application programs should test the PCB mask's status code field to detect errors that occur.

Segment I/O area

The *segment I/O area* is like a record I/O area for standard file processing. For input, DL/I places the retrieved segment in this area. For output, your program must place the segment data in this area before it issues the DL/I call.

```
01   CUSTOMER-SSA.
*
     05   FILLER              PIC X(19)   VALUE 'CUSTOMER(CUSTNO   ='.
     05   CUSTNO-SSA          PIC X(5).
     05   FILLER              PIC X       VALUE ')'.
```

Figure 3-8   A typical segment search argument description

Segment search argument

The *segment search argument*, or SSA, is the most complicated part of a DL/I call. It identifies which segment in a data base is to be processed. In the simplest case, an *unqualified* SSA supplies the eight-byte name of a segment type. For example, to add an INVOICE segment, you could supply an unqualified SSA containing the segment name INVOICE.

A *qualified* SSA specifies not only a segment name, but a search value as well. You can think of a qualified SSA as similar to the RIDFLD parameter required in a CICS file-control command. For example, a qualified SSA might indicate that an invoice segment whose invoice number field (named INVNO) is 10030 should be retrieved. That SSA would look like this:

```
INVOICE (INVNO     =10030)
```

Since DL/I segment and field names must be eight characters long in an SSA, blanks are required when the actual names are shorter. Also, one blank must separate the eight-character segment name from the equals sign in a qualified SSA.

When you code a DL/I CALL, you don't code an SSA directly. Instead, you specify a data name that contains the SSA. Figure 3-8 gives an example of a typical working-storage definition of an SSA. Here, the customer-number field is given its own data name. That way, you can move any value you wish to it before you issue the DL/I CALL. For example, this MOVE statement,

```
MOVE WS-CUSTOMER-NUMBER TO CUSTNO-SSA.
```

formats the SSA to specify the value in the field WS-CUSTOMER-NUMBER.

DISCUSSION

Quite frankly, DL/I is much more complicated than this topic might indicate. So if you feel confused about DL/I at this point, don't worry. The main point of this topic is to help you better understand the CICS material that's in the next topic. But a complete discussion of DL/I concepts and programming is a subject for another book.

Terminology

DL/I
Data Language/I
IMS/VS
Information Management System/Virtual Storage
DL/I DOS/VS
data base
segment
segment type
segment occurrence
root segment
data base record
segment dependence
parentage
child segment
parent segment
view
application data structure
Program Specification Block
PSB
Program Communication Block
PCB
sensitive segment
sensitive field
CALL interface
CBLTDLI
DL/I function
PCB mask
segment I/O area
segment search argument
SSA
unqualified SSA
qualified SSA

Objectives

1. Compare the hierarchical organization of a DL/I data base with a similarly organized structure of VSAM files.

2. Explain the distinction between the following pairs of terms:

    data base vs. base of data
    segment type vs. segment occurrence
    file record vs. data base record
    child segment vs. parent segment

3. Describe the function of the four basic parameters required on a DL/I call.

Topic 2 How to process a DL/I data base

In this topic, you'll learn how to code a CICS program that processes a DL/I data base. At the outset, I assume you're somewhat familiar with DL/I batch programming. If your only experience with DL/I is having read the last topic, you may not understand everything this topic presents. Nevertheless, you will have a basic understanding of how DL/I relates to CICS. If you're familiar with DL/I through a previous course or job experience, you should be able to write DL/I programs for execution under CICS when you complete this topic.

DL/I PROGRAMMING FOR CICS

If you've developed batch DL/I programs, you'll have little trouble learning how to code a DL/I program for execution under CICS. In fact, DL/I calls in a CICS program are identical to those in a batch program. But there are two differences you need to know about before you write a CICS DL/I program. First, your program must issue a special DL/I call—the *scheduling call*—before it can issue any other DL/I call. And second, DL/I error processing under CICS is a little different than it is in batch mode.

How to schedule a PSB

Before your program can issue a DL/I call to process a data base, it must have access to two areas of main storage. Figure 3-9 shows those areas. First, the *User Interface Block*, or *UIB*, is an interface area between your program and the CICS routines that communicate with DL/I. Each DL/I program requires a single UIB. Second, the Program Communication Block (PCB) is an interface area directly between your program and DL/I. There may be more than one PCB, depending on how many data base views are defined in the program's PSB. (Remember that each program has one PSB, which contains one or more PCBs that define data base views.)

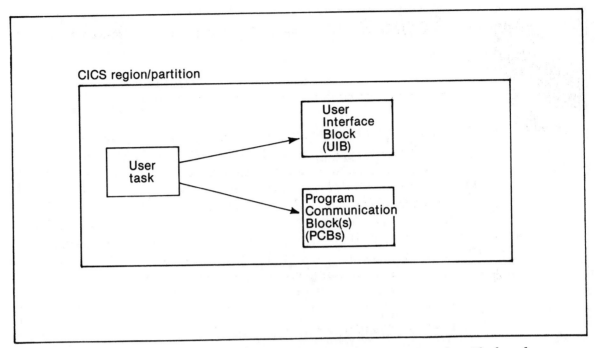

CICS region/partition

Figure 3-9   A DL/I task must establish addressability to the User Interface Block and one or
more Program Communication Blocks (PCBs)

Figure 3-10 shows an IBM-supplied copy book named DLIUIB
you can include in your program to define the UIB. If you'll study
it for a moment, you'll see that the User Interface Block consists of
just two fields. They're the 02-level items shaded in figure 3-10:
UIBPCBAL and UIBRCODE. You'll see how both of these fields
are used later in this topic.

As figure 3-9 indicates, the UIB and PCB are data areas that
exist outside of your program's storage. In other words, the UIB
and PCB are in storage that's owned by CICS rather than by your
application program. As a result, your program must use a special
technique, which I describe next, to access them.

How to use BLL cells to access CICS areas   In *Part 1: An
introductory course*, I introduced the notion of BLL cells by
showing you how to access a CICS area called the Common Work
Area, or CWA. The technique you use to access the UIB and PCB
is similar.

Because the UIB and PCB areas are located in storage that's
outside your program, you must define them in your program's
Linkage Section rather than in its Working-Storage Section. When

```
**************************************************************************
*                                                                        *
*         MODULE-NAME = DLIUIB                                           *
*                                                                        *
*         DESCRIPTIVE NAME = STRUCTURE FOR USER INTERFACE BLOCK         *
*                                                                        *
*         STATUS = VERSION 1.5                            @D15D38D*
*                                                                        *
*         FUNCTION = DESCRIBE USER INTERFACE BLOCK FIELDS.              *
*                    THE UIB CONTAINS SCHEDULING AND SYSTEM CALL        *
*                    STATUS INFORMATION RETURNED TO THE USER.           *
*                                                                        *
*         MODULE-TYPE = STRUCTURE                                       *
*                                                                        *
*         CHANGE ACTIVITY = @BCAC80A                                    *
*                                                                        *
**************************************************************************
   01    DLIUIB.
   *      DLIUIB      EXTENDED CALL USER INTERFACE BLOCK
          02 UIBPCBAL PICTURE S9(8) USAGE IS COMPUTATIONAL.
   *      UIBPCBAL       PCB ADDRESS LIST
          02 UIBRCODE.
   *      UIBRCODE       DL/I RETURN CODES
             03 UIBFCTR PICTURE X.
   *         UIBFCTR       RETURN CODES
             88   FCNORESP      VALUE ' '.
             88   FCNOTOPEN     VALUE ' '.
             88   FCINVREQ      VALUE ' '.
             03 UIBDLTR PICTURE X.
   *         UIBDLTR       ADDITIONAL INFORMATION
             88   DLPSBNF       VALUE ' '.
             88   DLTASKNA      VALUE ' '.
             88   DLPSBSCH      VALUE ' '.
             88   DLLANGCON     VALUE ' '.
             88   DLPSBFAIL     VALUE ' '.
             88   DLPSBNA       VALUE ' '.
             88   DLTERMNS      VALUE ' '.
             88   DLFUNCNS      VALUE ' '.
             88   DLINA         VALUE ' '.
```

Figure 3-10   The DLIUIB copy book

you define a field in your program's Linkage Section, you are *not* allocating storage for the field. Instead, you're defining how that field's contents are organized. The storage the field actually uses is allocated by CICS, outside of your program. In effect, entries in the Linkage Section act as *masks* for the actual storage areas associated with them. In fact, the Linkage Section description of a PCB is often called a PCB mask.

When CICS loads and executes your program, it expects to find two fields defined in the Linkage Section: the Execute

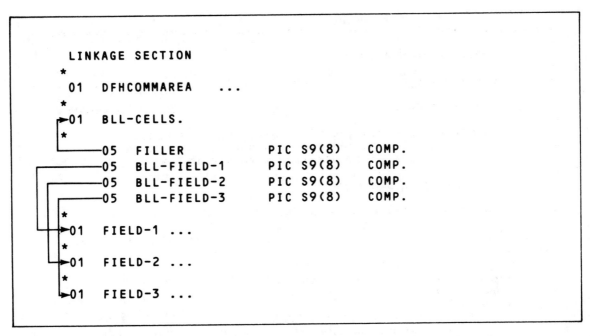

```
    LINKAGE SECTION
    *
    01   DFHCOMMAREA    ...
    *
►─01   BLL-CELLS.
│   *
└──────05   FILLER           PIC S9(8)   COMP.
┌──────05   BLL-FIELD-1      PIC S9(8)   COMP.
│ ┌────05   BLL-FIELD-2      PIC S9(8)   COMP.
│ │ ┌──05   BLL-FIELD-3      PIC S9(8)   COMP.
│ │ │ *
│ │ └►01   FIELD-1 ...
│ │   *
│ └──►01   FIELD-2 ...
│     *
└────►01   FIELD-3 ...
```

Figure 3-11   BLL cells are used to address data areas described in the Linkage Section

Interface Block (DFHEIB) and the Communication Area
(DFHCOMMAREA). As a result, CICS automatically provides
addressability to these two fields. However, if you define any other
fields in the Linkage Section (like the UIB and PCB), you must
establish addressability to them yourself. If you don't, your
program won't be able to access the information stored in those
fields.

To establish addressability to a field outside your program, you
use a convention called *Base Locator for Linkage* (or *BLL*). Figure
3-11 illustrates this convention. Quite simply, you must define an
01-level item in the Linkage Section following DFHCOMMAREA.
In figure 3-11, I call this item BLL-CELLS, but the name doesn't
matter. Each field in BLL-CELLS is a pointer that stores the
address of a subsequent Linkage Section field. These pointers must
be defined as binary full-words (PIC S9(8) COMP). The value of
the first pointer (FILLER) is the address of the BLL-CELLS item
itself. Then, each subsequent pointer contains the address of an
01-level item that follows in the Linkage Section. In figure 3-11,
the pointer named BLL-FIELD-1 is used to establish addressability
to FIELD-1. Similarly, BLL-FIELD-2 is used for FIELD-2 and
BLL-FIELD-3 is used for FIELD-3. The names of the BLL cells
don't matter; what does matter is the order in which you code
them.

How to obtain the address of the UIB and PCBs At this point, you should realize that you need to code Linkage Section entries for the UIB and PCBs. And you need to code entries for the BLL cells that will contain the addresses of those fields. But that's not enough. Before you can use any of those fields, you must first load the BLL-cell fields with the correct addresses. The question is, how do you obtain the addresses of the UIB and PCBs?

Figure 3-12 gives part of the answer. Here, you can see that one of the UIB fields (UIBPCBAL) points indirectly to the PCBs. I say indirectly because rather than containing the address of a PCB, UIBPCBAL contains the address of another data area that contains a list of PCB addresses. In other words, the UIB points to a PCB address list. And the PCB address list, in turn, points to all of the PCBs.

Why does PCB addressing work that way? To provide for a variable number of PCBs within a PSB. Although the User Interface Block is a fixed length area, it needs to point to a variable number of PCBs. That's why the PCB address list is used. The PCB address list is variable length: it contains one pointer for each PCB in the program's PSB. In figure 3-12, two PCBs are defined. So the PCB address list contains two pointers.

An implication of the addressing scheme in figure 3-12 is that you must define an additional Linkage Section field for the PCB address list. In fact, for the example shown in figure 3-12, you would define four Linkage Section fields: one for the UIB, one for the PCB address list, and one for each of the two PCBs. In addition, you would define four corresponding BLL cells to establish addressability to those fields.

Figure 3-12 shows that if you know the address of the UIB, you can establish addressability to the PCBs by using the pointer addresses in the PCB address list. The part of the addressing question left unanswered by figure 3-12 is how you get the address of the UIB itself. That's where the scheduling call comes in: its function is to acquire storage for the User Interface Block and return its address to your program. So once you've issued a scheduling call, you can address the UIB, the PCB address list, and the PCBs themselves.

Because I want to be sure you understand how PSB scheduling works, look at figure 3-13. The four parts of this figure show how your program establishes addressability to the required DL/I areas. The top section of each part shows the COBOL statement issued by the program. The bottom section shows the relationship of Linkage Section entries to the actual storage areas for DL/I control blocks. The areas that are addressable after the COBOL statement executes are shaded.

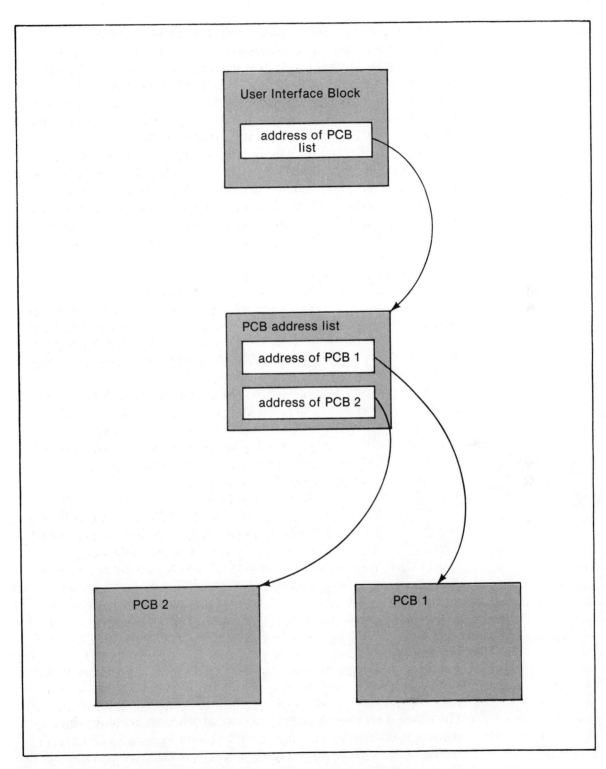

Figure 3-12   A field in the UIB points to a list of PCB addresses

Part 1 of figure 3-13 shows the scheduling call. DLI-SCHEDULE is the name of a four-character field defined in the Working-Storage Section. It contains the function code required to perform a scheduling call: PCB. PSB-NAME is an eight-character field that contains the name of the PSB this program uses. For the sake of the illustration, assume the PSB contains two PCBs, called PCB-1 and PCB-2. The scheduling call returns the address of the UIB in BLL-UIB. As the shading indicates, the Linkage Section field DLIUIB masks the actual UIB.

To establish addressability to the PCB address list, all you do is move the pointer (UIBPCBAL) to the BLL cell for the address list. That's what part 2 of figure 3-13 illustrates. Here, this MOVE statement:

```
MOVE UIBPCBAL TO BLL-PCB-AL
```

loads the address of the PCB address list into BLL-PCB-AL. As a result, PCB-ADDRESS-LIST now masks the actual address list.

Part 3 shows how to establish addressability to the first PCB: a MOVE statement loads the first pointer in the PCB address list into the BLL cell for PCB-1. After the MOVE statement executes, PCB-1 correctly masks the first PCB. In a similar manner, part 4 shows how addressability is established for the second PCB.

To summarize, the scheduling call places the UIB address in its BLL cell. Then, it's just a matter of moving pointers into appropriate BLL cells so that all of the required fields are addressable. Frankly, the COBOL coding required to establish addressability to all of the DL/I areas is simple. All you do is issue a CALL statement followed by a series of MOVE statements, like this:

```
CALL 'CBLTDLI' USING DLI-SCHEDULE
                     PSB-NAME
                     BLL-UIB.
MOVE UIBPCBAL    TO BLL-PCB-AL.
MOVE PCB-1-ADDR TO BLL-PCB-1.
MOVE PCB-2-ADDR TO BLL-PCB-2.
```

You'll see a complete example of how to schedule a PSB in the program example in this topic. With this background, though, you'll better understand what those simple COBOL elements really accomplish.

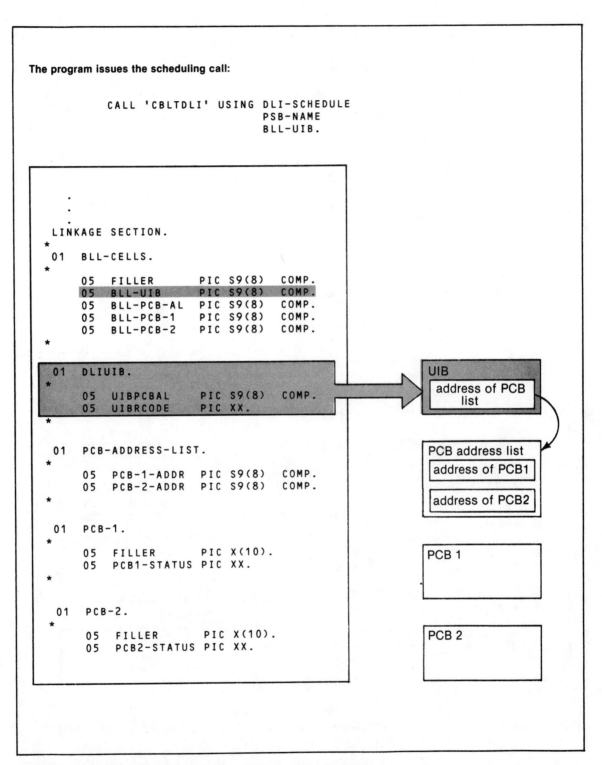

Figure 3-13   Addressing DL/I control blocks (part 1 of 4)

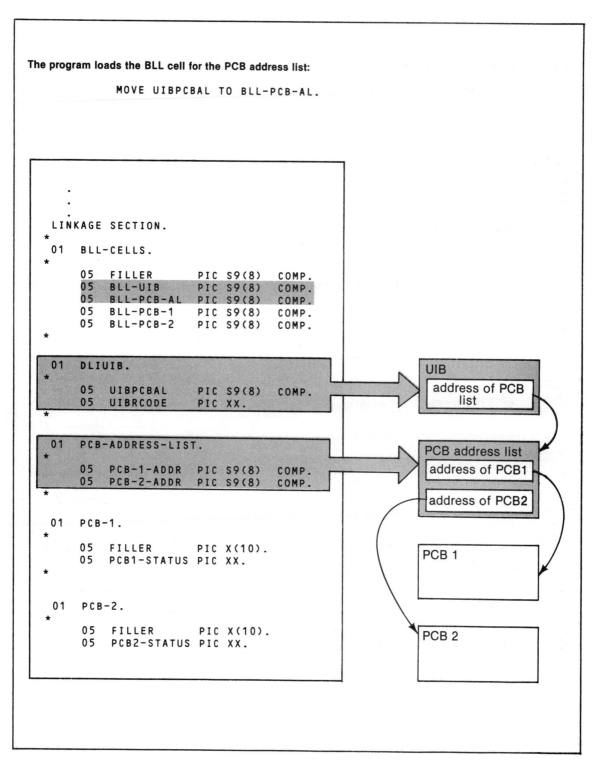

The program loads the BLL cell for the PCB address list:

```
          MOVE UIBPCBAL TO BLL-PCB-AL.
```

```
     .
     .
     .
  LINKAGE SECTION.
*
  01  BLL-CELLS.
*
      05  FILLER        PIC S9(8)  COMP.
      05  BLL-UIB       PIC S9(8)  COMP.
      05  BLL-PCB-AL    PIC S9(8)  COMP.
      05  BLL-PCB-1     PIC S9(8)  COMP.
      05  BLL-PCB-2     PIC S9(8)  COMP.
*

  01  DLIUIB.
*
      05  UIBPCBAL      PIC S9(8)  COMP.
      05  UIBRCODE      PIC XX.
*

  01  PCB-ADDRESS-LIST.
*
      05  PCB-1-ADDR    PIC S9(8)  COMP.
      05  PCB-2-ADDR    PIC S9(8)  COMP.
*

  01  PCB-1.
*
      05  FILLER        PIC X(10).
      05  PCB1-STATUS   PIC XX.
*

  01  PCB-2.
*
      05  FILLER        PIC X(10).
      05  PCB2-STATUS   PIC XX.
```

UIB
address of PCB list

PCB address list
address of PCB1
address of PCB2

PCB 1

PCB 2

Figure 3-13   Addressing DL/I control blocks (part 2 of 4)

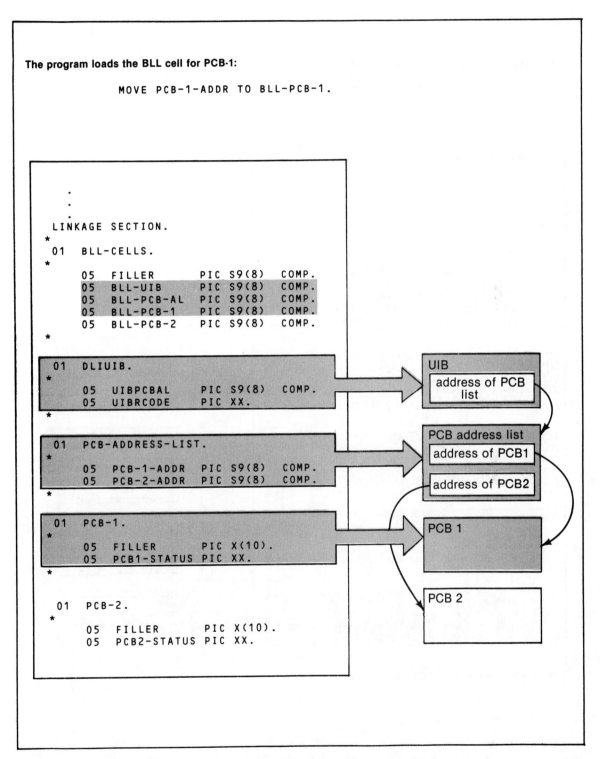

The program loads the BLL cell for PCB-1:

```
           MOVE PCB-1-ADDR TO BLL-PCB-1.
```

```
        .
        .
        .
  LINKAGE SECTION.
*
  01  BLL-CELLS.
*
      05  FILLER       PIC S9(8)  COMP.
      05  BLL-UIB      PIC S9(8)  COMP.
      05  BLL-PCB-AL   PIC S9(8)  COMP.
      05  BLL-PCB-1    PIC S9(8)  COMP.
      05  BLL-PCB-2    PIC S9(8)  COMP.
*

  01  DLIUIB.
*
      05  UIBPCBAL     PIC S9(8)  COMP.
      05  UIBRCODE     PIC XX.
*

  01  PCB-ADDRESS-LIST.
*
      05  PCB-1-ADDR   PIC S9(8)  COMP.
      05  PCB-2-ADDR   PIC S9(8)  COMP.
*

  01  PCB-1.
*
      05  FILLER       PIC X(10).
      05  PCB1-STATUS  PIC XX.
*

  01  PCB-2.
*
      05  FILLER       PIC X(10).
      05  PCB2-STATUS  PIC XX.
```

UIB
address of PCB list

PCB address list
address of PCB1
address of PCB2

PCB 1

PCB 2

Figure 3-13   Addressing DL/I control blocks (part 3 of 4)

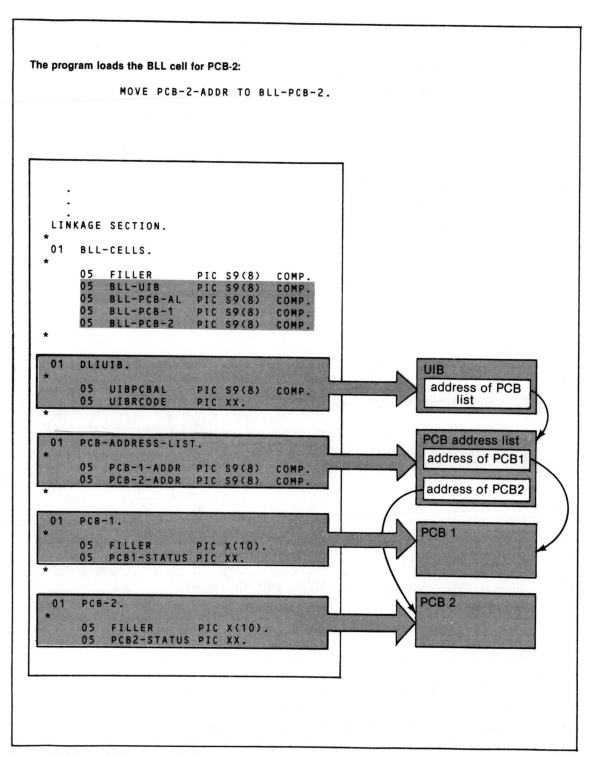

The program loads the BLL cell for PCB-2:

```
            MOVE PCB-2-ADDR TO BLL-PCB-2.
```

```
      .
      .
      .
  LINKAGE SECTION.
*
  01  BLL-CELLS.
*
      05  FILLER       PIC S9(8)  COMP.
      05  BLL-UIB      PIC S9(8)  COMP.
      05  BLL-PCB-AL   PIC S9(8)  COMP.
      05  BLL-PCB-1    PIC S9(8)  COMP.
      05  BLL-PCB-2    PIC S9(8)  COMP.
*
```

```
  01  DLIUIB.
*
      05  UIBPCBAL     PIC S9(8)  COMP.
      05  UIBRCODE     PIC XX.
*
```

UIB
address of PCB list

```
  01  PCB-ADDRESS-LIST.
*
      05  PCB-1-ADDR   PIC S9(8)  COMP.
      05  PCB-2-ADDR   PIC S9(8)  COMP.
*
```

PCB address list
address of PCB1
address of PCB2

```
  01  PCB-1.
*
      05  FILLER       PIC X(10).
      05  PCB1-STATUS PIC XX.
*
```

PCB 1

```
  01  PCB-2.
*
      05  FILLER       PIC X(10).
      05  PCB2-STATUS PIC XX.
```

PCB 2

Figure 3-13   Addressing DL/I control blocks (part 4 of 4)

Considerations for the VS COBOL II compiler   If your installation
is one of the few that's using the new VS COBOL II compiler
(that's the new IBM compiler based on the 198X COBOL
standards), you'll have to code your scheduling statements a little
differently than I've shown. That's because VS COBOL II doesn't
support the BLL-cell linkage convention for addressing Linkage
Section fields. Instead, it uses a new language feature: the
ADDRESS special register.

When you use the ADDRESS special register, you don't code
BLL-cell entries in the Linkage Section. And you code your
scheduling statements like this:

```
CALL 'CBLTDLI' USING DLI-SCHEDULE
                     PSB-NAME
                     ADDRESS OF DLIUIB.
MOVE UIBPCBAL   TO ADDRESS OF PCB-ADDRESS-LIST.
MOVE PCB-1-ADDR TO ADDRESS OF PCB-1.
MOVE PCB-2-ADDR TO ADDRESS OF PCB-2.
```

Because most shops aren't yet using VS COBOL II, however, you'll
probably code your scheduling statements using the BLL-cell
linkage convention.

How to handle DL/I errors

In a CICS DL/I program, as in a batch DL/I program, you are
responsible for checking for error conditions after each DL/I call
your program issues. To illustrate, consider the typical DL/I
module shown in figure 3-14. Here, a DL/I call tries to retrieve a
unique segment from a customer data base. The IF statements
following the CALL statement provide the required error
processing. To determine if a DL/I call is successful, your CICS
program must test two status fields: one in the UIB, the other in
the PCB.

How to test the UIB status code   The User Interface Block (figure
3-10) serves as an interface area between your program and the
CICS routines that communicate with DL/I. One of the fields in
the UIB, UIBRCODE, contains a status code that indicates
whether your DL/I call was successful. UIBRCODE contains two
subfields: UIBFCTR and UIBDLTR. UIBFCTR contains a one-byte
response code, while UIBDLTR contains a byte that provides

```
     1210-GET-CUSTOMER-SEGMENT SECTION.
 *
         MOVE OEM-D-CUSTOMER-NUMBER TO SSA-CUSTNO.
         CALL 'CBLTDLI' USING DLI-GET-UNIQUE
                              CUSTOMER-PCB
                              CUSTOMER-MASTER-SEGMENT
                              CUSTOMER-SSA.
         IF UIBFCTR NOT = LOW-VALUE
             EXEC CICS
                 ABEND ABCODE('DLI2')
             END-EXEC.
         IF CUSTOMER-STATUS-CODE = 'GE'
             MOVE 'N' TO CUSTOMER-FOUND-SW
             MOVE SPACE TO CM-NAME
         ELSE IF CUSTOMER-STATUS-CODE NOT = SPACE
             EXEC CICS
                 ABEND ABCODE('DLI3')
             END-EXEC.
```

Figure 3-14   A typical DL/I module

additional error information if UIBFCTR indicates an error.
Usually, you're only concerned with UIBFCTR.

UIBFCTR normally contains LOW-VALUE. If it does, there's
no error. If it contains any other value, there was a serious error
between your program and the CICS routine that handles DL/I
calls. Usually, the cause of this type of error is that the scheduling
call failed. An error indicated by UIBFCTR is always serious, so
you should issue an ABEND command to terminate the task, as I'll
explain in just a moment.

How to test the PCB status code   Following the test of UIBFCTR,
the DL/I module in figure 3-14 tests the status code field in the
PCB, CUSTOMER-STATUS-CODE. This error processing should
be familiar to you if you've written DL/I batch programs. If the
status code is 'GE', the requested customer segment doesn't exist, so
a switch is set accordingly. Any other non-blank value indicates a
serious error, so an ABEND command terminates the task.

Depending on the DL/I function, you may need to check the
PCB status code field for other values. At the very least, if you
don't expect an operation to cause any return codes to be
generated, you should test the status code field to make sure it
contains blanks.

The ABEND command   The ABEND command isn't commonly

The ABEND command

```
EXEC CICS
     ABEND [ABCODE(data-name|literal)]
END-EXEC
```

Explanation

ABCODE   Specifies that a transaction dump should be produced
                                and the one- to four character value supplied should be
                                used as the abend code.

Figure 3-15   The ABEND command

used in CICS programs. Simply put, it causes your program to
abend just as if CICS had detected some type of processing error: a
message is written to the terminal, an optional transaction dump is
created, and the task is terminated. I haven't mentioned the
ABEND command before because you seldom need to force your
task to abend. Normally, CICS abends your task automatically
when a serious error occurs. Not so for DL/I, though.

Figure 3-15 gives the format of the ABEND command. You use
the ABCODE option when you want to create a transaction dump;
the value you supply appears in the dump and in the message that's
written to the operator. I recommend you code the ABCODE
option for two reasons. First, you'll probably need the transaction
dump to determine the cause of the error. And second, if you use a
different code for each ABEND command, you can easily
determine which ABEND command terminated your program.

Unfortunately, using the ABEND command violates one of the
basic principles of structured programming—that every called
module must return to the module that called it. Although it's
possible to code a CICS DL/I program that adheres to this rule, I
think it would be foolish. It would involve major changes in nearly
all of the modules of the program. Since unrecoverable error
conditions are rare, I think it's best to issue an ABEND command
wherever such errors occur and not worry about returning to the
calling module.

A SAMPLE PROGRAM

Now that you know how to schedule a PSB for a CICS DL/I program and how to code DL/I requests under CICS, take a look at figures 3-16 through 3-21. Here, I present a DL/I version of the order-entry program I presented originally in *Part 1: An introductory course*. I'm not going to review all the details of this program; I'll just describe the DL/I programming implications. If you want a detailed description of this program, review chapter 9 of *Part 1*.

Figure 3-16 is the screen layout for this program. As you can see, the operator enters little information for an order: customer number, purchase order number, and up to ten line items, each consisting of an inventory item number and a quantity. Figure 3-17 shows the BMS mapset for this program, and figure 3-18 shows the symbolic map I created.

Figure 3-19 gives an overview of the two DL/I data bases this program accesses. The customer data base is the one topic 1 of this chapter describes. The inventory data base consists of just one segment type, with one occurrence for each inventory item on file. Of course, a data base for an actual application would probably be more complex than this one. But still, the structures in figure 3-19 are adequate for this example.

Figure 3-20 gives the structure chart for the order-entry program. This program structure is almost the same as the structure I used for the order-entry program in *Part 1*. The differences are: (1) I've added module 0500 to schedule the PSB, and (2) modules 1210, 1230, 2210, 2220, and 2230 are changed to reflect data base rather than file processing.

Figure 3-21 gives the complete source listing for this program. Because it's a long listing, I've shaded the parts that relate directly to DL/I processing. Now, I'll point out some of the highlights.

Module 0500 schedules the PSB. If you'll look to the Linkage Section, you'll see that the entries I coded are similar to those in figure 3-13. But instead of using generalized names like PCB-1 and PCB-2, I refer to the PCBs with specific names: CUSTOMER-PCB and INVENTORY-PCB.

Notice that I coded abbreviated versions of both PCB masks. The status code fields are the only ones I reference in the program. As a result, I only had to account for them and the fields that precede them in the PCBs. The subsequent fields in the PCBs are irrelevant for this program.

Module 0500 first issues a scheduling call to get the address of

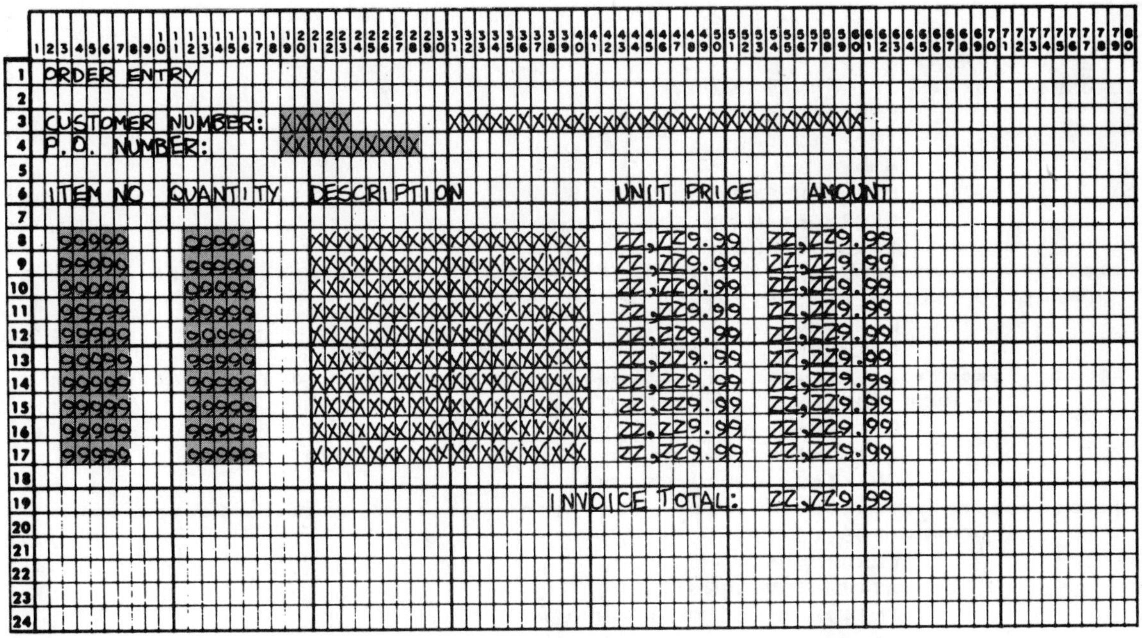

Figure 3-16   Screen layout for the DL/I version of the order-entry program

the UIB. Then, it tests UIBFCTR to make sure the scheduling call worked. If it didn't, an ABEND command terminates the program. Otherwise, three MOVE statements load addresses into the appropriate BLL cells so the PCB-POINTERS, CUSTOMER-PCB, and INVENTORY-PCB fields in the Linkage Section are addressable.

Module 1210 retrieves a specific customer segment from the customer data base. Here, the DL/I function is get unique, and CUSTOMER-SSA is used as a segment search argument to specify a particular customer. A CUSTOMER-STATUS-CODE of GE means the specified customer can't be found, so an appropriate switch is set. Module 1230 is similar to module 1210, only it retrieves a segment from the inventory data base using INVENTORY-SSA as a segment search argument.

Module 2200 calls module 2210 ten times to compute the total invoice amount for the current order. Then, module 2200 performs module 2220 to add an invoice segment to the customer data base.

Module 2220 first issues a LINK command to invoke the GETINV subprogram, which returns an invoice number via the communication area. Then, module 2220 formats the invoice

```
          PRINT NOGEN
ORDSET1   DFHMSD TYPE=&SYSPARM,                                                  X
                 LANG=COBOL,                                                     X
                 TERM=3270-2,                                                    X
                 MODE=INOUT,                                                     X
                 CTRL=FREEKB,                                                    X
                 STORAGE=AUTO,                                                   X
                 TIOAPFX=YES
****************************************************************************
ORDMAP1   DFHMDI SIZE=(24,80),                                                   X
                 LINE=1,                                                         X
                 COLUMN=1
****************************************************************************
          DFHMDF POS=(1,1),                                                      X
                 LENGTH=11,                                                      X
                 ATTRB=(BRT,PROT),                                               X
                 INITIAL='ORDER ENTRY'
****************************************************************************
          DFHMDF POS=(3,1),                                                      X
                 LENGTH=16,                                                      X
                 ATTRB=(BRT,PROT),                                               X
                 INITIAL='CUSTOMER NUMBER:'
CUSTNO    DFHMDF POS=(3,18),                                                     X
                 LENGTH=5,                                                       X
                 ATTRB=UNPROT
          DFHMDF POS=(3,24),                                                     X
                 LENGTH=1,                                                       X
                 ATTRB=ASKIP
****************************************************************************
NAME      DFHMDF POS=(3,30),                                                     X
                 LENGTH=30,                                                      X
                 ATTRB=PROT
****************************************************************************
          DFHMDF POS=(4,1),                                                      X
                 LENGTH=12,                                                      X
                 ATTRB=(BRT,PROT),                                               X
                 INITIAL='P.O. NUMBER:'
PO        DFHMDF POS=(4,18),                                                     X
                 LENGTH=10,                                                      X
                 ATTRB=UNPROT
          DFHMDF POS=(4,29),                                                     X
                 LENGTH=1,                                                       X
                 ATTRB=ASKIP
****************************************************************************
          DFHMDF POS=(6,1),                                                      X
                 LENGTH=30,                                                      X
                 ATTRB=(BRT,PROT),                                               X
                 INITIAL='ITEM NO   QUANTITY   DESCRIPTION'
          DFHMDF POS=(6,42),                                                     X
                 LENGTH=20,                                                      X
                 ATTRB=(BRT,PROT),                                               X
                 INITIAL='UNIT PRICE     AMOUNT'
```

Figure 3-17   Mapset listing for the DL/I version of the order-entry program (part 1 of 2)

```
************************************************************************
*          LINE ITEM 1                                                 *
************************************************************************
ITEMNO1    DFHMDF POS=(8,2),                                           X
                  LENGTH=5,                                            X
                  ATTRB=(UNPROT,NUM),                                  X
                  PICIN='9(5)'
           DFHMDF POS=(8,8),                                           X
                  LENGTH=1,                                            X
                  ATTRB=ASKIP
QTY1       DFHMDF POS=(8,11),                                          X
                  LENGTH=5,                                            X
                  ATTRB=(UNPROT,NUM),                                  X
                  PICIN='9(5)'
           DFHMDF POS=(8,17),                                          X
                  LENGTH=1,                                            X
                  ATTRB=ASKIP
DESCR1     DFHMDF POS=(8,20),                                          X
                  LENGTH=20,                                           X
                  ATTRB=PROT
UPRICE1    DFHMDF POS=(8,42),                                          X
                  LENGTH=9,                                            X
                  ATTRB=PROT,                                          X
                  PICOUT='ZZ,ZZ9.99'
AMOUNT1    DFHMDF POS=(8,53),                                          X
                  LENGTH=9,                                            X
                  ATTRB=PROT,                                          X
                  PICOUT='ZZ,ZZ9.99'
                  •          The BMS macro instructions that define line items
                  •          2 through 10 are similar to those that define
                  •          line item 1.
************************************************************************
           DFHMDF POS=(19,37),                                         X
                  LENGTH=14,                                           X
                  ATTRB=(BRT,PROT),                                    X
                  INITIAL='INVOICE TOTAL:'
TOTAL      DFHMDF POS=(19,53),                                         X
                  LENGTH=9,                                            X
                  ATTRB=PROT,                                          X
                  PICOUT='ZZ,ZZ9.99'
************************************************************************
MESSAGE    DFHMDF POS=(23,1),                                          X
                  LENGTH=79,                                           X
                  ATTRB=(BRT,PROT)
ERROR      DFHMDF POS=(24,1),                                          X
                  LENGTH=77,                                           X
                  ATTRB=(BRT,PROT)
DUMMY      DFHMDF POS=(24,79),                                         X
                  LENGTH=1,                                            X
                  ATTRB=(DRK,PROT,FSET),                               X
                  INITIAL=' '
************************************************************************
           DFHMSD TYPE=FINAL
           END
```

Figure 3-17   Mapset listing for the DL/I version of the order-entry program (part 2 of 2)

```
 01    ORDER-ENTRY-MAP.
 *
       05    FILLER                          PIC X(12).
 *
       05    OEM-L-CUSTOMER-NUMBER           PIC S9(4)    COMP.
       05    OEM-A-CUSTOMER-NUMBER           PIC X.
       05    OEM-D-CUSTOMER-NUMBER           PIC X(5).
 *
       05    OEM-L-NAME                      PIC S9(4)    COMP.
       05    OEM-A-NAME                      PIC X.
       05    OEM-D-NAME                      PIC X(30).
 *
       05    OEM-L-PO-NUMBER                 PIC S9(4)    COMP.
       05    OEM-A-PO-NUMBER                 PIC X.
       05    OEM-D-PO-NUMBER                 PIC X(10).
 *
       05    OEM-LINE-ITEM                   OCCURS 10.
 *
             10    OEM-L-ITEM-NUMBER         PIC S9(4)    COMP.
             10    OEM-A-ITEM-NUMBER         PIC X.
             10    OEM-D-ITEM-NUMBER         PIC 9(5).
 *
             10    OEM-L-QUANTITY            PIC S9(4)    COMP.
             10    OEM-A-QUANTITY            PIC X.
             10    OEM-D-QUANTITY            PIC 9(5).
 *
             10    OEM-L-ITEM-DESCRIPTION    PIC S9(4)    COMP.
             10    OEM-A-ITEM-DESCRIPTION    PIC X.
             10    OEM-D-ITEM-DESCRIPTION    PIC X(20).
 *
             10    OEM-L-UNIT-PRICE          PIC S9(4)    COMP.
             10    OEM-A-UNIT-PRICE          PIC X.
             10    OEM-D-UNIT-PRICE          PIC ZZ,ZZ9.99
                                             BLANK WHEN ZERO.
 *
             10    OEM-L-EXTENSION           PIC S9(4)    COMP.
             10    OEM-A-EXTENSION           PIC X.
             10    OEM-D-EXTENSION           PIC ZZ,ZZ9.99
                                             BLANK WHEN ZERO.
 *
       05    OEM-L-INVOICE-TOTAL             PIC S9(4)    COMP.
       05    OEM-A-INVOICE-TOTAL             PIC X.
       05    OEM-D-INVOICE-TOTAL             PIC ZZ,ZZ9.99
                                             BLANK WHEN ZERO.
 *
       05    OEM-L-OPERATOR-MESSAGE          PIC S9(4)    COMP.
       05    OEM-A-OPERATOR-MESSAGE          PIC X.
       05    OEM-D-OPERATOR-MESSAGE          PIC X(79).
 *
       05    OEM-L-ERROR-MESSAGE             PIC S9(4)    COMP.
       05    OEM-A-ERROR-MESSAGE             PIC X.
       05    OEM-D-ERROR-MESSAGE             PIC X(77).
 *
       05    OEM-L-DUMMY                     PIC S9(4)    COMP.
       05    OEM-A-DUMMY                     PIC X.
       05    OEM-D-DUMMY                     PIC X.
 *
```

Figure 3-18   Programmer-generated symbolic map for the DL/I version of the order-entry program (ORDSET1)

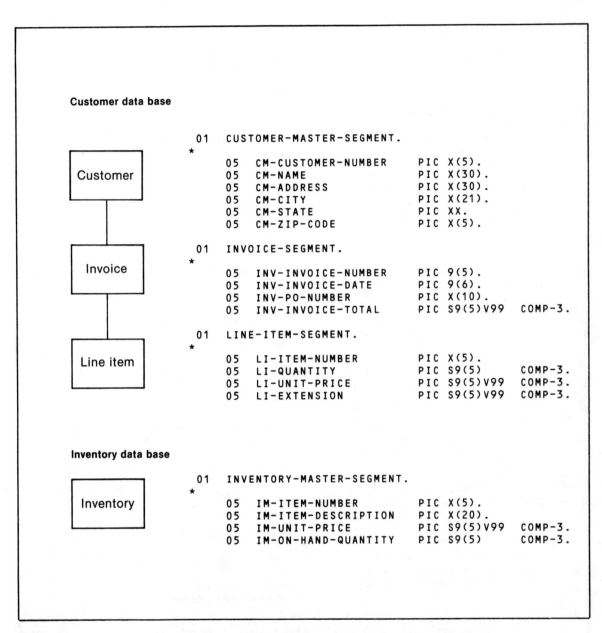

Customer data base

```
                          01   CUSTOMER-MASTER-SEGMENT.
                             *
                               05   CM-CUSTOMER-NUMBER     PIC X(5).
                               05   CM-NAME                PIC X(30).
                               05   CM-ADDRESS             PIC X(30).
                               05   CM-CITY                PIC X(21).
                               05   CM-STATE               PIC XX.
                               05   CM-ZIP-CODE            PIC X(5).

                          01   INVOICE-SEGMENT.
                             *
                               05   INV-INVOICE-NUMBER     PIC 9(5).
                               05   INV-INVOICE-DATE       PIC 9(6).
                               05   INV-PO-NUMBER          PIC X(10).
                               05   INV-INVOICE-TOTAL      PIC S9(5)V99    COMP-3.

                          01   LINE-ITEM-SEGMENT.
                             *
                               05   LI-ITEM-NUMBER         PIC X(5).
                               05   LI-QUANTITY            PIC S9(5)       COMP-3.
                               05   LI-UNIT-PRICE          PIC S9(5)V99    COMP-3.
                               05   LI-EXTENSION           PIC S9(5)V99    COMP-3.
```

Inventory data base

```
                          01   INVENTORY-MASTER-SEGMENT.
                             *
                               05   IM-ITEM-NUMBER         PIC X(5).
                               05   IM-ITEM-DESCRIPTION    PIC X(20).
                               05   IM-UNIT-PRICE          PIC S9(5)V99    COMP-3.
                               05   IM-ON-HAND-QUANTITY    PIC S9(5)       COMP-3.
```

Figure 3-19   Data structures used by the DL/I version of the order-entry program

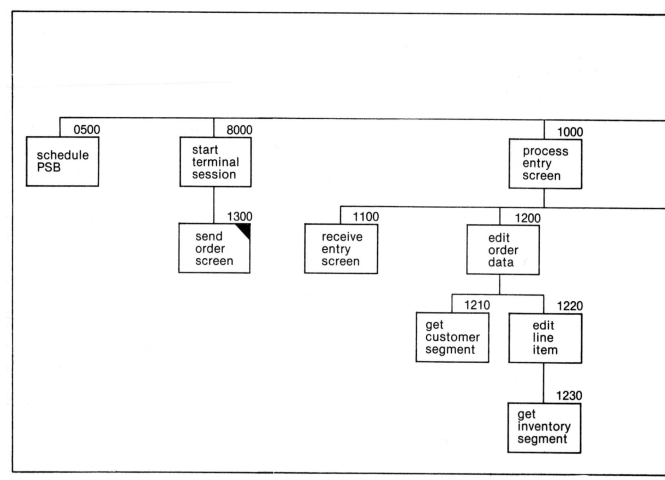

Figure 3-20   Structure chart for the DL/I version of the order-entry program

segment and issues a CALL statement to insert it in the data base. Notice that two segment search arguments are specified in the CALL statement. The first, CUSTOMER-SSA, tells DL/I to insert the invoice as a child of a particular customer segment. The second, UNQUALIFIED-SSA, tells DL/I that the segment being inserted is an INVOICE segment. DL/I determines the positioning for this segment by looking at the invoice number field within the invoice segment itself.

After module 2220 has added an invoice segment to the customer data base, module 2200 calls module 2230 ten times to add line item segments to the customer data base. Although module 2230 is performed ten times, a segment is added only when a line

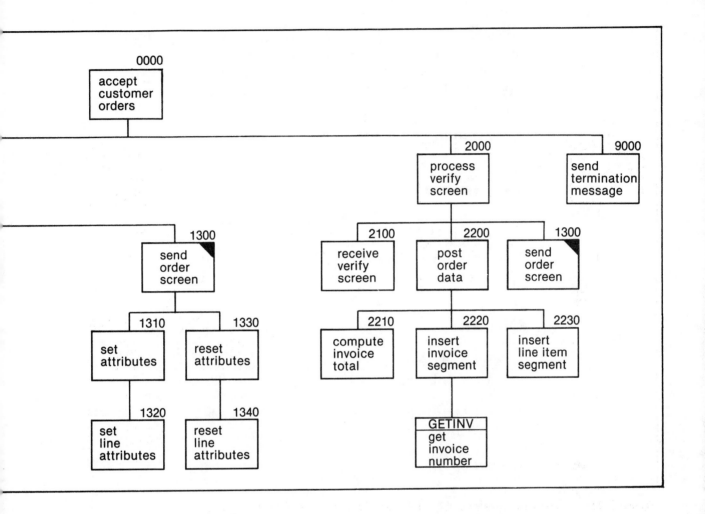

item actually exists. Three segment search arguments are specified
in the CALL statement in module 2230. The first two,
CUSTOMER-SSA and INVOICE-SSA, tell DL/I to insert the
segment as a child of a particular invoice segment that's a child of a
particular customer segment. And the unqualified SSA tells DL/I
that the segment being inserted is a LINEITEM segment.

DISCUSSION

DL/I programming is a complicated subject. Frankly, if this is your
first exposure to DL/I, you're not ready to start writing DL/I

programs. However, this chapter should put you in a good position to start learning DL/I in the context of CICS. And if you are an experienced DL/I programmer, this chapter should enable you to apply your DL/I batch programming skills in a CICS environment.

Terminology

scheduling call
User Interface Block
UIB
mask
addressability
Base Locator for Linkage
BLL

Objectives

1. Explain the function of the DL/I User Interface Block in a CICS DL/I program.

2. Explain how the scheduling call establishes addressability to the PCBs used by a CICS DL/I program.

3. Develop CICS DL/I programs.

```
         IDENTIFICATION DIVISION.
        *
         PROGRAM-ID. ORDREND.
        *
         ENVIRONMENT DIVISION.
        *
         DATA DIVISION.
        *
         WORKING-STORAGE SECTION.
        *
         01   SWITCHES.
        *
              05   END-SESSION-SW              PIC X     VALUE 'N'.
                   88   END-SESSION                      VALUE 'Y'.
              05   VALID-DATA-SW               PIC X     VALUE 'Y'.
                   88   VALID-DATA                       VALUE 'Y'.
              05   CUSTOMER-FOUND-SW           PIC X     VALUE 'Y'.
                   88   CUSTOMER-FOUND                   VALUE 'Y'.
              05   ITEM-FOUND-SW               PIC X     VALUE 'Y'.
                   88   ITEM-FOUND                       VALUE 'Y'.
              05   VALID-QUANTITY-SW           PIC X     VALUE 'Y'.
                   88   VALID-QUANTITY                   VALUE 'Y'.
        *
         01   FLAGS.
        *
              05   ORDER-VERIFICATION-FLAG     PIC X     VALUE '0'.
                   88   POST-ORDER                       VALUE '1'.
                   88   MODIFY-ORDER                     VALUE '2'.
                   88   CANCEL-ORDER                     VALUE '3'.
              05   ATTRIBUTE-CONTROL-FLAG      PIC X     VALUE '0'.
                   88   SET-PROTECTED                    VALUE '1'.
                   88   SET-UNPROTECTED                  VALUE '2'.
              05   SEND-CONTROL-FLAG           PIC X     VALUE '0'.
                   88   SEND-ALL                         VALUE '1'.
                   88   SEND-DATAONLY                    VALUE '2'.
        *
         01   WORK-FIELDS.
        *
              05   LINE-ITEM-SUB               PIC S9(4)     COMP.
              05   LINE-ITEM-COUNT             PIC S9(4)     COMP.
        *
         01   TOTAL-LINE.
        *
              05   TL-TOTAL-ORDERS    PIC ZZ9.
              05   FILLER             PIC X(15)     VALUE ' ORDERS ENTERED'.
              05   FILLER             PIC X(15)     VALUE '.  PRESS ENTER '.
              05   FILLER             PIC X(15)     VALUE 'TO RETURN TO ME'.
              05   FILLER             PIC X(3)      VALUE 'NU.'.
        *
```

Figure 3-21   Source listing for the DL/I version of the order-entry program (part 1 of 13)

```
   01   COMMUNICATION-AREA.
*
       05   CA-PROCESS-FLAG                PIC X.
            88   PROCESS-ENTRY-SCREEN      VALUE '1'.
            88   PROCESS-VERIFY-SCREEN     VALUE '2'.
       05   CA-UNIT-PRICE                  OCCURS 10
                                           PIC S9(5)V99    COMP-3.
       05   CA-TOTAL-ORDERS                PIC S9(3)       COMP-3
                                           VALUE ZERO.
*
   01   DLI-FUNCTION-CODES.
*
       05   DLI-GET-UNIQUE                 PIC X(4)     VALUE 'GU  '.
       05   DLI-INSERT                     PIC X(4)     VALUE 'ISRT'.
       05   DLI-SCHEDULE                   PIC X(4)     VALUE 'PCB '.
*
   01   PSB-NAME                           PIC X(8)     VALUE 'OEPSB   '.
*
   01   CUSTOMER-SSA.
*
       05   FILLER          PIC X(19)  VALUE 'CUSTOMER(CUSTNO  ='.
       05   SSA-CUSTNO      PIC X(5).
       05   FILLER          PIC X      VALUE ')'.
*
   01   INVOICE-SSA.
*
       05   FILLER          PIC X(19)  VALUE 'INVOICE (INVNO   ='.
       05   SSA-INVNO       PIC 9(5).
       05   FILLER          PIC X      VALUE ')'.
*
   01   INVENTORY-SSA.
*
       05   FILLER          PIC X(19)  VALUE 'INVNTORY(IMITEMNO='.
       05   SSA-IMITEMNO    PIC X(5).
       05   FILLER          PIC X      VALUE ')'.
*
   01   UNQUALIFIED-SSA.
*
       05   SEGMENT-NAME    PIC X(8).
       05   FILLER          PIC X      VALUE SPACE.
*
   01   CUSTOMER-MASTER-SEGMENT.
*
       05   CM-CUSTOMER-NUMBER             PIC X(5).
       05   CM-NAME                        PIC X(30).
       05   CM-ADDRESS                     PIC X(30).
       05   CM-CITY                        PIC X(21).
       05   CM-STATE                       PIC XX.
       05   CM-ZIP-CODE                    PIC X(5).
*
```

Figure 3-21   Source listing for the DL/I version of the order-entry program (part 2 of 13)

Edwin N. Strickland

```
01    INVOICE-SEGMENT.
*
      05    INV-INVOICE-NUMBER              PIC 9(5).
      05    INV-INVOICE-DATE               PIC 9(6).
      05    INV-PO-NUMBER                  PIC X(10).
      05    INV-INVOICE-TOTAL              PIC S9(5)V99    COMP-3.
*
01    LINE-ITEM-SEGMENT.
*
      05    LI-ITEM-NUMBER                 PIC X(5).
      05    LI-QUANTITY                    PIC S9(5)       COMP-3.
      05    LI-UNIT-PRICE                  PIC S9(5)V99    COMP-3.
      05    LI-EXTENSION                   PIC S9(5)V99    COMP-3.
*
01    INVENTORY-MASTER-SEGMENT.
*
      05    IM-ITEM-NUMBER                 PIC X(5).
      05    IM-ITEM-DESCRIPTION            PIC X(20).
      05    IM-UNIT-PRICE                  PIC S9(5)V99    COMP-3.
      05    IM-ON-HAND-QUANTITY            PIC S9(5)       COMP-3.
*
COPY ORDSET1.
*
COPY FACDEFN.
*
LINKAGE SECTION.
*
01    DFHCOMMAREA                          PIC X(43).
*
01    BLL-CELLS.
*
      05    FILLER                         PIC S9(8)       COMP.
      05    BLL-CWA                        PIC S9(8)       COMP.
      05    BLL-UIB                        PIC S9(8)       COMP.
      05    BLL-PCB-POINTERS               PIC S9(8)       COMP.
      05    BLL-CUSTOMER-PCB               PIC S9(8)       COMP.
      05    BLL-INVENTORY-PCB              PIC S9(8)       COMP.
*
01    COMMON-WORK-AREA.
*
      05    CWA-DATE                       PIC 9(6).
*
COPY DLIUIB.
*
01    PCB-POINTERS.
*
      05    CUSTOMER-PCB-POINTER           PIC S9(8)       COMP.
      05    INVENTORY-PCB-POINTER          PIC S9(8)       COMP.
*
```

Figure 3-21   Source listing for the DL/I version of the order-entry program (part 3 of 13)

```
01    CUSTOMER-PCB.
*
      05   FILLER                      PIC X(10).
      05   CUSTOMER-STATUS-CODE        PIC XX.
*
01    INVENTORY-PCB.
*
      05   FILLER                      PIC X(10).
      05   INVENTORY-STATUS-CODE       PIC XX.
*
PROCEDURE DIVISION.
*
0000-ACCEPT-CUSTOMER-ORDERS SECTION.
*
      MOVE LOW-VALUE TO ORDER-ENTRY-MAP.
      EXEC CICS
          ADDRESS CWA(BLL-CWA)
      END-EXEC.
      IF EIBCALEN = ZERO
          PERFORM 8000-START-TERMINAL-SESSION
      ELSE
          PERFORM 0500-SCHEDULE-PSB
          MOVE DFHCOMMAREA TO COMMUNICATION-AREA
          IF PROCESS-ENTRY-SCREEN
              PERFORM 1000-PROCESS-ENTRY-SCREEN
          ELSE IF PROCESS-VERIFY-SCREEN
              PERFORM 2000-PROCESS-VERIFY-SCREEN.
      IF END-SESSION
          PERFORM 9000-SEND-TERMINATION-MESSAGE
          EXEC CICS
              RETURN TRANSID('MENU')
          END-EXEC
      ELSE
          EXEC CICS
              RETURN TRANSID('ORDD')
                     COMMAREA(COMMUNICATION-AREA)
                     LENGTH(43)
          END-EXEC.
*
0500-SCHEDULE-PSB SECTION.
*
      CALL 'CBLTDLI' USING DLI-SCHEDULE
                           PSB-NAME
                           BLL-UIB.
      IF UIBFCTR NOT = LOW-VALUE
          EXEC CICS
              ABEND ABCODE('DLI1')
          END-EXEC.
      MOVE UIBPCBAL                 TO BLL-PCB-POINTERS.
      MOVE CUSTOMER-PCB-POINTER  TO BLL-CUSTOMER-PCB.
      MOVE INVENTORY-PCB-POINTER TO BLL-INVENTORY-PCB.
*
```

Figure 3-21   Source listing for the DL/I version of the order-entry program (part 4 of 13)

```
1000-PROCESS-ENTRY-SCREEN SECTION.
*

    PERFORM 1100-RECEIVE-ENTRY-SCREEN.
    IF NOT END-SESSION
        IF VALID-DATA
            PERFORM 1200-EDIT-ORDER-DATA.
    IF NOT END-SESSION
        IF VALID-DATA
            MOVE 'PRESS ENTER TO POST ORDER, PF1 TO MODIFY ORDER,
                ' OR CLEAR TO CANCEL ORDER'
                TO OEM-D-OPERATOR-MESSAGE
            MOVE SPACE TO OEM-D-ERROR-MESSAGE
            MOVE '1' TO ATTRIBUTE-CONTROL-FLAG
            MOVE '2' TO SEND-CONTROL-FLAG
            PERFORM 1300-SEND-ORDER-SCREEN
            MOVE '2' TO CA-PROCESS-FLAG
        ELSE
            MOVE 'ERRORS DETECTED--MAKE CORRECTIONS OR PRESS CLEA
                'R TO END SESSION' TO OEM-D-OPERATOR-MESSAGE
            MOVE '0' TO ATTRIBUTE-CONTROL-FLAG
            MOVE '2' TO SEND-CONTROL-FLAG
            PERFORM 1300-SEND-ORDER-SCREEN
            MOVE '1' TO CA-PROCESS-FLAG.
*
 1100-RECEIVE-ENTRY-SCREEN SECTION.
*
    EXEC CICS
        HANDLE AID CLEAR(1100-CLEAR-KEY)
                   ANYKEY(1100-ANYKEY)
    END-EXEC.
    EXEC CICS
        RECEIVE MAP('ORDMAP1')
                MAPSET('ORDSET1')
                INTO(ORDER-ENTRY-MAP)
    END-EXEC.
    GO TO 1100-EXIT.
*
 1100-CLEAR-KEY.
*
    MOVE 'Y' TO END-SESSION-SW.
    GO TO 1100-EXIT.
*
 1100-ANYKEY.
*
    MOVE -1 TO OEM-L-CUSTOMER-NUMBER.
    MOVE 'N' TO VALID-DATA-SW.
    MOVE 'INVALID KEY PRESSED' TO OEM-D-ERROR-MESSAGE.
*
 1100-EXIT.
*
    EXIT.
*
```

Figure 3-21   Source listing for the DL/I version of the order-entry program (part 5 of 13)

```
 1200-EDIT-ORDER-DATA SECTION.
*
     MOVE FAC-UNPROT-NUM-MDT TO OEM-A-CUSTOMER-NUMBER.
*
     MOVE ZERO TO LINE-ITEM-COUNT
                  INV-INVOICE-TOTAL.
     PERFORM 1220-EDIT-LINE-ITEM
         VARYING LINE-ITEM-SUB FROM 10 BY -1
         UNTIL LINE-ITEM-SUB < 1.
     MOVE INV-INVOICE-TOTAL TO OEM-D-INVOICE-TOTAL.
     IF LINE-ITEM-COUNT = ZERO
         MOVE FAC-UNPROT-NUM-BRT-MDT TO OEM-A-ITEM-NUMBER(1)
         MOVE -1 TO OEM-L-ITEM-NUMBER(1)
         MOVE 'YOU MUST ENTER AT LEAST ONE LINE ITEM'
             TO OEM-D-ERROR-MESSAGE.
*
     IF OEM-L-CUSTOMER-NUMBER = ZERO
         MOVE FAC-UNPROT-NUM-BRT-MDT TO OEM-A-CUSTOMER-NUMBER
         MOVE -1 TO OEM-L-CUSTOMER-NUMBER
         MOVE 'YOU MUST ENTER A CUSTOMER NUMBER'
             TO OEM-D-ERROR-MESSAGE
         MOVE SPACE TO OEM-D-NAME
     ELSE
         PERFORM 1210-GET-CUSTOMER-SEGMENT
         IF CUSTOMER-FOUND
             MOVE CM-NAME TO OEM-D-NAME
         ELSE
             MOVE FAC-UNPROT-NUM-BRT-MDT TO OEM-A-CUSTOMER-NUMBER
             MOVE -1 TO OEM-L-CUSTOMER-NUMBER
             MOVE 'CUSTOMER NOT IN FILE' TO OEM-D-ERROR-MESSAGE
             MOVE SPACE TO OEM-D-NAME.
*
     IF OEM-D-ERROR-MESSAGE NOT = LOW-VALUE
         MOVE 'N' TO VALID-DATA-SW.
*
 1210-GET-CUSTOMER-SEGMENT SECTION.
*
     MOVE OEM-D-CUSTOMER-NUMBER TO SSA-CUSTNO.
     CALL 'CBLTDLI' USING DLI-GET-UNIQUE
                   CUSTOMER-PCB
                   CUSTOMER-MASTER-SEGMENT
                   CUSTOMER-SSA.
     IF UIBFCTR NOT = LOW-VALUE
         EXEC CICS
             ABEND ABCODE('DLI2')
         END-EXEC.
     IF CUSTOMER-STATUS-CODE = 'GE'
         MOVE 'N' TO CUSTOMER-FOUND-SW
         MOVE SPACE TO CM-NAME
     ELSE IF CUSTOMER-STATUS-CODE NOT = SPACE
         EXEC CICS
             ABEND ABCODE('DLI3')
         END-EXEC.
```

Figure 3-21   Source listing for the DL/I version of the order-entry program (part 6 of 13)

```
*
  1220-EDIT-LINE-ITEM SECTION.
*
      MOVE 'N' TO ITEM-FOUND-SW.
      MOVE 'Y' TO VALID-QUANTITY-SW.
      MOVE FAC-UNPROT-NUM-MDT TO OEM-A-ITEM-NUMBER(LINE-ITEM-SUB)
                                  OEM-A-QUANTITY(LINE-ITEM-SUB).
*
      IF OEM-L-ITEM-NUMBER(LINE-ITEM-SUB) = ZERO
          IF OEM-L-QUANTITY(LINE-ITEM-SUB) NOT = ZERO
              MOVE FAC-UNPROT-NUM-BRT-MDT
                  TO OEM-A-QUANTITY(LINE-ITEM-SUB)
              MOVE -1 TO OEM-L-QUANTITY(LINE-ITEM-SUB)
              MOVE 'QUANTITY INVALID WITHOUT ITEM NUMBER'
                  TO OEM-D-ERROR-MESSAGE.
*
      IF OEM-L-ITEM-NUMBER(LINE-ITEM-SUB) NOT = ZERO
          IF OEM-L-QUANTITY(LINE-ITEM-SUB) = ZERO
              MOVE 'N' TO VALID-QUANTITY-SW
              MOVE FAC-UNPROT-NUM-BRT-MDT
                  TO OEM-A-QUANTITY(LINE-ITEM-SUB)
              MOVE -1 TO OEM-L-QUANTITY(LINE-ITEM-SUB)
              MOVE 'YOU MUST ENTER A QUANTITY'
                  TO OEM-D-ERROR-MESSAGE
          ELSE IF OEM-D-QUANTITY(LINE-ITEM-SUB) NOT NUMERIC
              MOVE 'N' TO VALID-QUANTITY-SW
              MOVE FAC-UNPROT-NUM-BRT-MDT
                  TO OEM-A-QUANTITY(LINE-ITEM-SUB)
              MOVE -1 TO OEM-L-QUANTITY(LINE-ITEM-SUB)
              MOVE 'QUANTITY MUST BE NUMERIC'
                  TO OEM-D-ERROR-MESSAGE
          ELSE IF OEM-D-QUANTITY(LINE-ITEM-SUB) NOT > ZERO
              MOVE 'N' TO VALID-QUANTITY-SW
              MOVE FAC-UNPROT-NUM-BRT-MDT
                  TO OEM-A-QUANTITY(LINE-ITEM-SUB)
              MOVE -1 TO OEM-L-QUANTITY(LINE-ITEM-SUB)
              MOVE 'QUANTITY MUST BE GREATER THAN ZERO'
                  TO OEM-D-ERROR-MESSAGE.
*
      IF OEM-L-ITEM-NUMBER(LINE-ITEM-SUB) = ZERO
          MOVE SPACE TO OEM-D-ITEM-DESCRIPTION(LINE-ITEM-SUB)
          MOVE ZERO  TO OEM-D-UNIT-PRICE(LINE-ITEM-SUB)
                        OEM-D-EXTENSION(LINE-ITEM-SUB)
      ELSE
          ADD 1 TO LINE-ITEM-COUNT
          PERFORM 1230-GET-INVENTORY-SEGMENT
          IF ITEM-FOUND
              MOVE IM-ITEM-DESCRIPTION
                  TO OEM-D-ITEM-DESCRIPTION(LINE-ITEM-SUB)
              MOVE IM-UNIT-PRICE
                  TO OEM-D-UNIT-PRICE(LINE-ITEM-SUB)
                     CA-UNIT-PRICE(LINE-ITEM-SUB)
```

Figure 3-21   Source listing for the DL/I version of the order-entry program (part 7 of 13)

```
          ELSE
              MOVE SPACE TO OEM-D-ITEM-DESCRIPTION(LINE-ITEM-SUB)
              MOVE ZERO  TO OEM-D-UNIT-PRICE(LINE-ITEM-SUB)
                            OEM-D-EXTENSION(LINE-ITEM-SUB)
              MOVE FAC-UNPROT-NUM-BRT-MDT
                  TO OEM-A-ITEM-NUMBER(LINE-ITEM-SUB)
              MOVE -1 TO OEM-L-ITEM-NUMBER(LINE-ITEM-SUB)
              MOVE 'ITEM NOT IN INVENTORY FILE'
                  TO OEM-D-ERROR-MESSAGE.
*
      IF        ITEM-FOUND
          AND VALID-QUANTITY
          MULTIPLY OEM-D-QUANTITY(LINE-ITEM-SUB)
              BY IM-UNIT-PRICE
              GIVING OEM-D-EXTENSION(LINE-ITEM-SUB)
                     LI-EXTENSION
              ON SIZE ERROR
                  MOVE 'N' TO VALID-QUANTITY-SW
                  MOVE ZERO TO OEM-D-EXTENSION(LINE-ITEM-SUB)
                  MOVE FAC-UNPROT-NUM-BRT-MDT
                      TO OEM-A-QUANTITY(LINE-ITEM-SUB)
                  MOVE -1 TO OEM-L-QUANTITY(LINE-ITEM-SUB)
                  MOVE 'QUANTITY TOO LARGE'
                      TO OEM-D-ERROR-MESSAGE.
*
      IF        ITEM-FOUND
          AND VALID-QUANTITY
          ADD LI-EXTENSION
              TO INV-INVOICE-TOTAL
              ON SIZE ERROR
                  MOVE 99999.99 TO INV-INVOICE-TOTAL
                  MOVE -1 TO OEM-L-ITEM-NUMBER(1)
                  MOVE 'INVOICE TOTAL TOO LARGE'
                      TO OEM-D-ERROR-MESSAGE.
*
  1230-GET-INVENTORY-SEGMENT SECTION.
*
      MOVE 'Y' TO ITEM-FOUND-SW.
      MOVE OEM-D-ITEM-NUMBER(LINE-ITEM-SUB) TO SSA-IMITEMNO.
      CALL 'CBLTDLI' USING DLI-GET-UNIQUE
                          INVENTORY-PCB
                          INVENTORY-MASTER-SEGMENT
                          INVENTORY-SSA.
      IF UIBFCTR NOT = LOW-VALUE
          EXEC CICS
              ABEND ABCODE('DLI4')
          END-EXEC.
      IF INVENTORY-STATUS-CODE = 'GE'
          MOVE SPACE TO IM-ITEM-DESCRIPTION
          MOVE ZERO  TO IM-UNIT-PRICE
          MOVE 'N' TO ITEM-FOUND-SW
```

Figure 3-21   Source listing for the DL/I version of the order-entry program (part 8 of 13)

```
      ELSE IF INVENTORY-STATUS-CODE NOT = SPACE
          EXEC CICS
              ABEND ABCODE('DLI5')
          END-EXEC.
 *
 1300-SEND-ORDER-SCREEN SECTION.
 *
      IF SET-PROTECTED
          PERFORM 1310-SET-ATTRIBUTES
      ELSE IF SET-UNPROTECTED
          PERFORM 1330-RESET-ATTRIBUTES.
      IF SEND-ALL
          EXEC CICS
              SEND MAP('ORDMAP1')
                   MAPSET('ORDSET1')
                   FROM(ORDER-ENTRY-MAP)
                   ERASE
                   CURSOR
          END-EXEC
      ELSE IF SEND-DATAONLY
          EXEC CICS
              SEND MAP('ORDMAP1')
                   MAPSET('ORDSET1')
                   FROM(ORDER-ENTRY-MAP)
                   DATAONLY
                   CURSOR
          END-EXEC.
 *
 1310-SET-ATTRIBUTES SECTION.
 *
      MOVE FAC-PROT-MDT TO OEM-A-CUSTOMER-NUMBER
                          OEM-A-PO-NUMBER.
      PERFORM 1320-SET-LINE-ATTRIBUTES
          VARYING LINE-ITEM-SUB FROM 1 BY 1
          UNTIL LINE-ITEM-SUB > 10.
 *
 1320-SET-LINE-ATTRIBUTES SECTION.
 *
      MOVE FAC-PROT-MDT TO OEM-A-ITEM-NUMBER(LINE-ITEM-SUB)
                          OEM-A-QUANTITY(LINE-ITEM-SUB).
 *
 1330-RESET-ATTRIBUTES SECTION.
 *
      MOVE FAC-UNPROT-MDT TO OEM-A-CUSTOMER-NUMBER
                            OEM-A-PO-NUMBER.
      PERFORM 1340-RESET-LINE-ATTRIBUTES
          VARYING LINE-ITEM-SUB FROM 1 BY 1
          UNTIL LINE-ITEM-SUB > 10.
 *
```

Figure 3-21   Source listing for the DL/I version of the order-entry program (part 9 of 13)

```
   1340-RESET-LINE-ATTRIBUTES SECTION.
*
       MOVE FAC-UNPROT-NUM-MDT TO OEM-A-ITEM-NUMBER(LINE-ITEM-SUB)
                                  OEM-A-QUANTITY(LINE-ITEM-SUB).
*
   2000-PROCESS-VERIFY-SCREEN SECTION.
*
       PERFORM 2100-RECEIVE-VERIFY-SCREEN.
       IF POST-ORDER
           PERFORM 2200-POST-ORDER-DATA
           MOVE LOW-VALUE TO ORDER-ENTRY-MAP
           MOVE -1 TO OEM-L-CUSTOMER-NUMBER
           MOVE 'ORDER POSTED--ENTER NEXT ORDER OR PRESS CLEAR TO EN
               'D SESSION' TO OEM-D-OPERATOR-MESSAGE
           MOVE '0' TO ATTRIBUTE-CONTROL-FLAG
           MOVE '1' TO SEND-CONTROL-FLAG
           PERFORM 1300-SEND-ORDER-SCREEN
           MOVE '1' TO CA-PROCESS-FLAG
       ELSE IF MODIFY-ORDER
           MOVE LOW-VALUE TO ORDER-ENTRY-MAP
           MOVE -1 TO OEM-L-CUSTOMER-NUMBER
           MOVE 'ENTER MODIFICATIONS OR PRESS CLEAR TO END SESSION'
               TO OEM-D-OPERATOR-MESSAGE
           MOVE '2' TO ATTRIBUTE-CONTROL-FLAG
           MOVE '2' TO SEND-CONTROL-FLAG
           PERFORM 1300-SEND-ORDER-SCREEN
           MOVE '1' TO CA-PROCESS-FLAG
       ELSE IF CANCEL-ORDER
           MOVE LOW-VALUE TO ORDER-ENTRY-MAP
           MOVE -1 TO OEM-L-CUSTOMER-NUMBER
           MOVE 'ORDER CANCELLED--ENTER NEXT ORDER OR PRESS CLEAR TO
               ' END SESSION' TO OEM-D-OPERATOR-MESSAGE
           MOVE '0' TO ATTRIBUTE-CONTROL-FLAG
           MOVE '1' TO SEND-CONTROL-FLAG
           PERFORM 1300-SEND-ORDER-SCREEN
           MOVE '1' TO CA-PROCESS-FLAG
       ELSE
           MOVE LOW-VALUE TO ORDER-ENTRY-MAP
           MOVE 'PRESS ENTER TO POST ORDER, PF1 TO MODIFY ORDER, OR
               'CLEAR TO CANCEL ORDER' TO OEM-D-OPERATOR-MESSAGE
           MOVE 'INVALID KEY PRESSED' TO OEM-D-ERROR-MESSAGE
           MOVE '0' TO ATTRIBUTE-CONTROL-FLAG
           MOVE '2' TO SEND-CONTROL-FLAG
           PERFORM 1300-SEND-ORDER-SCREEN
           MOVE '2' TO CA-PROCESS-FLAG.
*
   2100-RECEIVE-VERIFY-SCREEN SECTION.
*
       EXEC CICS
           HANDLE AID PF1(2100-PF1-KEY)
                      CLEAR(2100-CLEAR-KEY)
                      ANYKEY(2100-ANYKEY)
       END-EXEC.
       MOVE '1' TO ORDER-VERIFICATION-FLAG.
```

Figure 3-21   Source listing for the DL/I version of the order-entry program (part 10 of 13)

```
        EXEC CICS
            RECEIVE MAP('ORDMAP1')
                    MAPSET('ORDSET1')
                    INTO(ORDER-ENTRY-MAP)
        END-EXEC.
        GO TO 2100-EXIT.
*
    2100-PF1-KEY.
*
        MOVE '2' TO ORDER-VERIFICATION-FLAG.
        GO TO 2100-EXIT.
*
    2100-CLEAR-KEY.
*
        MOVE '3' TO ORDER-VERIFICATION-FLAG.
        GO TO 2100-EXIT.
*
    2100-ANYKEY.
*
        MOVE '0' TO ORDER-VERIFICATION-FLAG.
*
    2100-EXIT.
*
        EXIT.
*
    2200-POST-ORDER-DATA SECTION.
*
        MOVE ZERO TO INV-INVOICE-TOTAL.
        PERFORM 2210-COMPUTE-INVOICE-TOTAL
            VARYING LINE-ITEM-SUB FROM 1 BY 1
            UNTIL LINE-ITEM-SUB > 10.
        PERFORM 2220-INSERT-INVOICE-SEGMENT.
        PERFORM 2230-INSERT-LINE-ITEM-SEGMENT
            VARYING LINE-ITEM-SUB FROM 1 BY 1
            UNTIL LINE-ITEM-SUB > 10.
        ADD 1 TO CA-TOTAL-ORDERS.
*
    2210-COMPUTE-INVOICE-TOTAL SECTION.
*
        IF OEM-L-ITEM-NUMBER(LINE-ITEM-SUB) NOT = ZERO
            COMPUTE INV-INVOICE-TOTAL = INV-INVOICE-TOTAL +
                OEM-D-QUANTITY(LINE-ITEM-SUB) *
                CA-UNIT-PRICE(LINE-ITEM-SUB).
*
    2220-INSERT-INVOICE-SEGMENT SECTION.
*
        EXEC CICS
            LINK PROGRAM('GETINV')
                 COMMAREA(INV-INVOICE-NUMBER)
                 LENGTH(5)
        END-EXEC.
```

Figure 3-21   Source listing for the DL/I version of the order-entry program (part 11 of 13)

```
            MOVE CWA-DATE                    TO INV-INVOICE-DATE.
            MOVE OEM-D-PO-NUMBER             TO INV-PO-NUMBER.
            MOVE OEM-D-CUSTOMER-NUMBER TO SSA-CUSTNO.
            MOVE 'INVOICE'                   TO SEGMENT-NAME.
            CALL 'CBLTDLI' USING DLI-INSERT
                          CUSTOMER-PCB
                          INVOICE-SEGMENT
                          CUSTOMER-SSA
                          UNQUALIFIED-SSA.
        IF        UIBFCTR NOT = LOW-VALUE
            OR CUSTOMER-STATUS-CODE NOT = SPACE
            EXEC CICS
                ABEND ABCODE('DLI6')
            END-EXEC.
    *
    2230-INSERT-LINE-ITEM-SEGMENT SECTION.
    *
        IF OEM-L-ITEM-NUMBER(LINE-ITEM-SUB) NOT = ZERO
            MOVE OEM-D-ITEM-NUMBER(LINE-ITEM-SUB)
                TO LI-ITEM-NUMBER
            MOVE OEM-D-QUANTITY(LINE-ITEM-SUB)
                TO LI-QUANTITY
            MOVE CA-UNIT-PRICE(LINE-ITEM-SUB)
                TO LI-UNIT-PRICE
            COMPUTE LI-EXTENSION = LI-QUANTITY * LI-UNIT-PRICE
            MOVE INV-INVOICE-NUMBER TO SSA-INVNO
            MOVE 'LINEITEM' TO SEGMENT-NAME
            CALL 'CBLTDLI' USING DLI-INSERT
                              CUSTOMER-PCB
                              LINE-ITEM-SEGMENT
                              CUSTOMER-SSA
                              INVOICE-SSA
                              UNQUALIFIED-SSA
        IF        UIBFCTR NOT = LOW-VALUE
            OR CUSTOMER-STATUS-CODE NOT = SPACE
            EXEC CICS
                ABEND ABCODE('DLI7')
            END-EXEC.
    *
    8000-START-TERMINAL-SESSION SECTION.
    *
        MOVE LOW-VALUE TO ORDER-ENTRY-MAP.
        MOVE -1 TO OEM-L-CUSTOMER-NUMBER.
        MOVE 'PRESS CLEAR TO END SESSION' TO OEM-D-OPERATOR-MESSAGE.
        MOVE '0' TO ATTRIBUTE-CONTROL-FLAG.
        MOVE '1' TO SEND-CONTROL-FLAG.
        PERFORM 1300-SEND-ORDER-SCREEN.
        MOVE '1' TO CA-PROCESS-FLAG.
    *
```

Figure 3-21   Source listing for the DL/I version of the order-entry program (part 12 of 13)

```
    9000-SEND-TERMINATION-MESSAGE SECTION.
*
        MOVE CA-TOTAL-ORDERS TO TL-TOTAL-ORDERS.
        EXEC CICS
            SEND TEXT FROM(TOTAL-LINE)
                      LENGTH(51)
                      ERASE
                      FREEKB
        END-EXEC.
```

Figure 3-21   Source listing for the DL/I version of the order-entry program (part 13 of 13)

Part 2

Queue management features

In part 1 of this book, you learned how to use the file and data base management capabilities of CICS. The chapters in this part show you how to use two related CICS features: temporary storage and transient data. Both let you store and retrieve data in ways not practical using typical VSAM files. In chapter 4, you'll learn how to use temporary storage, and in chapter 5, you'll learn how to create and retrieve transient data. Because these chapters are independent, you can read either one first.

I want to warn you that it's easy to become confused about the distinction between temporary storage and transient data. That's because they use similar commands and the IBM literature uses similar terminology to describe them. Their differences and similarities should become apparent as you read these chapters.

Chapter 4

Temporary storage control

Many CICS programs have to be able to process data outside their Working-Storage Sections. For example, pseudo-conversational programs often need to save data between executions during a single terminal session. The storage area in which you place data like that is sometimes called a *scratchpad*. You already know one way to implement a scratchpad: the communication area. Now, you'll learn how *temporary storage control* provides a more sophisticated scratchpad facility than the communication area.

After I present the temporary storage concepts you need to know, I'll show you three temporary storage commands that let you read, write, and delete temporary storage data. Then, I'll present a sample program that shows you how to use temporary storage.

TEMPORARY STORAGE CONCEPTS

Temporary storage is just what it says: a place CICS provides that programs can use to store data temporarily. Temporary storage is divided into *temporary storage queues*, or just *TS queues*. Each TS queue contains one or more *records*, sometimes called *items*, that contain data stored by application programs. Although TS queues contain records, don't think of those records in file-processing terms. Usually, a TS queue consists of just one record, and the data elements in that record aren't necessarily related in the way data elements in a file record are.

Queues and queue names

A temporary storage queue is identified by a unique one- to eight-character *queue name* (sometimes called a *data-id*). You don't have to define TS queue names in a CICS table. Instead, queues are created dynamically. When an application program tries to write a record using a queue name that doesn't exist, temporary storage control creates a new TS queue.

I want you to realize that CICS does provide a *Temporary Storage Table* (or *TST*) in which you can define TS queue names. But the only reason you use the TST is to specify which TS queues CICS should make recoverable. Since it's unusual to require that a TS queue be recoverable, you probably don't need to worry about the TST.

Because many users can create temporary storage queues at once, it's important to use a unique name when you create a TS queue. To ensure that TS queue names are unique, you can use the value in the Execute Interface Block's terminal-identification field as part of the queue name. Since each terminal within a CICS system has a unique term-id, queue names based on EIBTRMID are also unique. However, if your shop has other standards that dictate how queues should be named, by all means follow them.

Items and item numbers

Within a queue, each record is assigned an *item number*. The first record written to a queue is item 1, the second is item 2, and so on. CICS automatically assigns an item number to each record you add to a queue, so you only need to specify an item number when you retrieve or update a record. Unlike the record key of a VSAM key-sequenced file, a temporary storage item number is *not* a part of the record it's associated with.

Although you can store many records in a TS queue, it's uncommon to store more than one. In most applications, you'll use temporary storage as a scratchpad. And for that purpose, you'll usually store a single record that the next execution of your pseudo-conversational program can retrieve.

An application program can retrieve records from a temporary storage queue in two ways: sequentially and randomly. For sequential retrieval, records are retrieved in item number sequence. For random retrieval, you specify the item number of the TS queue record you want to retrieve. Because most scratchpad applications need only one record, you'll typically use random retrieval, specifying item 1.

An application program can also rewrite a record in a TS queue. For scratchpad applications, that's a common requirement. Usually, a pseudo-conversational program writes one record to a TS queue when the operator invokes the program for the first time. Then, on subsequent executions of the program during the same terminal session, the program rewrites the existing TS record—it doesn't add additional records.

How temporary storage queues are stored

Normally, temporary storage control maintains TS queues in a single VSAM entry-sequenced data set called the *temporary storage file*, or *DFHTEMP*. For pseudo-conversational programs, that's an efficient way to store data between program executions. In fact, that's one of the advantages temporary storage has over the communication area: it makes better use of your system's resources by not tying up main storage for long periods of time.

In cases where you want to store and retrieve a temporary storage record within a single task execution, however, the additional overhead of disk processing can be a drawback. So temporary storage control lets you choose between disk storage and virtual storage. If you specify main storage rather than disk, temporary storage saves your records in main storage. That results in faster processing, but bear in mind that main storage is a critical resource in a CICS system. For a routine scratchpad application (that is, where a TS queue exists between task executions), you should place the queue on disk rather than in main storage.

CICS COMMANDS FOR TEMPORARY STORAGE QUEUES

To process a temporary storage queue, you use three CICS commands. You use the WRITEQ TS command to add a record to a TS queue. You use the READQ TS command to retrieve a record from a TS queue. And you use the DELETEQ TS command to delete a TS queue.

The WRITEQ TS command

```
EXEC CICS
    WRITEQ TS QUEUE(data-name|literal)
              FROM(data-name)
              LENGTH(data-name|literal)
             [ITEM(data-name)
              REWRITE]
             [{MAIN     }]
             [{AUXILIARY}]
END-EXEC
```

Explanation

QUEUE	The one- to eight-character name of the temporary storage queue to which data is written.
FROM	The data area that contains the record to be written.
LENGTH	The length of the FROM area. Must be numeric. If you use a data-name, it must be a binary half-word (PIC S9(4) COMP).
ITEM	The item number of the record to be updated. Must be a binary half-word (PIC S9(4) COMP).
REWRITE	An existing record in the TS queue should be updated.
MAIN	The temporary storage queue will reside in main storage.
AUXILIARY	The temporary storage queue will reside on disk in the temporary storage file (DFHTEMP).

Figure 4-1   The WRITEQ TS command

The WRITEQ TS command

Figure 4-1 gives the format of the WRITEQ TS command. Depending on how you code it, the WRITEQ TS command either adds a new record to a TS queue or updates an existing record in a queue.

How to add a record to a queue   To add a record to a temporary storage queue, you code the WRITEQ TS command like this:

```
EXEC CICS
    WRITEQ TS QUEUE(TS-QUEUE-NAME)
              FROM(TS-QUEUE-RECORD)
              LENGTH(TS-QUEUE-LENGTH)
END-EXEC
```

Here, the contents of TS-QUEUE-RECORD, whose length is specified by TS-QUEUE-LENGTH, are written to a queue whose name is in TS-QUEUE-NAME. You should define the LENGTH field as a binary half-word (PIC S9(4) COMP).

If a TS queue with the name you specify already exists, your record is added to the end of that queue. If no queue with that name exists, CICS automatically creates a queue, then adds your record as the queue's first record. As a result, no special processing is required to create a temporary storage queue.

You indicate whether the queue is stored in main storage or on disk by coding AUXILIARY or MAIN. If you code AUXILIARY (or let it default), the queue is stored in the temporary storage file. If you code MAIN, the queue is kept in main storage.

There aren't any errors that are likely to occur when you issue a WRITEQ TS command to add a record to a TS queue. So you don't need to issue a HANDLE CONDITION command before the WRITEQ TS command.

How to update an existing record   If you code REWRITE on a WRITEQ TS command, an existing record in the TS queue is replaced. In that case, you must specify the ITEM parameter to indicate which record should be updated. For example, suppose the value of TS-ITEM-NUMBER is 1. Then, if you issue the command

```
EXEC CICS
    WRITEQ TS QUEUE(TS-QUEUE-NAME)
              FROM(TS-QUEUE-RECORD)
              LENGTH(TS-QUEUE-LENGTH)
              ITEM(TS-ITEM-NUMBER)
              REWRITE
END-EXEC
```

item 1 is replaced by the contents of TS-QUEUE-RECORD. In other words, this command updates the first queue record.

When you update a temporary storage record, one of two exceptional conditions might be raised. If you specify a queue that doesn't exist, the QIDERR condition is raised. And if you specify an item number that doesn't exist within the queue, the ITEMERR condition is raised. Note that the ITEMERR condition is never raised if you're updating item 1. That's because if item 1 doesn't exist, the queue doesn't exist. So the QIDERR condition is raised instead. The default action for both the QIDERR condition and the ITEMERR condition is to terminate your task. So depending on your application's requirements, you may need to provide for one or both of these conditions in a HANDLE CONDITION command.

The READQ TS command

To retrieve records from a temporary storage queue, you use the READQ TS command, shown in figure 4-2. Typically, you code it like this:

```
EXEC CICS
    READQ TS QUEUE(TS-QUEUE-NAME)
             INTO(TS-QUEUE-RECORD)
             LENGTH(TS-QUEUE-LENGTH)
             ITEM(TS-ITEM-NUMBER)
END-EXEC
```

Here, the record whose item number is indicated by TS-ITEM-NUMBER is read. Normally, you'll assign a value of 1 to the item number field to retrieve the first—and only—record in your queue.

If the item you specify doesn't exist, the ITEMERR condition is raised. And if the queue doesn't exist, the QIDERR condition is raised. You may need to handle one or both of these conditions, depending on your application's requirements. Remember that ITEMERR won't occur when you attempt to read item 1, because a queue doesn't exist until at least one record has been written to it.

For a READQ TS command, the initial value of the LENGTH field gives the maximum record length your program can process. If CICS reads a queue record that's longer than this maximum, the LENGERR condition is raised and your task is terminated. You can handle the LENGERR condition if you wish, but it probably represents a serious error if it occurs. So you may as well let CICS abend your task. Assuming the LENGERR condition doesn't occur, CICS places the actual length of the record that's read in the LENGTH field after the READQ TS command executes.

If you're processing a queue that contains more than one item, you can specify NEXT rather than ITEM to retrieve the queue

The READQ TS command

```
EXEC CICS
      READQ TS QUEUE(data-name|literal)
               INTO(data-name)
               LENGTH(data-name)
              [{ITEM(data-name|literal)}]
              [{NEXT                    }]
END-EXEC
```

Explanation

QUEUE	The one- to eight-character name of the temporary storage queue from which data is read.
INTO	The data area that will contain the record.
LENGTH	The length of the INTO area. Must be a binary half-word (PIC S9(4) COMP).
ITEM	The item number of the record to be read. Must be numeric. If you use a data-name, it must be a binary half-word (PIC S9(4) COMP).
NEXT	The next record in sequence should be read.

Figure 4-2   The READQ TS command

items in sequence. Quite simply, NEXT means that CICS should retrieve the next record in sequence following the most recently read record. However, you must realize that *any* task in a CICS system can affect the positioning of a READQ TS/NEXT command by issuing a READQ TS command for the same queue. So if your task is reading queue records sequentially while another task is retrieving records from the same queue, your program won't work properly.

Normally, you won't run into contention problems when you process a TS queue. That's because a typical TS queue has a unique name that uses the terminal-id field from the Execute Interface Block. If your application requires that two or more tasks have access to a common TS queue, you'll need to use two CICS commands that let you reserve exclusive access to a CICS resource: ENQ and DEQ. Because it's not common for several tasks to share access to a TS queue, I'm not going to show you how to use the

---

The DELETEQ TS command

```
EXEC CICS
    DELETEQ TS QUEUE(data-name|literal)
END-EXEC
```

Explanation

QUEUE   The one- to eight-character name of the temporary storage
                           queue to be deleted.

Figure 4-3   The DELETEQ TS command

ENQ and DEQ commands in this chapter. But you'll find a complete description of them in chapter 11, so feel free to look ahead to that chapter if you need to.

The DELETEQ TS command

Figure 4-3 gives the format of the DELETEQ TS command. You must issue a DELETEQ TS command to delete a TS queue when you're finished processing it. If you don't, the queue remains indefinitely, wasting valuable disk or main storage space. Note that the DELETEQ TS command deletes an entire TS queue—there's no way to delete a single record. Since most queues contain just one record anyway, that shouldn't be a problem.

If you try to delete a queue that doesn't exist, the QIDERR condition is raised. As a result, you should provide a HANDLE CONDITION command for the QIDERR condition. In many cases, you can simply ignore the error condition. That's because QIDERR means the queue you specify doesn't exist—and your DELETEQ TS command is trying to delete the queue anyway.

A SAMPLE PROGRAM

Figures 4-4 through 4-8 present a program that maintains records in a customer file, allowing additions, deletions, or changes to records in the file. As you can see in figure 4-4, the customer-maintenance program uses two screens. On the first one, the

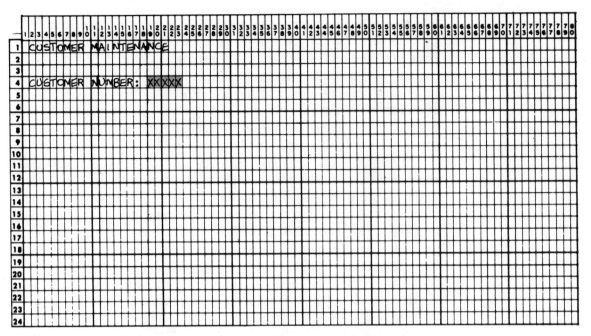

Figure 4-4   Screen layout for the enhanced customer-maintenance program (part 1 of 2)

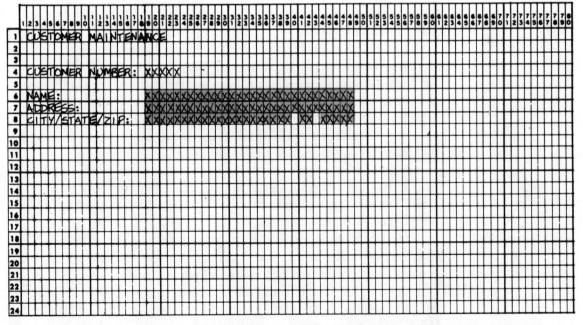

Figure 4-4   Screen layout for the enhanced customer-maintenance program (part 2 of 2)

operator enters a customer number. If a corresponding customer record exists, the program displays the second screen along with the data from the record. Then, the operator can change the data or press PF1 to delete the record. If the record doesn't exist, the program displays the second screen with no initial data, and the operator enters data for the record to be added. Figure 4-5 shows the mapset for the customer-maintenance program, and figure 4-6 shows the symbolic map I created.

If you've read *Part 1: An introductory course*, you'll recognize right away that this program is an enhancement of the customer-maintenance program presented in chapter 9 of that book. In fact, the screen layouts, mapset, and symbolic map in figures 4-4, 4-5, and 4-6 are nearly identical to those for the customer-maintenance program *Part 1* presents.

The enhanced version of the customer-maintenance program uses a temporary storage queue to insure data integrity when two operators try to update the same record at the same time. Although it's true that the READ/UPDATE command holds a record for update until a REWRITE, DELETE, or UNLOCK command is issued, that only applies during a single task. CICS provides no way to hold a record for update *between* tasks in a pseudo-conversational session. So in a pseudo-conversational program, while the data for update is displayed on the screen, the record in the file isn't held for update because the task isn't active. As a result, it's possible for a second operator to modify or delete the record before the first operator's task is restarted.

I solved that problem in this version of the customer-maintenance program by saving an image of the customer record between program executions in a temporary storage queue. After the program issues its READ/UPDATE command, it retrieves the saved record from temporary storage and compares it with the customer record just read. If the records differ, it means someone has changed the customer record.

Figure 4-7 presents the structure chart for this program. You'll find a detailed discussion of this program's structure in *Part 1*. Here, I want you to concentrate on the modules that process the temporary storage queue: 8100, 1220, 2330, and 3000.

Module 8100 is invoked by module 8000 the first time the maintenance program is executed during a terminal session. It creates a temporary storage queue by issuing a WRITEQ TS command. The data the module writes to the queue doesn't matter; its only purpose is to create a record that can be updated by the WRITEQ TS command in module 1220.

```
          PRINT NOGEN
MNTSET1   DFHMSD TYPE=&SYSPARM,                                          X
                 LANG=COBOL,                                             X
                 MODE=INOUT,                                             X
                 TERM=3270-2,                                            X
                 CTRL=FREEKB,                                            X
                 STORAGE=AUTO,                                           X
                 TIOAPFX=YES
*************************************************************************
*************************************************************************
MNTMAP1   DFHMDI SIZE=(24,80),                                          X
                 LINE=1,                                                 X
                 COLUMN=1
*************************************************************************
          DFHMDF POS=(1,1),                                             X
                 LENGTH=20,                                              X
                 ATTRB=(BRT,PROT),                                       X
                 INITIAL='CUSTOMER MAINTENANCE'
*************************************************************************
          DFHMDF POS=(4,1),                                             X
                 LENGTH=16,                                              X
                 ATTRB=(BRT,PROT),                                       X
                 INITIAL='CUSTOMER NUMBER:'
NUMBER1   DFHMDF POS=(4,18),                                            X
                 LENGTH=5,                                               X
                 ATTRB=(UNPROT,IC)
          DFHMDF POS=(4,24),                                            X
                 LENGTH=1,                                               X
                 ATTRB=PROT
*************************************************************************
MESSAG1   DFHMDF POS=(23,1),                                            X
                 LENGTH=79,                                              X
                 ATTRB=(BRT,PROT)
ERROR1    DFHMDF POS=(24,1),                                            X
                 LENGTH=77,                                              X
                 ATTRB=(BRT,PROT)
DUMMY1    DFHMDF POS=(24,79),                                           X
                 LENGTH=1,                                               X
                 ATTRB=(DRK,PROT,FSET),                                  X
                 INITIAL=' '
*************************************************************************
*************************************************************************
MNTMAP2   DFHMDI SIZE=(24,80),                                          X
                 LINE=1,                                                 X
                 COLUMN=1
*************************************************************************
          DFHMDF POS=(1,1),                                             X
                 LENGTH=20,                                              X
                 ATTRB=(BRT,PROT),                                       X
                 INITIAL='CUSTOMER MAINTENANCE'
*************************************************************************
```

Figure 4-5   Mapset listing for the enhanced customer-maintenance program (part 1 of 3)

```
          DFHMDF POS=(4,1),                                               X
                 LENGTH=16,                                               X
                 ATTRB=(BRT,PROT),                                        X
                 INITIAL='CUSTOMER NUMBER:'
NUMBER2   DFHMDF POS=(4,18),                                              X
                 LENGTH=5,                                                X
                 ATTRB=(PROT,FSET)
***********************************************************************************
          DFHMDF POS=(6,1),                                               X
                 LENGTH=5,                                                X
                 ATTRB=(BRT,PROT),                                        X
                 INITIAL='NAME:'
NAME      DFHMDF POS=(6,18),                                              X
                 LENGTH=30,                                               X
                 ATTRB=(UNPROT,FSET)
          DFHMDF POS=(6,49),                                              X
                 LENGTH=1,                                                X
                 ATTRB=ASKIP
***********************************************************************************
          DFHMDF POS=(7,1),                                               X
                 LENGTH=8,                                                X
                 ATTRB=(BRT,PROT),                                        X
                 INITIAL='ADDRESS:'
ADDRESS   DFHMDF POS=(7,18),                                              X
                 LENGTH=30,                                               X
                 ATTRB=(UNPROT,FSET)
          DFHMDF POS=(7,49),                                              X
                 LENGTH=1,                                                X
                 ATTRB=ASKIP
***********************************************************************************
          DFHMDF POS=(8,1),                                               X
                 LENGTH=15,                                               X
                 ATTRB=(BRT,PROT),                                        X
                 INITIAL='CITY/STATE/ZIP:'
CITY      DFHMDF POS=(8,18),                                              X
                 LENGTH=21,                                               X
                 ATTRB=(UNPROT,FSET)
STATE     DFHMDF POS=(8,40),                                              X
                 LENGTH=2,                                                X
                 ATTRB=(UNPROT,FSET)
ZIP       DFHMDF POS=(8,43),                                              X
                 LENGTH=5,                                                X
                 ATTRB=(UNPROT,FSET)
          DFHMDF POS=(8,49),                                              X
                 LENGTH=1,                                                X
                 ATTRB=ASKIP
***********************************************************************************
MESSAG2   DFHMDF POS=(23,1),                                              X
                 LENGTH=79,                                               X
                 ATTRB=(BRT,PROT)
```

Figure 4-5   Mapset listing for the enhanced customer-maintenance program (part 2 of 3)

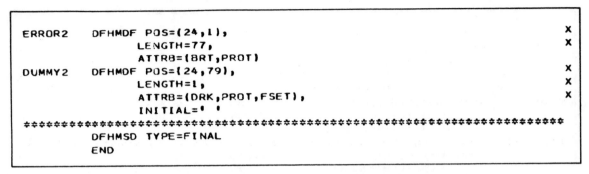

```
ERROR2      DFHMDF POS=(24,1),                                                  X
                   LENGTH=77,                                                   X
                   ATTRB=(BRT,PROT)
DUMMY2      DFHMDF POS=(24,79),                                                 X
                   LENGTH=1,                                                    X
                   ATTRB=(DRK,PROT,FSET),                                       X
                   INITIAL=' '
************************************************************************************
            DFHMSD TYPE=FINAL
            END
```

Figure 4-5   Mapset listing for the enhanced customer-maintenance program (part 3 of 3)

Module 1200 performs two modules. First, it performs module 1210 to read a customer record. Then, it performs module 1220 to rewrite the temporary storage record so it contains an image of the customer record just read. Later, when module 2320 is invoked to read the customer's record for update, module 2330 is also invoked to read the record image stored in the queue. And module 3000 deletes the TS queue when the operator ends the terminal session.

Figure 4-8 shows the complete source listing for the enhanced customer-maintenance program. Again, you'll find a detailed description of how this program works in *Part 1*. Here, I just want to describe how the temporary storage queue is used in this program. The shading in figure 4-8 highlights the sections of the maintenance program that relate directly to the temporary storage queue.

In the Working-Storage Section, I defined an 01-level item for the fields used to process the temporary storage queue. TS-QUEUE-NAME provides the name of the TS queue. The first four bytes of the name are the terminal-id extracted from the Execute Interface Block. The second four bytes of the name are MNT2, indicating which transaction uses the queue. Next, TS-ITEM-NUMBER identifies which queue record is processed. Because this queue always contains just one record, I gave TS-ITEM-NUMBER a value of 1. The program won't change that value as it executes. TS-CUSTOMER-RECORD will contain the record that's read from the queue. It's 93 bytes long, as indicated by the last field: TS-RECORD-LENGTH.

The first statement in the Procedure Division is:

```
MOVE EIBTRMID TO TS-TERMINAL-ID.
```

That moves the terminal-id field from the Execute Interface Block to the queue-name field. That way, the queue name is unique for each operator who uses this program.

```
01   KEY-MAP.
*
     05   FILLER                       PIC X(12).
*
     05   KM-L-CUSTOMER-NUMBER         PIC S9(4)     COMP.
     05   KM-A-CUSTOMER-NUMBER         PIC X.
     05   KM-D-CUSTOMER-NUMBER         PIC X(5).
*
     05   KM-L-OPERATOR-MESSAGE        PIC S9(4)     COMP.
     05   KM-A-OPERATOR-MESSAGE        PIC X.
     05   KM-D-OPERATOR-MESSAGE        PIC X(79).
*
     05   KM-L-ERROR-MESSAGE           PIC S9(4)     COMP.
     05   KM-A-ERROR-MESSAGE           PIC X.
     05   KM-D-ERROR-MESSAGE           PIC X(77).
*
     05   KM-L-DUMMY                   PIC S9(4)     COMP.
     05   KM-A-DUMMY                   PIC X.
     05   KM-D-DUMMY                   PIC X.
*
01   CUSTOMER-DATA-MAP.
*
     05   FILLER                       PIC X(12).
*
     05   CDM-L-CUSTOMER-NUMBER        PIC S9(4)     COMP.
     05   CDM-A-CUSTOMER-NUMBER        PIC X.
     05   CDM-D-CUSTOMER-NUMBER        PIC X(5).
*
     05   CDM-L-NAME                   PIC S9(4)     COMP.
     05   CDM-A-NAME                   PIC X.
     05   CDM-D-NAME                   PIC X(30).
*
     05   CDM-L-ADDRESS                PIC S9(4)     COMP.
     05   CDM-A-ADDRESS                PIC X.
     05   CDM-D-ADDRESS                PIC X(30).
*
     05   CDM-L-CITY                   PIC S9(4)     COMP.
     05   CDM-A-CITY                   PIC X.
     05   CDM-D-CITY                   PIC X(21).
*
     05   CDM-L-STATE                  PIC S9(4)     COMP.
     05   CDM-A-STATE                  PIC X.
     05   CDM-D-STATE                  PIC XX.
*
     05   CDM-L-ZIP-CODE               PIC S9(4)     COMP.
     05   CDM-A-ZIP-CODE               PIC X.
     05   CDM-D-ZIP-CODE               PIC X(5).
*
     05   CDM-L-OPERATOR-MESSAGE       PIC S9(4)     COMP.
     05   CDM-A-OPERATOR-MESSAGE       PIC X.
     05   CDM-D-OPERATOR-MESSAGE       PIC X(79).
```

Figure 4-6   Programmer-generated symbolic map for the enhanced customer-maintenance
program (MNTSET1) (part 1 of 2)

```
*
       05    CDM-L-ERROR-MESSAGE              PIC  S9(4)      COMP.
       05    CDM-A-ERROR-MESSAGE              PIC  X.
       05    CDM-D-ERROR-MESSAGE             PIC  X(77).
*
       05    CDM-L-DUMMY                          PIC  S9(4)      COMP.
       05    CDM-A-DUMMY                          PIC  X.
       05    CDM-D-DUMMY                          PIC  X.
*
```

Figure 4-6   Programmer-generated symbolic map for the enhanced customer-maintenance program (MNTSET1) (part 2 of 2)

Module 8000, invoked when the operator starts the program, performs module 8100. There, a WRITEQ TS command writes a record containing LOW-VALUE to the TS queue. That creates the queue with one record. Subsequent temporary storage commands will retrieve and update that record.

Module 1200 invokes two modules. First, module 1210 reads a customer record. Then, if a customer record is found, module 1220 updates the temporary storage record so it contains an image of the customer record. Because the WRITEQ TS command specifies item 1, the record created by module 8100 is updated. I don't provide a HANDLE CONDITION command for the QIDERR condition here because if it occurs, I want the task to abend anyway. And a HANDLE CONDITION command for the ITEMERR condition is unnecessary because the TS queue contains only one record.

Module 2330, invoked from module 2310, reads the temporary storage record. The READQ TS command specifies item 1 to ensure that the first queue record is read. Then, an IF statement compares the queue record with the actual customer record. If there's a difference, it means another operator has updated the record. Again, I don't handle the QIDERR condition here because if it occurs, I want the task to abend.

Module 3000 deletes the temporary storage queue. It's invoked when the operator ends the terminal session by pressing the clear key.

DISCUSSION

I mentioned at the start of this chapter that you'll often use temporary storage rather than the communication area to save data between executions of a pseudo-conversational program. Now that

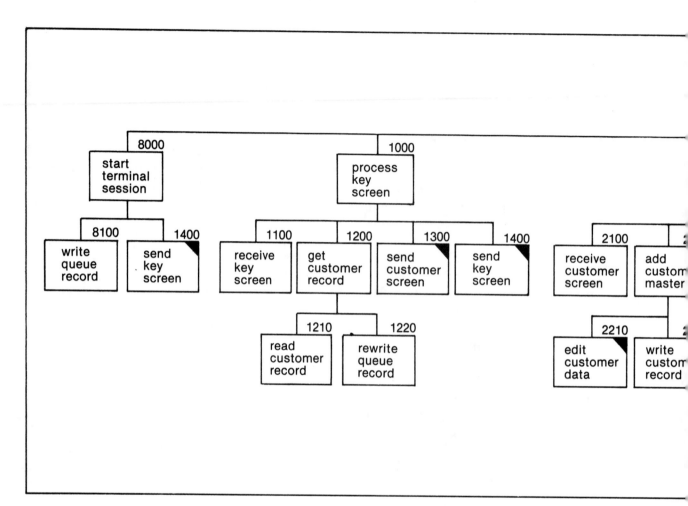

Figure 4-7   Structure chart for the enhanced customer-maintenance program

you know how to process a temporary storage queue, you may be wondering how to decide whether to use temporary storage or the communication area. In general, I recommend you use temporary storage unless the amount of data you want to save is small—say, 50 bytes or less. When the amount of data is that small, you're probably better off using the communication area because a temporary storage record on disk requires almost that much main storage as overhead.

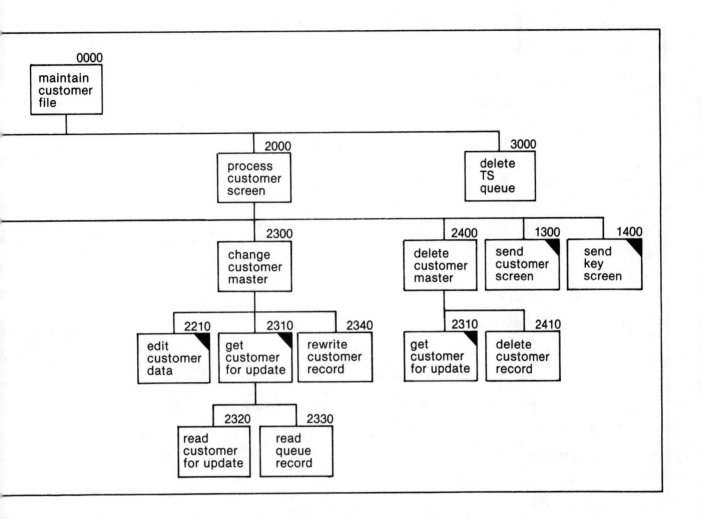

Terminology

scratchpad	data-id
temporary storage control	Temporary Storage Table
temporary storage queue	TST
TS queue	item number
record	temporary storage file
item	DFHTEMP
queue name	

Objective

Given a programming problem requiring the use of a temporary storage queue, code a program for its solution using the features this chapter presents.

```
       IDENTIFICATION DIVISION.
*
       PROGRAM-ID.  CUSTMNT2.
*
       ENVIRONMENT DIVISION.
*
       DATA DIVISION.
*
       WORKING-STORAGE SECTION.
*
       01  SWITCHES.
*
           05   END-SESSION-SW               PIC X       VALUE 'N'.
                88   END-SESSION                          VALUE 'Y'.
           05   CANCEL-ENTRY-SW              PIC X       VALUE 'N'.
                88   CANCEL-ENTRY                         VALUE 'Y'.
           05   VALID-DATA-SW               PIC X       VALUE 'Y'.
                88   VALID-DATA                           VALUE 'Y'.
           05   PF-KEY-1-SW                 PIC X       VALUE 'N'.
                88   PF-KEY-1                             VALUE 'Y'.
*
       01  COMMUNICATION-AREA.
*
           05   CA-PROCESS-FLAG             PIC X.
                88   PROCESS-KEY-SCREEN                   VALUE '1'.
                88   PROCESS-CUSTOMER-SCREEN              VALUE '2'.
           05   CA-CUSTOMER-FOUND-SW        PIC X       VALUE 'Y'.
                88   CA-CUSTOMER-FOUND                    VALUE 'Y'.
*
       COPY MNTSET1.
*
       01  CUSTOMER-MASTER-RECORD.
*
           05   CM-CUSTOMER-NUMBER          PIC X(5).
           05   CM-NAME                     PIC X(30).
           05   CM-ADDRESS                  PIC X(30).
           05   CM-CITY                     PIC X(21).
           05   CM-STATE                    PIC XX.
           05   CM-ZIP-CODE                 PIC X(5).
*
       01  TEMPORARY-STORAGE-FIELDS.
*
           05   TS-QUEUE-NAME.
                10   TS-TERMINAL-ID         PIC X(4).
                10   FILLER                 PIC X(4)    VALUE 'MNT2'.
           05   TS-ITEM-NUMBER             PIC S9(4)  COMP    VALUE +1.
           05   TS-CUSTOMER-RECORD         PIC X(93).
           05   TS-RECORD-LENGTH           PIC S9(4)  COMP    VALUE +93.
*
       LINKAGE SECTION.
*
       01  DFHCOMMAREA                     PIC X(2).
*
```

Figure 4-8   Source listing for the enhanced customer-maintenance program (part 1 of 8)

```
PROCEDURE DIVISION.
*
 0000-MAINTAIN-CUSTOMER-FILE SECTION.
*
        MOVE EIBTRMID TO TS-TERMINAL-ID.
        MOVE LOW-VALUE TO KEY-MAP
                          CUSTOMER-DATA-MAP.
        IF EIBCALEN = ZERO
            PERFORM 8000-START-TERMINAL-SESSION
        ELSE
            MOVE DFHCOMMAREA TO COMMUNICATION-AREA
            IF PROCESS-KEY-SCREEN
                PERFORM 1000-PROCESS-KEY-SCREEN
            ELSE
                PERFORM 2000-PROCESS-CUSTOMER-SCREEN.
        IF END-SESSION
            PERFORM 3000-DELETE-TS-QUEUE
            EXEC CICS
                XCTL PROGRAM('INVMENU')
            END-EXEC
        ELSE
            EXEC CICS
                RETURN TRANSID('MNT2')
                       COMMAREA(COMMUNICATION-AREA)
                       LENGTH(2)
            END-EXEC.
*
 1000-PROCESS-KEY-SCREEN SECTION.
*
        PERFORM 1100-RECEIVE-KEY-SCREEN.
        IF NOT END-SESSION
            IF NOT VALID-DATA
                PERFORM 1400-SEND-KEY-SCREEN
            ELSE
                IF       KM-D-CUSTOMER-NUMBER = SPACE
                   OR KM-L-CUSTOMER-NUMBER = ZERO
                    MOVE 'YOU MUST ENTER A CUSTOMER NUMBER'
                       TO KM-D-ERROR-MESSAGE
                    PERFORM 1400-SEND-KEY-SCREEN
                ELSE
                    PERFORM 1200-GET-CUSTOMER-RECORD
                    MOVE KM-D-CUSTOMER-NUMBER TO CDM-D-CUSTOMER-NUMBER
                    MOVE CM-NAME              TO CDM-D-NAME
                    MOVE CM-ADDRESS           TO CDM-D-ADDRESS
                    MOVE CM-CITY              TO CDM-D-CITY
                    MOVE CM-STATE             TO CDM-D-STATE
                    MOVE CM-ZIP-CODE          TO CDM-D-ZIP-CODE
                    MOVE -1 TO CDM-L-NAME
                    MOVE '2' TO CA-PROCESS-FLAG
                    PERFORM 1300-SEND-CUSTOMER-SCREEN.
*
```

Figure 4-8   Source listing for the enhanced customer-maintenance program (part 2 of 8)

```
  1100-RECEIVE-KEY-SCREEN SECTION.
*
      EXEC CICS
          HANDLE AID CLEAR(1100-CLEAR-KEY)
                     ANYKEY(1100-ANYKEY)
      END-EXEC.
      EXEC CICS
          RECEIVE MAP('MNTMAP1')
                  MAPSET('MNTSET1')
                  INTO(KEY-MAP)
      END-EXEC.
      GO TO 1100-EXIT.
*
  1100-CLEAR-KEY.
*
      MOVE 'Y' TO END-SESSION-SW.
      GO TO 1100-EXIT.
*
  1100-ANYKEY.
*
      MOVE 'N' TO VALID-DATA-SW.
      MOVE 'INVALID KEY PRESSED' TO KM-D-ERROR-MESSAGE.
*
  1100-EXIT.
*
      EXIT.
*
  1200-GET-CUSTOMER-RECORD SECTION.
*
      PERFORM 1210-READ-CUSTOMER-RECORD.
      IF CA-CUSTOMER-FOUND
          PERFORM 1220-REWRITE-QUEUE-RECORD.
*
  1210-READ-CUSTOMER-RECORD SECTION.
*
      MOVE 'Y' TO CA-CUSTOMER-FOUND-SW.
      EXEC CICS
          HANDLE CONDITION NOTFND(1210-NOTFND)
      END-EXEC.
      EXEC CICS
          READ DATASET('CUSTMAS')
               INTO(CUSTOMER-MASTER-RECORD)
               RIDFLD(KM-D-CUSTOMER-NUMBER)
      END-EXEC.
      MOVE 'ENTER CHANGES OR PRESS PF1 TO DELETE CUSTOMER OR CLEAR
-         'TO START OVER' TO CDM-D-OPERATOR-MESSAGE.
      MOVE SPACE TO CDM-D-ERROR-MESSAGE.
      GO TO 1210-EXIT.
*
  1210-NOTFND.
*
      MOVE SPACE TO CUSTOMER-MASTER-RECORD.
      MOVE 'N' TO CA-CUSTOMER-FOUND-SW.
      MOVE 'ENTER DATA FOR NEW CUSTOMER OR PRESS CLEAR TO START OVE
-         'R' TO CDM-D-OPERATOR-MESSAGE.
```

Figure 4-8   Source listing for the enhanced customer-maintenance program (part 3 of 8)

```
        MOVE SPACE TO COM-D-ERROR-MESSAGE.
*
 1210-EXIT.
*
     EXIT.
*
 1220-REWRITE-QUEUE-RECORD SECTION.
*
     EXEC CICS
         WRITEQ TS QUEUE(TS-QUEUE-NAME)
                    FROM(CUSTOMER-MASTER-RECORD)
                    LENGTH(TS-RECORD-LENGTH)
                    ITEM(TS-ITEM-NUMBER)
                    REWRITE
     END-EXEC.
*
 1300-SEND-CUSTOMER-SCREEN SECTION.
*
     EXEC CICS
         SEND MAP('MNTMAP2')
              MAPSET('MNTSET1')
              FROM(CUSTOMER-DATA-MAP)
              CURSOR
     END-EXEC.
*
 1400-SEND-KEY-SCREEN SECTION.
*
     MOVE 'PRESS CLEAR TO END SESSION' TO KM-D-OPERATOR-MESSAGE.
     EXEC CICS
         SEND MAP('MNTMAP1')
              MAPSET('MNTSET1')
              FROM(KEY-MAP)
              ERASE
     END-EXEC.
*
 2000-PROCESS-CUSTOMER-SCREEN SECTION.
*
     PERFORM 2100-RECEIVE-CUSTOMER-SCREEN.
     IF VALID-DATA
         IF NOT CANCEL-ENTRY
             IF CA-CUSTOMER-FOUND
                 IF PF-KEY-1
                     PERFORM 2400-DELETE-CUSTOMER-MASTER
                 ELSE
                     PERFORM 2300-CHANGE-CUSTOMER-MASTER
             ELSE
                 PERFORM 2200-ADD-CUSTOMER-MASTER
         ELSE
             MOVE 'NO ACTION TAKEN' TO KM-D-ERROR-MESSAGE.
     IF VALID-DATA
         PERFORM 1400-SEND-KEY-SCREEN
         MOVE '1' TO CA-PROCESS-FLAG
     ELSE
         PERFORM 1300-SEND-CUSTOMER-SCREEN
         MOVE '2' TO CA-PROCESS-FLAG.
```

Figure 4-8   Source listing for the enhanced customer-maintenance program (part 4 of 8)

```
✿
 2100-RECEIVE-CUSTOMER-SCREEN SECTION.
✿
     EXEC CICS
         HANDLE AID CLEAR(2100-CLEAR-KEY)
                    PF1(2100-PF1-KEY)
                    ANYKEY(2100-ANYKEY)
     END-EXEC.
     EXEC CICS
         RECEIVE MAP('MNTMAP2')
                 MAPSET('MNTSET1')
                 INTO(CUSTOMER-DATA-MAP)
     END-EXEC.
     GO TO 2100-EXIT.
✿
 2100-CLEAR-KEY.
✿
     MOVE 'Y' TO CANCEL-ENTRY-SW.
     GO TO 2100-EXIT.
✿
 2100-PF1-KEY.
✿
     IF CA-CUSTOMER-FOUND
         MOVE 'Y' TO PF-KEY-1-SW
     ELSE
         MOVE 'N' TO VALID-DATA-SW
         MOVE 'INVALID KEY PRESSED' TO CDM-D-ERROR-MESSAGE.
     GO TO 2100-EXIT.
✿
 2100-ANYKEY.
✿
     MOVE 'N' TO VALID-DATA-SW.
     MOVE 'INVALID KEY PRESSED' TO CDM-D-ERROR-MESSAGE.
✿
 2100-EXIT.
✿
     EXIT.
✿
 2200-ADD-CUSTOMER-MASTER SECTION.
✿
     PERFORM 2210-EDIT-CUSTOMER-DATA.
     IF VALID-DATA
         MOVE CDM-D-CUSTOMER-NUMBER TO CM-CUSTOMER-NUMBER
         MOVE CDM-D-NAME              TO CM-NAME
         MOVE CDM-D-ADDRESS           TO CM-ADDRESS
         MOVE CDM-D-CITY              TO CM-CITY
         MOVE CDM-D-STATE             TO CM-STATE
         MOVE CDM-D-ZIP-CODE          TO CM-ZIP-CODE
         MOVE 'RECORD ADDED' TO KM-D-ERROR-MESSAGE
         PERFORM 2220-WRITE-CUSTOMER-RECORD.
✿
```

Figure 4-8   Source listing for the enhanced customer-maintenance program (part 5 of 8)

```
  2210-EDIT-CUSTOMER-DATA SECTION.
*
      IF         CDM-D-ZIP-CODE = SPACE
          OR CDM-L-ZIP-CODE = ZERO
        MOVE -1 TO CDM-L-ZIP-CODE
        MOVE 'YOU MUST ENTER A ZIP CODE'
            TO CDM-D-ERROR-MESSAGE.
*
      IF          CDM-D-STATE = SPACE
          OR CDM-L-STATE = ZERO
        MOVE -1 TO CDM-L-STATE
        MOVE 'YOU MUST ENTER A STATE'
            TO CDM-D-ERROR-MESSAGE.
*
      IF         CDM-D-CITY = SPACE
          OR CDM-L-CITY = ZERO
        MOVE -1 TO CDM-L-CITY
        MOVE 'YOU MUST ENTER A CITY'
            TO CDM-D-ERROR-MESSAGE.
*
      IF         CDM-D-ADDRESS = SPACE
          OR CDM-L-ADDRESS = ZERO
        MOVE -1 TO CDM-L-ADDRESS
        MOVE 'YOU MUST ENTER AN ADDRESS'
            TO CDM-D-ERROR-MESSAGE.
*
      IF         CDM-D-NAME = SPACE
          OR CDM-L-NAME = ZERO
        MOVE -1 TO CDM-L-NAME
        MOVE 'YOU MUST ENTER A NAME'
            TO CDM-D-ERROR-MESSAGE.
*
      IF CDM-D-ERROR-MESSAGE NOT = LOW-VALUE
          MOVE 'N' TO VALID-DATA-SW.
*
  2220-WRITE-CUSTOMER-RECORD SECTION.
*
      EXEC CICS
          HANDLE CONDITION DUPREC(2220-DUPREC)
      END-EXEC.
      EXEC CICS
          WRITE DATASET('CUSTMAS')
              FROM(CUSTOMER-MASTER-RECORD)
              RIDFLD(CM-CUSTOMER-NUMBER)
      END-EXEC.
      GO TO 2220-EXIT.
*
  2220-DUPREC.
*
      MOVE 'ERROR--CUSTOMER RECORD ALREADY EXISTS'
          TO KM-D-ERROR-MESSAGE.
*
  2220-EXIT.
*
      EXIT.
```

Figure 4-8   Source listing for the enhanced customer-maintenance program (part 6 of 8)

```
*
 2300-CHANGE-CUSTOMER-MASTER SECTION.
*
     PERFORM 2210-EDIT-CUSTOMER-DATA.
     IF VALID-DATA
         PERFORM 2310-GET-CUSTOMER-FOR-UPDATE
         IF CA-CUSTOMER-FOUND
             MOVE CDM-D-NAME          TO CM-NAME
             MOVE CDM-D-ADDRESS       TO CM-ADDRESS
             MOVE CDM-D-CITY          TO CM-CITY
             MOVE CDM-D-STATE         TO CM-STATE
             MOVE CDM-D-ZIP-CODE      TO CM-ZIP-CODE
             PERFORM 2340-REWRITE-CUSTOMER-RECORD
             MOVE 'RECORD UPDATED' TO KM-D-ERROR-MESSAGE.
*
 2310-GET-CUSTOMER-FOR-UPDATE SECTION.
*
     PERFORM 2320-READ-CUSTOMER-FOR-UPDATE.
     IF CA-CUSTOMER-FOUND
         PERFORM 2330-READ-QUEUE-RECORD.
*
 2320-READ-CUSTOMER-FOR-UPDATE SECTION.
*
     EXEC CICS
         HANDLE CONDITION NOTFND(2320-NOTFND)
     END-EXEC.
     EXEC CICS
         READ DATASET('CUSTMAS')
             INTO(CUSTOMER-MASTER-RECORD)
             RIDFLD(CDM-D-CUSTOMER-NUMBER)
             UPDATE
     END-EXEC.
     MOVE 'Y' TO CA-CUSTOMER-FOUND-SW.
     GO TO 2320-EXIT.
*
 2320-NOTFND.
*
     MOVE 'ERROR--CUSTOMER RECORD DOES NOT EXIST'
         TO KM-D-ERROR-MESSAGE.
     MOVE 'N' TO CA-CUSTOMER-FOUND-SW.
*
 2320-EXIT.
*
     EXIT.
*
 2330-READ-QUEUE-RECORD SECTION.
*
     EXEC CICS
         READQ TS QUEUE(TS-QUEUE-NAME)
                  INTO(TS-CUSTOMER-RECORD)
                  LENGTH(TS-RECORD-LENGTH)
                  ITEM(TS-ITEM-NUMBER)
     END-EXEC.
```

Figure 4-8   Source listing for the enhanced customer-maintenance program (part 7 of 8)

```
            IF TS-CUSTOMER-RECORD NOT = CUSTOMER-MASTER-RECORD
                MOVE 'ERROR--ANOTHER OPERATOR HAS UPDATED THAT CUSTOMER'
                    TO KM-D-ERROR-MESSAGE
                MOVE 'N' TO CA-CUSTOMER-FOUND-SW.
*
 2340-REWRITE-CUSTOMER-RECORD SECTION.
*
     EXEC CICS
         REWRITE DATASET('CUSTMAS')
                     FROM(CUSTOMER-MASTER-RECORD)
     END-EXEC.
*
 2400-DELETE-CUSTOMER-MASTER SECTION.
*
     PERFORM 2310-GET-CUSTOMER-FOR-UPDATE.
     IF CA-CUSTOMER-FOUND
         PERFORM 2410-DELETE-CUSTOMER-RECORD
         MOVE 'RECORD DELETED' TO KM-D-ERROR-MESSAGE.
*
 2410-DELETE-CUSTOMER-RECORD SECTION.
*
     EXEC CICS
         DELETE DATASET('CUSTMAS')
     END-EXEC.
*
 3000-DELETE-TS-QUEUE SECTION.
*
     EXEC CICS
         DELETEQ TS QUEUE(TS-QUEUE-NAME)
     END-EXEC.
*
 8000-START-TERMINAL-SESSION SECTION.
*
     PERFORM 8100-WRITE-QUEUE-RECORD.
     PERFORM 1400-SEND-KEY-SCREEN.
     MOVE '1' TO CA-PROCESS-FLAG.
*
 8100-WRITE-QUEUE-RECORD SECTION.
*
     MOVE LOW-VALUE TO TS-CUSTOMER-RECORD.
     EXEC CICS
         WRITEQ TS QUEUE(TS-QUEUE-NAME)
                   FROM(TS-CUSTOMER-RECORD)
                   LENGTH(TS-RECORD-LENGTH)
     END-EXEC.
```

Figure 4-8   Source listing for the enhanced customer-maintenance program (part 8 of 8)

Chapter 5

Transient data control

The *transient data control* module of CICS provides a convenient way to do simple sequential processing. With it, you can store data sequentially and retrieve it later in the same sequence in which it was stored. Although you can implement that kind of processing using VSAM entry-sequenced files, transient data control is often a better choice for reasons you'll learn in this chapter.

One of the most common uses of transient data control is for programs that produce output on 3270 printers. Using transient data control, those programs can store print data that's eventually directed to a printer. The advantage of using transient data control for printing is that you don't have to worry about the complex formatting requirements of 3270 printers. You'll see a printing application that uses transient data control in this chapter.

Before you learn how to process transient data, you need to learn some important concepts. After I present those concepts, I'll show you the commands you use to process transient data. Then, I'll present a sample program that shows you how to use transient data for a typical printing application.

TRANSIENT DATA CONCEPTS

Transient means passing quickly into and out of existence. That
aptly describes the nature of a *transient data queue*, or *TD queue*.
A record passes into a transient data queue when you write it to the
queue. That record passes out of the queue—and out of
existence—when you read it. As a result, data in a transient data
queue is truly transient.

You process records in a transient data queue sequentially.
Each record you write is placed at the end of the queue. And when
you perform a read operation for the queue, the first record in the
queue is retrieved and deleted. Because a record is deleted as it's
read, you can't read the same record twice. Nor can you update a
record. So all you can do with a transient data queue is write
records to it and read records from it. Although that may seem like
a limitation, it's really one of the advantages of transient data: you
don't have to worry about deleting data that's already been
processed. In contrast, you must explicitly delete records from a
VSAM file when they're no longer needed.

Transient data queues are often called *destinations*. In fact,
you can use the terms interchangeably. All transient data queues
must be defined in the *Destination Control Table*, or *DCT*. Each
DCT entry defines a queue's name, or *destination-id*, along with
the queue's characteristics. The systems programmer normally
maintains the DCT, so you don't need to worry about the format of
DCT entries. But you do need to know a queue's destination-id and
characteristics to use it effectively.

Extrapartition and intrapartition transient data queues

Transient data control provides two types of transient data queues:
extrapartition and intrapartition. An *extrapartition transient data
queue* lets CICS tasks access sequential files that are managed by
the host system's sequential access method (SAM for DOS, QSAM
for OS). An extrapartition destination doesn't have to be a disk file;
it can reside on any device that's valid for SAM or QSAM, such as a
tape drive, a printer, or even a card unit.

Extrapartition destinations are used mostly to collect data that's
entered on-line but processed later by a batch program. For
example, an order-entry program might write order records to an
extrapartition destination on disk or tape. Then, on a nightly basis,
the orders can be processed by a standard batch COBOL program.

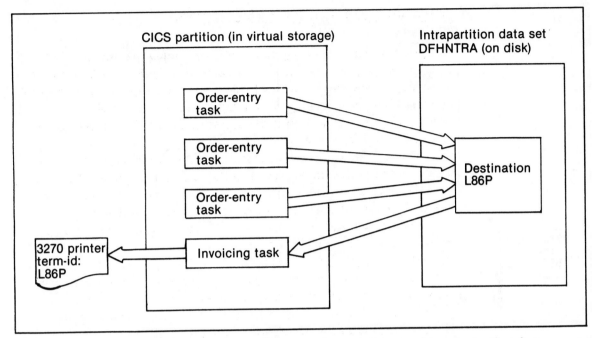

Figure 5-1   An order-entry program writes records to an intrapartition destination for subsequent processing by an invoicing program

Because of efficiency problems that can be associated with transient data, however, it's usually better to collect batches of data in standard VSAM entry-sequenced files. Because extrapartition transient data queues aren't frequently used, the rest of this chapter applies just to intrapartition destinations. You shouldn't have any problems learning how to process an extrapartition destination should the need arise, however, because you use the same commands for both types of destinations.

Intrapartition transient data queues are used more commonly than extrapartition destinations. Figure 5-1 shows how an order-entry application might use an intrapartition destination to store order data entered by terminal operators. Here, several operators run an order-entry program that writes records to an intrapartition transient data queue. And an invoicing program reads records from the queue to print invoices.

As figure 5-1 indicates, CICS stores an intrapartition TD queue in a VSAM file named *DFHNTRA*. Regardless of how many intrapartition transient data queues are in use at one time, they're all stored in DFHNTRA. So you don't have to create a new file to create a new TD queue. However, unlike temporary storage queues, which are also maintained in a single data set, you must make an entry in the DCT for each transient data queue.

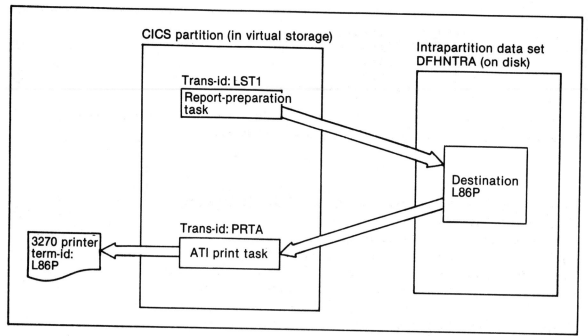

Figure 5-2   A typical generalized printing facility that uses an intrapartition destination to store print lines

Automatic transaction initiation

One of the most useful features of intrapartition transient data queues is *automatic transaction initiation*, or *ATI*. ATI provides a convenient way to start a task automatically. To use ATI, you assign a transaction identifier and a *trigger level* to a transient data queue by making appropriate entries in the DCT. When the number of records in the queue reaches the trigger level, the specified transaction is automatically started. Because the presence of data in a transient data queue triggers the task, an ATI transaction is often called a *data-driven transaction*.

To illustrate, figure 5-2 shows how an intrapartition destination is used in a typical printing application. Here, a user-initiated reporting program (trans-id LST1) prepares a report by writing records to an intrapartition destination named L86P. Figure 5-3 shows the DCT entry for the L86P destination. Because the entry specifies a trigger level of 1, a special print program—identified by the trans-id PRTA—is automatically started when a record is written to the destination. The print task reads records from the destination, formats the print data for a 3270 printer, and

```
DFHDCT TYPE=INTRA,
       DESTID=L86P,
       TRANSID=PRTA,
       TRIGLEV=1,
       DESTFAC=TERMINAL
```

Figure 5-3   Destination Control Table entry for the L86P destination

sends the formatted data to its attached terminal: a 3270 printer whose terminal-id is L86P.

In this case, the queue's destination-id is the same as a terminal-id. As a result, I was able to associate the ATI task for the queue with the terminal L86P by coding DESTFAC = TERMINAL in the queue's DCT entry. Although you probably won't have to code DCT entries, this example should help you understand how an intrapartition destination can be used for a printing application.

Indirect destinations

An *indirect destination* lets a single transient data queue be identified by more than one destination-id. The DCT entry for an indirect destination simply specifies the name of a destination defined elsewhere in the DCT. The name specified for the indirect destination may itself be an indirect destination, but ultimately each indirect destination must lead to an intrapartition or extrapartition destination.

One common reason for using indirect destinations is to shelter application programs from actual destination-ids. By using an indirect destination, you can change a destination-id without having to change and recompile every application program that refers to that destination. That's a valuable feature when a destination is associated with a terminal, because terminal configurations are likely to change.

To illustrate how an indirect destination is defined, figure 5-4 shows the DCT entries for two destinations. The first defines the intrapartition destination L86P. It's just like the table entry in figure 5-3. The second defines an indirect destination (TYPE = INDIRECT) named PRT1. The INDDEST parameter relates PRT1 to L86P. As a result, output written to destination PRT1 will be processed through destination L86P by a task running

```
DFHDCT TYPE=INTRA,
       DESTID=L86P,
       TRANSID=PRTA,
       TRIGLEV=1,
       DESTFAC=TERMINAL


DFHDCT TYPE=INDIRECT,
       DESTID=PRT1,
       INDDEST=L86P
```

Figure 5-4   Destination Control Table entries for the indirect destination PRT1

at terminal L86P. If you want to route the output to a different terminal, you just change the DCT entries—not the application program. Because of the indirect destination, programs that write data to PRT1 don't have to know what the final destination is.

Reserving a destination for exclusive use

One minor drawback of transient data is that CICS doesn't automatically ensure that only one task writes records to a destination at one time. So, if two users simultaneously execute a program that writes records to a common destination, those records will be mixed. Although that's not always a problem, in a printing application it is.

Fortunately, CICS provides a facility that lets you reserve—or *enqueue*—a resource for exclusive use: the ENQ and DEQ commands. You'll learn more about the ENQ and DEQ commands in chapter 11. For now, I want you to realize that when you write more than one record to a transient data queue, you may need to use the ENQ and DEQ commands to make sure another user doesn't mix records with the ones you write. You'll see an example of how to do that later in this chapter.

CICS COMMANDS
FOR TRANSIENT DATA QUEUES

To process a transient data queue, you use three CICS commands. You use the WRITEQ TD command to add a record to a transient

```
The WRITEQ TD command

EXEC CICS
     WRITEQ TD QUEUE(data-name|literal)
               FROM(data-name)
               LENGTH(data-name|literal)
END-EXEC


Explanation

QUEUE          The one- to eight-character name of the transient data queue
               to which data is written.

FROM           The data area that contains the record to be written.

LENGTH         The length of the FROM area. Must be numeric. If you use a
               data-name, it must be a binary half-word (PIC S9(4) COMP).
```

Figure 5-5   The WRITEQ TD command

data queue. You use the READQ TD command to retrieve a record
from a TD queue. And you use the DELETEQ TD command to
delete a TD queue. In addition, you use two other commands—
ENQ and DEQ—when you need exclusive access to a destination.

The WRITEQ TD command

You normally code the WRITEQ TD command, whose format is
given in figure 5-5, like this:

```
EXEC CICS
     WRITEQ TD QUEUE('L86P')
               FROM(PRINT-AREA)
               LENGTH(133)
END-EXEC
```

Here, the 133 bytes of data contained in the field named PRINT-
AREA are written to a transient data queue named L86P.

Although several exceptional conditions might be raised when
your program executes a WRITEQ TD command, all of them
represent serious error conditions—like hardware errors—that your

---

The READQ TD command

```
EXEC CICS
     READQ TD QUEUE(data-name|literal)
              INTO(data-name)
              LENGTH(data-name)
END-EXEC
```

Explanation

QUEUE   The one- to eight-character name of the transient data queue
                      from which data is read.

INTO   The data area that will contain the record.

LENGTH   The length of the INTO area. Must be a binary half-word
                      (PIC S9(4) COMP).

Figure 5-6   The READQ TD command

program probably can't correct. As a result, I don't recommend you provide for them in a HANDLE CONDITION command unless your shop has a standard that says otherwise.

The READQ TD command

Figure 5-6 gives the format of the READQ TD command. You usually code it like this:

```
EXEC CICS
     READQ TD QUEUE('L86P')
              INTO(PRINT-AREA)
              LENGTH(PRINT-AREA-LENGTH)
END-EXEC
```

Notice that for a READQ TD command, you must specify a data-name in the LENGTH option. The initial value of the LENGTH field indicates the length of the largest record your program will accept. After the READQ TD command completes, the LENGTH field is updated to indicate the actual length of the record that was

read. You should define the LENGTH field as a half-word binary
field (PIC S9(4) COMP).

If your program reads a record that's longer than the
maximum length you specify, the LENGERR condition is raised.
Depending on your application's requirements, you might want to
provide for this condition in a HANDLE CONDITION command.
When the LENGERR condition occurs, as much of the input data
as will fit is placed in the INTO field. The rest of the data is
discarded. As a result, your program can process some of the data,
provided you allow for LENGERR with a HANDLE CONDITION
command.

The QZERO condition is a destination's equivalent of the
ENDFILE condition encountered during a browse operation on a
VSAM file. When you issue a READQ TD command for a queue
that has no records, the QZERO command is raised. As a result,
you should always provide for the QZERO condition when you use
a READQ TD command.

The DELETEQ TD command

When you read a record from a transient data queue, that record is
deleted. As a result, you can read a TD record only once. However,
depending on how the DCT entry for the queue is coded, the disk
space occupied by that record may still be reserved, even though
the record itself is unavailable. As a result, you may need to
reclaim that disk space. In other cases, you may need to delete all
of the records remaining in a queue because of an error condition
or some other application requirement.

The DELETEQ TD command, shown in figure 5-7, reclaims
unused space and deletes all remaining records in a queue. You
issue the DELETEQ TD command like this:

```
EXEC CICS
    DELETEQ TD QUEUE('L86P')
END-EXEC
```

Here, the queue named L86P is deleted. All disk space allocated to
its records, whether they've been read or not, is released.

Note that a DELETEQ TD command doesn't remove the
queue's DCT entry or disable the queue. It just removes all the
queue's records and returns the space they occupied to the system.
You can still add records to the queue by issuing a WRITEQ TD
command.

The DELETEQ TD command

```
EXEC CICS
     DELETEQ TD QUEUE(data-name|literal)
END-EXEC
```

Explanation

QUEUE   The one- to eight-character name of the transient data queue
                         to be deleted.

Figure 5-7   The DELETEQ TD command

The ENQ and DEQ commands

Strictly speaking, the ENQ and DEQ commands aren't transient
data control commands. Nevertheless, you'll often use them when
you process a transient data queue, so I'll describe them briefly
here. You'll find a more detailed description of how these
commands work in chapter 11.

Figures 5-8 and 5-9 give the formats of the ENQ and DEQ
commands. If your program writes more than one record to a
destination, you should issue an ENQ command to enqueue the
destination. That way, other tasks won't be able to write records to
it as long as you have it enqueued.

DEQ releases an enqueued resource. If you don't issue a DEQ
command before your task ends, CICS releases the enqueued
resource automatically. Still, it's a good idea to issue a DEQ
command as soon as possible after you're finished processing the
destination. Otherwise, you'll tie up the destination longer than
necessary.

In the RESOURCE option of the ENQ and DEQ commands,
you provide the name of a field that contains a 1- to 255-character
resource name. The resource name identifies the resource—in this
case a transient data queue—that you want to enqueue. Usually,
you just supply the destination-id of the queue you want to
enqueue. But check first to see if your shop has standards for
forming resource names.

The ENQ command

```
EXEC CICS
    ENQ RESOURCE(data-name)
        LENGTH(data-name|literal)
END-EXEC
```

Explanation

RESOURCE   A 1- to 255-byte character string that identifies the resource to
                be reserved.

LENGTH   The length of the RESOURCE field. Must be numeric. If you
                use a data-name, it must be a binary half-word (PIC S9(4)
                COMP).

Figure 5-8   The ENQ command

The DEQ command

```
EXEC CICS
    DEQ RESOURCE(data-name)
        LENGTH(data-name|literal)
END-EXEC
```

Explanation

RESOURCE   A 1- to 255-byte character string that identifies the resource to
                be released.

LENGTH   The length of the RESOURCE field. Must be numeric. If you
                use a data-name, it, must be a binary half-word (PIC S9(4)
                COMP).

Figure 5-9   The DEQ command

A SAMPLE PROGRAM

Figure 5-10 gives the print chart for a program that lists the contents of a file of inventory records. For each inventory record, four fields are printed: item number, item description, unit price, and quantity on hand. After all the inventory records have been listed, a total line showing the number of records in the file is printed.

The inventory-listing program doesn't create its output directly on a printer. Instead, it uses the generalized printing facility in figure 5-2 that lets you write print records to a transient data queue. The queue has a trigger level of one and is associated with a printer terminal and an ATI task. When the inventory-listing program writes records to the queue, the ATI task reads and prints them. In chapter 8, you'll see the program that reads the queue records and prints them. For now, though, you don't need to worry about how that program works.

The generalized printing facility I describe here uses a subset of standard ASA control characters to control printer spacing. The inventory-listing program places one of the characters in figure 5-11 in the first byte of each output record it writes to the transient data queue. A space means advance the printer to the next line before printing the data. A 0 (zero) causes double spacing, and a hyphen (-) causes triple spacing. A 1 in the first byte causes the printer to skip to the first line of the next page.

I want you to realize that this printing facility is by no means a standard facility. Each installation creates its own printing facility, and not all of them use the standard ASA control characters in figure 5-11. I know of one installation that uses an F to skip to the top of a new form and a digit (1-9) to skip one to nine lines before printing data. The point is this: if your installation implements a printing facility using transient data, you'll have to find out how it works.

Figure 5-12 gives the structure chart for the inventory-listing program. This structure is similar to what you'd use for a standard batch report-preparation program. Module 1000 starts a browse operation for the inventory file. Then, module 2000 is executed once for each record in the file. It invokes module 2100 to read an inventory record and module 2200 to print the record. Module 2200, in turn, invokes module 2210 to print heading lines when necessary and module 2220 to write a record to the transient data queue. Because module 2210 needs to write records to the queue as well, it also invokes module 2220. Finally, after all records in the

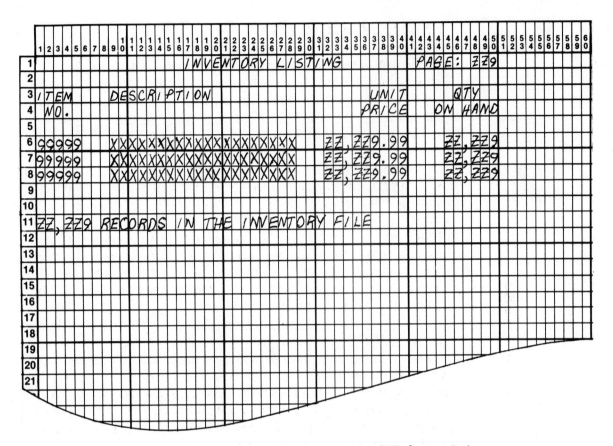

Figure 5-10   Print chart for the inventory-listing program (TD destination)

Character	Resulting printer action
blank	Skip one line before printing.
0	Skip two lines before printing.
–	Skip three lines before printing.
1	Skip to the top of the next page before printing.

Figure 5-11   ASA control characters

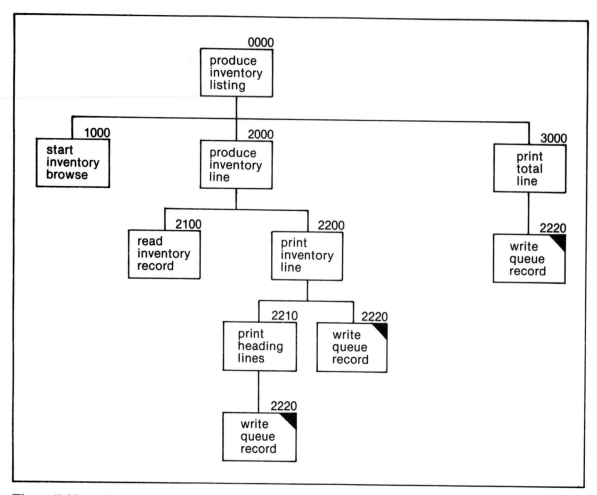

Figure 5-12 Structure chart for the inventory-listing program (TD destination)

inventory file have been processed, module 3000 is performed to print the total line. Don't let the word "print" in the module names confuse you. This program writes all of its print output to a transient data queue—not directly to a printer.

Figure 5-13 gives the complete source listing for this program. I don't think you'll have any trouble understanding how it works. In fact, there are only three points I want you to notice. First, each of the print lines defined in the Working-Storage Section (HDG-LINE-1, HDG-LINE-2, HDG-LINE-3, INVENTORY-LINE, and TOTAL-LINE) includes a print control character in the first position. That way, proper printer spacing is ensured for each print line written to the queue.

```
       IDENTIFICATION DIVISION.
      *
       PROGRAM-ID.   INVLST1.
      *
       ENVIRONMENT DIVISION.
      *
       DATA DIVISION.
      *
       WORKING-STORAGE SECTION.
      *
       01   SWITCHES.
      *
           05   INVMAST-EOF-SW    PIC X          VALUE 'N'.
                88  INVMAST-EOF                   VALUE 'Y'.
      *
       01   WORK-FIELDS.
      *
           05   RECORD-COUNT      PIC S9(5)  VALUE ZERO   COMP-3.
      *
       01   PRINT-FIELDS.
      *
           05   LINE-COUNT        PIC S99    VALUE +50    COMP-3.
           05   LINES-ON-PAGE     PIC S99    VALUE +50    COMP-3.
           05   PAGE-NO           PIC S999   VALUE +1     COMP-3.
           05   PRINT-AREA        PIC X(133).
           05   LINE-LENGTH       PIC S9(4)               COMP.
      *
       01   HDG-LINE-1.
      *
           05   HDG1-CC           PIC X          VALUE '1'.
           05   FILLER            PIC X(20)  VALUE '             INVE'.
           05   FILLER            PIC X(20)  VALUE 'NTORY LISTING     '.
           05   FILLER            PIC X(7)   VALUE ' PAGE: '.
           05   HDG1-PAGE-NO      PIC ZZ9.
      *
       01   HDG-LINE-2.
      *
           05   HDG2-CC           PIC X          VALUE '0'.
           05   FILLER            PIC X(20)  VALUE 'ITEM     DESCRIPTION '.
           05   FILLER            PIC X(20)  VALUE '                UNIT'.
           05   FILLER            PIC X(8)   VALUE '     QTY'.
      *
       01   HDG-LINE-3.
      *
           05   HDG3-CC           PIC X          VALUE ' '.
           05   FILLER            PIC X(20)  VALUE ' NO.              '.
           05   FILLER            PIC X(20)  VALUE '           PRICE'.
           05   FILLER            PIC X(10)  VALUE '   ON HAND'.
      *
```

Figure 5-13   Source listing for the inventory-listing program (TD destination) (part 1 of 4)

```
    01   INVENTORY-LINE.
    *
         05   IL-CC                PIC X             VALUE SPACE.
         05   IL-ITEM-NUMBER       PIC 9(5).
         05   FILLER               PIC X(3)          VALUE SPACE.
         05   IL-ITEM-DESCRIPTION  PIC X(20).
         05   FILLER               PIC X(3)          VALUE SPACE.
         05   IL-UNIT-PRICE        PIC ZZ,ZZ9.99.
         05   FILLER               PIC X(4)          VALUE SPACE.
         05   IL-ON-HAND-QUANTITY  PIC ZZ,ZZ9.
    *
    01   TOTAL-LINE.
    *
         05   TL-CC                PIC X        VALUE '-'.
         05   TL-RECORD-COUNT      PIC ZZ,ZZ9.
         05   FILLER               PIC X(20)    VALUE ' RECORDS IN THE INVE'.
         05   FILLER               PIC X(10)    VALUE 'NTORY FILE'.
    *
    01   EOJ-MESSAGE.
    *
         05   FILLER               PIC X(20)    VALUE 'INVENTORY LISTING PR'.
         05   FILLER               PIC X(6)     VALUE 'INTED.'.
    *
    01   INVENTORY-MASTER-RECORD.
    *
         05   IM-ITEM-NUMBER       PIC X(5).
         05   IM-ITEM-DESCRIPTION  PIC X(20).
         05   IM-UNIT-PRICE        PIC S9(5)V99    COMP-3.
         05   IM-ON-HAND-QUANTITY  PIC S9(5)       COMP-3.
    *
    01   DESTINATION-ID           PIC X(4)          VALUE 'L86P'.
    *
    PROCEDURE DIVISION.
    *
    0000-PRODUCE-INVENTORY-LISTING SECTION.
    *
        PERFORM 1000-START-INVENTORY-BROWSE.
        EXEC CICS
            HANDLE CONDITION ENDFILE(2100-ENDFILE)
        END-EXEC.
        EXEC CICS
            ENQ RESOURCE(DESTINATION-ID)
                LENGTH(4)
        END-EXEC.
        PERFORM 2000-PRODUCE-INVENTORY-LINE
            UNTIL INVMAST-EOF.
        PERFORM 3000-PRINT-TOTAL-LINE.
        EXEC CICS
            DEQ RESOURCE(DESTINATION-ID)
                LENGTH(4)
        END-EXEC.
```

Figure 5-13   Source listing for the inventory-listing program (TD destination) (part 2 of 4)

```
        EXEC CICS
            SEND TEXT FROM(EOJ-MESSAGE)
                        LENGTH(26)
                        ERASE
                        FREEKB
        END-EXEC.
        EXEC CICS
            RETURN
        END-EXEC.
    *
    1000-START-INVENTORY-BROWSE SECTION.
    *
        EXEC CICS
            HANDLE CONDITION NOTFND(1000-NOTFND)
        END-EXEC.
        MOVE ZERO TO IM-ITEM-NUMBER.
        EXEC CICS
            STARTBR DATASET('INVMAST')
                    RIDFLD(IM-ITEM-NUMBER)
        END-EXEC.
        GO TO 1000-EXIT.
    *
    1000-NOTFND.
    *
        MOVE 'Y' TO INVMAST-EOF-SW.
    *
    1000-EXIT.
    *
        EXIT.
    *
    2000-PRODUCE-INVENTORY-LINE SECTION.
    *
        PERFORM 2100-READ-INVENTORY-RECORD.
        IF NOT INVMAST-EOF
            PERFORM 2200-PRINT-INVENTORY-LINE.
    *
    2100-READ-INVENTORY-RECORD SECTION.
    *
        EXEC CICS
            READNEXT DATASET('INVMAST')
                    INTO(INVENTORY-MASTER-RECORD)
                    RIDFLD(IM-ITEM-NUMBER)
        END-EXEC.
        ADD 1 TO RECORD-COUNT.
        GO TO 2100-EXIT.
    *
    2100-ENDFILE.
    *
        MOVE 'Y' TO INVMAST-EOF-SW.
    *
    2100-EXIT.
    *
        EXIT.
```

Figure 5-13   Source listing for the inventory-listing program (TD destination) (part 3 of 4)

```
 *
  2200-PRINT-INVENTORY-LINE SECTION.
 *
        IF LINE-COUNT = LINES-ON-PAGE
            PERFORM 2210-PRINT-HEADING-LINES.
        MOVE IM-ITEM-NUMBER       TO IL-ITEM-NUMBER.
        MOVE IM-ITEM-DESCRIPTION TO IL-ITEM-DESCRIPTION.
        MOVE IM-UNIT-PRICE        TO IL-UNIT-PRICE.
        MOVE IM-ON-HAND-QUANTITY TO IL-ON-HAND-QUANTITY.
        MOVE INVENTORY-LINE TO PRINT-AREA.
        MOVE 51 TO LINE-LENGTH.
        PERFORM 2220-WRITE-QUEUE-RECORD.
        ADD 1 TO LINE-COUNT.
        MOVE SPACE TO IL-CC.
 *
  2210-PRINT-HEADING-LINES SECTION.
 *
        MOVE PAGE-NO TO HDG1-PAGE-NO.
        MOVE HDG-LINE-1 TO PRINT-AREA.
        MOVE 51 TO LINE-LENGTH.
        PERFORM 2220-WRITE-QUEUE-RECORD.
        ADD 1 TO PAGE-NO.
        MOVE HDG-LINE-2 TO PRINT-AREA.
        MOVE 49 TO LINE-LENGTH.
        PERFORM 2220-WRITE-QUEUE-RECORD.
        MOVE HDG-LINE-3 TO PRINT-AREA.
        MOVE 51 TO LINE-LENGTH.
        PERFORM 2220-WRITE-QUEUE-RECORD.
        MOVE '0' TO IL-CC.
        MOVE ZERO TO LINE-COUNT.
 *
  2220-WRITE-QUEUE-RECORD SECTION.
 *
        EXEC CICS
            WRITEQ TD QUEUE(DESTINATION-ID)
                      FROM(PRINT-AREA)
                      LENGTH(LINE-LENGTH)
        END-EXEC.
 *
  3000-PRINT-TOTAL-LINE SECTION.
 *
        MOVE RECORD-COUNT TO TL-RECORD-COUNT.
        MOVE TOTAL-LINE TO PRINT-AREA.
        MOVE 37 TO LINE-LENGTH.
        PERFORM 2220-WRITE-QUEUE-RECORD.
```

Figure 5-13   Source listing for the inventory-listing program (TD destination) (part 4 of 4)

Second, notice the ENQ and DEQ commands in module 0000. They prevent other tasks from writing to the L86P queue while the inventory-listing program is executing. In chapter 11, you'll learn more about these commands.

Third, notice the two MOVE statements I coded before the PERFORM statements that invoke module 2220. They format two working-storage fields: PRINT-AREA and LINE-LENGTH. For example, to print the third heading line, I code these statements:

```
MOVE HDG-LINE-3 TO PRINT-AREA.
MOVE 51 TO LINE-LENGTH.
PERFORM 2220-WRITE-QUEUE-RECORD.
```

Here, HDG-LINE-3 is moved to PRINT-AREA and its length (51 bytes) is moved to LINE-LENGTH. Then, module 2220 is performed. If you'll look at module 2220, you'll see that the WRITEQ TD command specifies PRINT-AREA in the FROM option and LINE-LENGTH in the LENGTH option. By coding the WRITEQ TD command in this way, I can use it for each print line that's written to the queue, even though they're not all the same length.

DISCUSSION

I hope by now you appreciate the value of transient data as a generalized queuing facility—especially for printing applications. There are other ways to implement printing applications, and you'll see variations of the inventory-listing program later in this book. When you do, remember that printing applications are usually implemented using the transient data control elements this chapter presents.

The sample program in this chapter shows you how to write records to a transient data queue but doesn't show you how to read records from a queue. That's fair enough, because you're more likely to develop a program that writes records to a queue than one that reads records from a queue. Still, you shouldn't have any problems reading records from a TD queue, because the format of the READQ TD command is simple. If you want to see a program that reads records from a transient data queue, look ahead to chapter 8. There, you'll see the program that reads print records from the L86P queue and actually prints them on a 3270 printer.

Terminology

transient data control
transient data queue
TD queue
destination
Destination Control Table
DCT
destination-id
extrapartition transient data queue
intrapartition transient data queue
DFHNTRA
automatic transaction initiation
ATI
trigger level
data-driven transaction
indirect destination
enqueue
resource name

Objective

Given a programming problem that requires reading or writing
transient data records, code an acceptable program for its solution.

Part 3

Advanced terminal processing features

In *Part 1: An introductory course*, you learned how to use Basic Mapping Support (BMS) facilities to process simple terminal input and output. The chapters in this part show you how to use a variety of CICS facilities to process more complicated forms of terminal input and output. In chapter 6, you'll learn how to use BMS commands to create a logical message: a single unit of terminal output built by one or more SEND MAP or SEND TEXT commands that can be directed to one or more display or printer terminals. In chapter 7, you'll learn about BMS features that support color display and extended highlighting capabilities of some 3270 terminals. And in chapter 8, you'll learn how to use terminal control commands to bypass BMS so you can communicate directly with terminal devices.

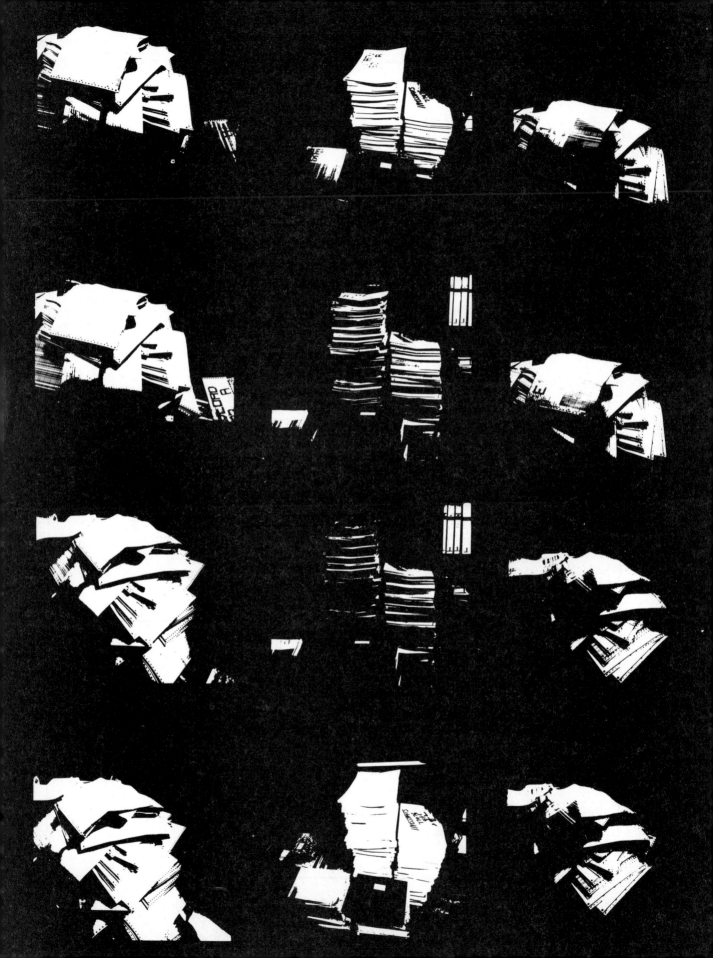

Chapter 6

BMS features
for logical message building

In this chapter, you'll learn how to create logical messages. Logical messages are typically used for reports that are displayed or printed on 3270 terminal devices. For example, a terminal operator may want to display a listing of all items in an inventory file to see which ones need to be reordered. Or, the operator may need a printed copy of the listing. In this example, the inventory listing would be created as a logical message and displayed or printed as necessary.

This chapter has three topics. Topic 1 presents the concepts and terms you need to know before you can code a program that creates a logical message. Then, topic 2 presents two techniques you can use to create a logical message; one uses the SEND TEXT command, the other uses SEND MAP. Finally, topic 3 shows you how to build a logical message that's intended for a printer.

As you study the chapters in this part, I want you to understand that logical message building is one of the less commonly used facilities of CICS. In fact, many installations don't use it at all. Still, logical message building is a powerful facility that you should know about, even if you won't use it as often as other CICS facilities.

Topic 1   Logical message building concepts and terminology

A *logical message* is a single unit of output that's created from one or more SEND TEXT or SEND MAP commands. When you use SEND TEXT and SEND MAP commands for normal display output as I presented in *Part 1: An introductory course*, you do *not* create a logical message because the output from each SEND TEXT or SEND MAP command is treated separately. In contrast, when you use SEND TEXT or SEND MAP commands to build a logical message, BMS collects the output from one or more of those commands and treats it as a single logical unit.

Don't let the term "logical message" confuse you. Although the term implies that there's also a "physical message" you should know about, there isn't. And in addition, the word "message" suggests that a logical message is brief—just one or two lines of information. Although logical messages can be that short, they often contain many pages of information.

When you use logical message building, BMS automatically provides many features for you. For example, BMS handles the complex formatting requirements of different types of terminals, including 3270 printers. And BMS provides a set of message retrieval commands that you'll learn later in this topic.

I want you to realize, though, that logical message building does *not* provide many of the features of spooling systems like JES2, JES3, and VSE/POWER. As a result, many installations have either purchased a CICS-based spooling system or developed one of their own. If that's the case at your installation, some or all of the concepts this topic presents may not apply. So keep that in mind as you read on.

MESSAGE BUILDING AND DELIVERY

The process of creating a logical message is usually called *logical message building*, or just *message building*. Unfortunately, that term isn't clearly defined in the IBM literature. And you'll often encounter other terms, like *terminal paging* and *page building*, that mean the same thing. In any event, you code a *message building program* to create a logical message. In the message building program, you issue SEND TEXT or SEND MAP commands with special options to build the message. You'll learn how to do that in the next topic.

Message delivery is the BMS process of sending a logical message to a terminal. Three factors affect how message building and message delivery work: message disposition, terminal status, and message routing.

Message disposition

A logical message can have one of two *dispositions*: terminal or paging. You specify the disposition option you want with the SEND TEXT or SEND MAP commands that build the message, as you'll see in the next topic.

Terminal disposition   When you specify *terminal disposition*, your logical message is sent directly to your terminal as it's created. You'll normally use terminal disposition when your task is attached directly to a printer. That way, your logical message is printed as it's created. To attach a task to a printer, you use the START command, which you'll learn in chapter 9.

Figure 6-1 shows how BMS handles logical messages with terminal disposition. Here, a user task issues multiple SEND TEXT or SEND MAP commands. The BMS module that processes those commands, the *page and text build program*, formats your data in an intermediate storage area called the *page buffer*. As you issue successive SEND TEXT or SEND MAP commands, data is added to the page buffer until the buffer is full. Then, another BMS module, the *terminal page processor*, transfers the data from the page buffer to the terminal and clears the page buffer so your program can continue. As a result, your logical message is built and delivered one *page* at a time.

Paging disposition   When you specify *paging disposition*, your logical message isn't sent directly to a terminal. Instead, the entire message is held in temporary storage until an operator retrieves it. Typically, you use paging disposition when the output terminal is a display device.

A logical message with paging disposition is built much like one with terminal disposition, as figure 6-2 shows. Each time your program issues a SEND TEXT or SEND MAP command, data is formatted in the page buffer. However, when the page buffer is full, the page is written to temporary storage instead of the

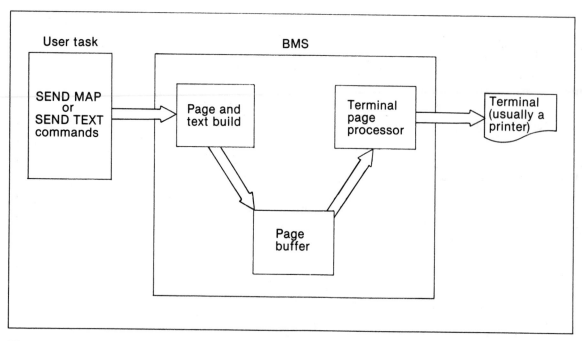

Figure 6-1 BMS sends logical messages with terminal disposition directly to the terminal

terminal. The result is that your logical message is stored as a collection of pages in temporary storage.

When you specify paging disposition, you can use *message routing* to direct a message to other terminals. I'll describe message routing in more detail in a moment. Whether or not you use message routing, though, a logical message in temporary storage is eventually delivered to one or more terminals. How a message is delivered to a terminal depends on that terminal's status.

Terminal status

Each terminal in a CICS system is assigned a *terminal status* that affects how messages with paging disposition are delivered to it. If a message is created with terminal disposition, terminal status doesn't affect how it's delivered. BMS provides two options for terminal status: paging and autopage.

Paging status For a terminal with *paging status*, usually a display station, BMS delivers pages one at a time as an operator requests them. Figure 6-3 shows how BMS delivers a logical message with paging disposition to a terminal with paging status. To view a page

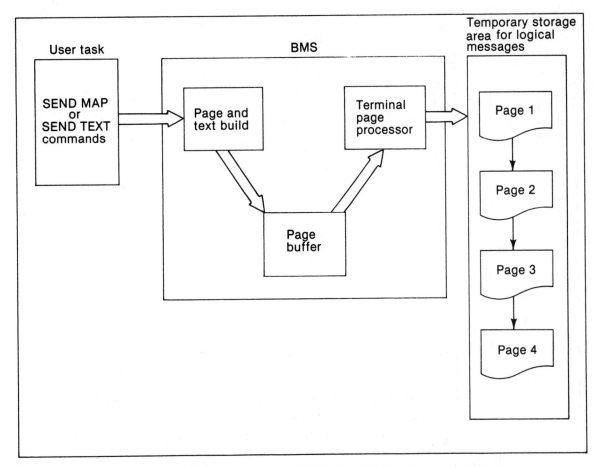

Figure 6-2 BMS stores logical messages with paging disposition in temporary storage

of the logical message, the terminal operator enters a *message retrieval command*. Then, a BMS module called the *page retrieval program* retrieves the requested page from temporary storage and displays it at the terminal.

Don't confuse paging status with paging disposition. Paging status indicates that operators can request pages one at a time by issuing message retrieval commands. In contrast, paging disposition means a logical message is written to temporary storage for later delivery. Remember, paging status is meaningful only for output with paging disposition.

Autopage status For a terminal with *autopage status*, usually a printer, the entire message is delivered automatically as soon as the terminal is ready. For an autopage terminal, BMS also uses the

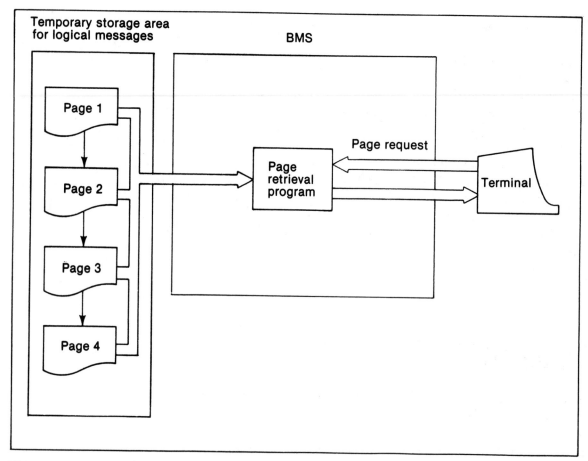

Figure 6-3 BMS retrieves pages from temporary storage under operator control

page retrieval program. But instead of processing message retrieval commands, the page retrieval program transfers pages one at a time, in order, to the autopage device. Although BMS lets any terminal have paging or autopage status, printer terminals almost always have autopage status. That way, logical messages sent to them are automatically printed.

The effect of paging disposition and autopage status together is similar to terminal disposition. The difference is that terminal disposition causes BMS to send your message directly to the terminal, while paging disposition and autopage status causes BMS to store the message in temporary storage before sending it to the terminal. Because terminal disposition is more efficient for printing applications, I recommend you use it unless you're directing a logical message to more than one printer by using message routing.

Message routing

So far, I've assumed that all logical messages are intended for the terminal where the message building task is attached. And that's normally the case: when an operator starts a message building program, its output is displayed at that operator's terminal. And for printer output, it's common to use an interval control START command to start a task attached to a particular printer.

It's not unusual, though, for a program to send a logical message to terminals other than the one the message building task is attached to. For example, consider an invoicing application that requires orders to be printed on two printers: one in the billing department, the other in the shipping department. In this case, the same logical message (an invoice) is routed to two terminals. You'll learn how to use message routing in topic 3.

OPERATOR COMMANDS FOR MESSAGE RETRIEVAL

When a logical message with paging disposition is delivered to a terminal with paging status (a display terminal), only one page is displayed at a time. To tell BMS what page to display, you use message retrieval commands. Figure 6-4 shows the two most commonly used message retrieval commands: getpage and msgterm. You use getpage to retrieve pages, and you use msgterm to end a message retrieval session. Although there are other message retrieval commands, you're not likely to use them.

Each message retrieval command begins with a prefix that's assigned by your systems programmer. In figure 6-4, the prefix for the getpage command is P/, and the prefix for the msgterm command is T/. Although your installation may use different prefixes, the ones in figure 6-4 are common. And although the prefixes may vary, the values that follow them are always the same. As a result, you always code L on a getpage command to retrieve the last page of a message, regardless of what prefix is assigned to the getpage command.

Entering a page retrieval command is simple. When the first page of your message is displayed (that's automatic), press the clear key, key in a page retrieval command, and press the enter key. If you enter a valid page retrieval command prefix, CICS invokes the page retrieval program to process your command.

The getpage command

P/n	Retrieve page n.
P/ + n	Retrieve the page that's n pages past the current page.
P/ − n	Retrieve the page that's n pages before the current page.
P/L	Retrieve the last page.
P/N	Retrieve the next page.
P/P	Retrieve the previous page.

The msgterm command

T/B	Terminate the page retrieval session and purge the message being displayed.

Figure 6-4   Message retrieval commands

How to retrieve pages

You use the getpage command (prefix P/ in figure 6-4) to display a specific page. For example, to retrieve the third page of a message, you enter:

    P / 3

You can move forward through a logical message by entering a command like this:

    P / +2

Here, the page that's two pages beyond the current page is displayed. So if you enter that command when page 3 is displayed, the page retrieval program displays page 5. To display a page that's before the current page, use a minus sign, as in:

    P / −1

The effect of this command is to retrieve the previous page.

Three special forms of the getpage command let you retrieve the last page of a message, the next page, and the previous page. To display the last page, enter P/L. To display the next page, you enter P/N (that's the same as P/+1), and to display the previous page, you enter P/P (that's the same as P/ − 1). Although there's no special option to retrieve the first page of a message, you can do that by entering P/1.

How to end a page-retrieval session

When you've finished displaying a logical message, you must purge it before you can do other work on your terminal. To do that, you enter a msgterm command. Figure 6-4 shows the version of the msgterm command you're most likely to use: T/B. When you enter T/B, the message you're retrieving is deleted.

Single-keystroke retrieval

Some installations use a feature called *single-keystroke retrieval*, or *SKR*, to simplify page retrieval. When SKR is used, PF keys are associated with specific paging commands. For example, suppose five PF keys are assigned like this:

PF1	P/1
PF2	P/L
PF3	P/P
PF4	P/N

Then, you can display the first page of a logical message by pressing PF1 or the last page by pressing PF2. And you can use PF3 and PF4 to move forward or backward through the message one page at a time.

You can still use PF keys in application programs when SKR is used. The PF keys take on their SKR meanings only during a message retrieval session.

DISCUSSION

I hope you realize by now that logical message building is not simple. Because its programming requirements are difficult to learn, many CICS installations use other techniques for report preparation—especially when printers are involved. In particular, transient data queues are often used for printer output. If such facilities are available at your installation, by all means use them.

Terminology

logical message
logical message building
message building
terminal paging
page building
message building program
message delivery
disposition
terminal disposition
page and text build program
page buffer
terminal page processor
page
paging disposition
message routing
terminal status
paging status
message retrieval command
page retrieval program
autopage status
single keystroke retrieval
SKR

Objectives

1. Explain the meaning of the following terms:

    a. logical message
    b. message building
    c. message routing

2. Distinguish between:

    a. terminal and paging disposition
    b. paging and autopage status

3. Describe the function of the getpage and msgterm paging commands.

Topic 2   Two techniques for building a logical message

In this topic, you'll learn two techniques for building a logical message. The first uses the SEND TEXT command and doesn't require a mapset; the second uses the SEND MAP command and *does* require a mapset. In most cases, I think it's easier to use the SEND TEXT technique, although there are cases where it's better to use the SEND MAP technique. So you need to know about both.

Throughout this topic, I assume that your logical message is delivered to a display terminal, not to a printer. In the next topic, you'll learn how directing a logical message to a printer affects the way you code the SEND TEXT and SEND MAP commands.

Figure 6-5 presents the screen layout for two programs that display a listing of data from a file of inventory records. Although both programs produce identical output, they use different message building techniques. The first version uses the SEND TEXT command, and the other uses the SEND MAP command.

If you've read chapter 5, you'll recognize that the screen layout in figure 6-5 is a variation of the print chart for the inventory-listing program I presented there. One difference between the print chart and the screen layout you should notice is that the first position of each screen line is left blank. That's because the first position is required for an attribute byte.

Also, notice the groupings of output lines I've marked in figure 6-5. The first five lines of each output page are the *header*. Following the header are 17 occurrences of the inventory detail line. At the bottom of each output page except the last is a two-line *trailer* with a message that tells the operator that the listing continues on the next page. And on the last page of the inventory listing, a total line shows the number of records in the inventory file. As you read on, you'll see that a significant difference between the SEND TEXT and SEND MAP techniques is in how you place headers and trailers on each page.

THE INVENTORY-LISTING PROGRAM: SEND TEXT VERSION

The structure chart for the SEND TEXT version of the inventory-listing program, shown in figure 6-6, is easy to understand. After

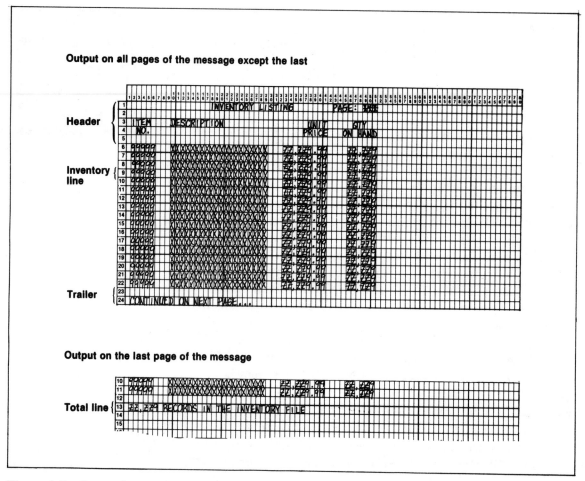

Figure 6-5 Screen layout for the inventory-listing programs

module 1000 starts a browse operation on the inventory file, module 2000 is invoked repeatedly to produce inventory lines. It calls module 2100 to read an inventory record and module 2200 to add lines to the logical message. After all the inventory records have been processed, module 3000 is invoked to send the total line.

As you've probably noticed, the structure chart in figure 6-6 provides no modules to format and send header or trailer lines, even though the screen layout in figure 6-5 calls for both. There's no need for separate modules to handle those functions because BMS provides them automatically when you code the SEND TEXT command to build a logical message. That's one of the main advantages of using SEND TEXT rather than SEND MAP for

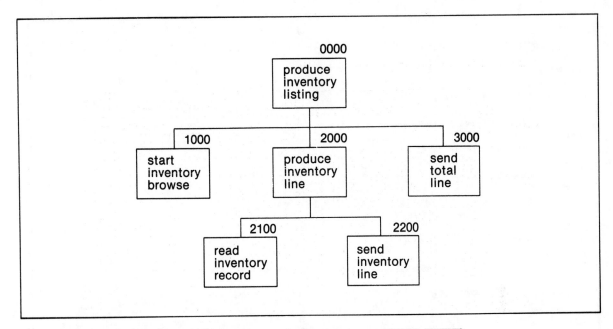

Figure 6-6 Structure chart for the inventory-listing program (SEND TEXT)

message building: the SEND MAP command does *not* automatically format header and trailer lines.

Figure 6-7 gives the source listing for the SEND TEXT version of the inventory-listing program. Because this program is easy to understand, I'll focus on those elements that relate directly to logical message building. In the Procedure Division, I've shaded three commands: the SEND TEXT commands in modules 2200 and 3000 and the SEND PAGE command in module 0000. Once you understand how those commands work, you'll have no trouble understanding this program.

The SEND TEXT command

In *Part 1: An introductory course*, you learned how to use the SEND TEXT command to send a short message to the terminal. Figure 6-8 gives a more complete format for the SEND TEXT command, showing the options you can code for message building. You already know about the FROM and LENGTH options: they identify the location and length of the data that's to be sent. And the ERASE option works the same way it does for a non-message building SEND TEXT command: it erases the previous contents of

```
     IDENTIFICATION DIVISION.
 *
 PROGRAM-ID.   INVLST2.
 *
 ENVIRONMENT DIVISION.
 *
 DATA DIVISION.
 *
 WORKING-STORAGE SECTION.
 *
 01  SWITCHES.
 *
     05  INVMAST-EOF-SW   PIC X        VALUE 'N'.
         88  INVMAST-EOF               VALUE 'Y'.
 *
 01  WORK-FIELDS.
 *
     05  RECORD-COUNT     PIC S9(5)  VALUE ZERO     COMP-3.
 *
 01  HEADER-AREA.
 *
     05  HA-PREFIX.
         10  HA-LENGTH     PIC S9(4)  VALUE +153     COMP.
         10  HA-PAGE-CODE PIC X       VALUE '*'.
         10  FILLER        PIC X       VALUE SPACE.
     05  HEADER-LINE-1.
         10  FILLER        PIC X(20)  VALUE '                    INVE'.
         10  FILLER        PIC X(20)  VALUE 'NTORY LISTING           '.
         10  FILLER        PIC X(10)  VALUE ' PAGE: ***'.
         10  HA1-NL        PIC XX     VALUE ' '.
     05  HEADER-LINE-2.
         10  FILLER        PIC X(20)  VALUE 'ITEM      DESCRIPTION '.
         10  FILLER        PIC X(20)  VALUE '                  UNIT'.
         10  FILLER        PIC X(8)   VALUE '     QTY'.
         10  HA2-NL        PIC X      VALUE ' '.
     05  HEADER-LINE-3.
         10  FILLER        PIC X(20)  VALUE ' NO.                 '.
         10  FILLER        PIC X(20)  VALUE '                 PRICE'.
         10  FILLER        PIC X(10)  VALUE '    ON HAND'.
         10  HA3-NL        PIC X(2)   VALUE ' '.
 *
 01  INVENTORY-LINE.
 *
     05  IL-ITEM-NUMBER      PIC 9(5).
     05  FILLER              PIC X(3)          VALUE SPACE.
     05  IL-ITEM-DESCRIPTION PIC X(20).
     05  FILLER              PIC X(3)          VALUE SPACE.
     05  IL-UNIT-PRICE       PIC ZZ,ZZ9.99.
     05  FILLER              PIC X(4)          VALUE SPACE.
     05  IL-ON-HAND-QUANTITY PIC ZZ,ZZ9.
     05  IL-NL               PIC X             VALUE ' '.
 *
```

Figure 6-7   Source listing for the inventory-listing program (SEND TEXT) (part 1 of 4)

```
01   TOTAL-LINE.
*
     05   TL-NL               PIC X          VALUE ' '.
     05   TL-RECORD-COUNT     PIC ZZ,ZZ9.
     05   FILLER              PIC X(20)   VALUE ' RECORDS IN THE INVE'.
     05   FILLER              PIC X(10)   VALUE 'NTORY FILE'.
*
01   TRAILER-AREA.
*
     05   TA-PREFIX.
          10   TA-LENGTH      PIC S9(4)   VALUE +26      COMP.
          10   FILLER         PIC X(2)    VALUE SPACE.
     05   TRAILER-LINE.
          10   TA-NL          PIC X       VALUE ' '.
          10   FILLER         PIC X(20)   VALUE 'CONTINUED ON NEXT PA'.
          10   FILLER         PIC X(5)    VALUE 'GE...'.
*
01   INVENTORY-MASTER-RECORD.
*
     05   IM-ITEM-NUMBER       PIC X(5).
     05   IM-ITEM-DESCRIPTION  PIC X(20).
     05   IM-UNIT-PRICE        PIC S9(5)V99      COMP-3.
     05   IM-ON-HAND-QUANTITY  PIC S9(5)         COMP-3.
*
 PROCEDURE DIVISION.
*
 0000-PRODUCE-INVENTORY-LISTING SECTION.
*
     PERFORM 1000-START-INVENTORY-BROWSE.
     EXEC CICS
          HANDLE CONDITION ENDFILE(2100-ENDFILE)
     END-EXEC.
     PERFORM 2000-PRODUCE-INVENTORY-LINE
          UNTIL INVMAST-EOF.
     PERFORM 3000-SEND-TOTAL-LINE.
     EXEC CICS
          SEND PAGE
               OPERPURGE
     END-EXEC.
     EXEC CICS
          RETURN
     END-EXEC.
*
 1000-START-INVENTORY-BROWSE SECTION.
*
     EXEC CICS
          HANDLE CONDITION NOTFND(1000-NOTFND)
     END-EXEC.
     MOVE ZERO TO IM-ITEM-NUMBER.
     EXEC CICS
          STARTBR DATASET('INVMAST')
                  RIDFLD(IM-ITEM-NUMBER)
     END-EXEC.
     GO TO 1000-EXIT.
```

Figure 6-7   Source listing for the inventory-listing program (SEND TEXT) (part 2 of 4)

```
*
 1000-NOTFND.
*
     MOVE 'Y' TO INVMAST-EOF-SW.
*
 1000-EXIT.
*
     EXIT.
*
 2000-PRODUCE-INVENTORY-LINE SECTION.
*
     PERFORM 2100-READ-INVENTORY-RECORD.
     IF NOT INVMAST-EOF
         PERFORM 2200-SEND-INVENTORY-LINE.
*
 2100-READ-INVENTORY-RECORD SECTION.
*
     EXEC CICS
         READNEXT DATASET('INVMAST')
                  INTO(INVENTORY-MASTER-RECORD)
                  RIDFLD(IM-ITEM-NUMBER)
     END-EXEC.
     ADD 1 TO RECORD-COUNT.
     GO TO 2100-EXIT.
*
 2100-ENDFILE.
*
     MOVE 'Y' TO INVMAST-EOF-SW.
*
 2100-EXIT.
*
     EXIT.
*
 2200-SEND-INVENTORY-LINE SECTION.
*
     MOVE IM-ITEM-NUMBER       TO IL-ITEM-NUMBER.
     MOVE IM-ITEM-DESCRIPTION TO IL-ITEM-DESCRIPTION.
     MOVE IM-UNIT-PRICE        TO IL-UNIT-PRICE.
     MOVE IM-ON-HAND-QUANTITY TO IL-ON-HAND-QUANTITY.
     EXEC CICS
         SEND TEXT FROM(INVENTORY-LINE)
                   LENGTH(51)
                   ACCUM
                   PAGING
                   ERASE
                   HEADER(HEADER-AREA)
                   TRAILER(TRAILER-AREA)
     END-EXEC.
*
```

Figure 6-7 Source listing for the inventory-listing program (SEND TEXT) (part 3 of 4)

```
    3000-SEND-TOTAL-LINE SECTION.
*
        MOVE RECORD-COUNT TO TL-RECORD-COUNT.
        EXEC CICS
            SEND TEXT FROM(TOTAL-LINE)
                      LENGTH(37)
                      ACCUM
                      PAGING
                      ERASE
        END-EXEC.
```

Figure 6-7   Source listing for the inventory-listing program (SEND TEXT) (part 4 of 4)

the screen. (You should always specify ERASE.) So the only new
options are ACCUM, PAGING, HEADER, and TRAILER. After I
describe the special formatting considerations for data you specify
in the FROM option, I'll describe those options.

How to control vertical spacing in SEND TEXT output data
When you use a SEND TEXT command, the field you specify in
the FROM option can provide one or more lines of output. To
indicate where line endings fall in your output, you use *new-line
characters*. To understand, look at the coding for the inventory
detail line (INVENTORY-LINE) in figure 6-7. Here, you can see
that the last item in the group is this:

```
05   IL-NL     PIC X      VALUE ' '.
```

Although it's not apparent from the source listing, the VALUE
clause of this item contains a new-line character (hex 15). The
name I gave this field tells me that it contains a new-line character
(NL stands for New Line). Because hex 15 isn't part of the COBOL
character set, you'll have to use the hexadecimal editing feature of
your text editor to enter the new-line character in your source
program.

   Figure 6-9 shows a more complex example of formatting data
for a SEND TEXT command. Here, each SEND TEXT command
will send the six lines in the screen layout. Of the six, two are
blank, and four contain data showing a customer's number, name,
address, city, state, and zip code. Notice how I coded two
consecutive new-line characters at the end of CUSTOMER-LINE-1
and CUSTOMER-LINE-4 to force blank lines.

   In the IBM-supplied copy member DFHBMSCA, there's an
entry named DFHBMPNL that contains a new-line character. If

The SEND TEXT command

```
EXEC CICS
    SEND TEXT FROM(data-name)
              LENGTH(data-name|literal)
              [ACCUM]
              [PAGING]
              [ERASE]
              [HEADER(data-name)]
              [TRAILER(data-name)]
END-EXEC
```

Explanation

FROM	Specifies the name of the field that contains the data to be added to the logical message.
LENGTH	The length of the FROM field. Must be numeric. If you use a data-name, it must be a binary half-word (PIC S9(4) COMP).
ACCUM	Specifies that this SEND TEXT command is used to build a logical message.
PAGING	Specifies that output pages should be written to temporary storage for later retrieval under operator control.
ERASE	Specifies that the terminal's buffer should be erased as each page of the message is sent during page retrieval.
HEADER	Specifies the name of a field that contains header information to be placed at the top of each page.
TRAILER	Specifies the name of a field that contains trailer information to be placed at the bottom of each page.

Figure 6-8   The SEND TEXT command

you wish, you can use this entry by copying DFHBMSCA into your program. Then, near the start of your program, you can move DFHBMPNL to each field that should contain a new-line character like this:

```
MOVE DFHBMPNL TO IL-NL.
```

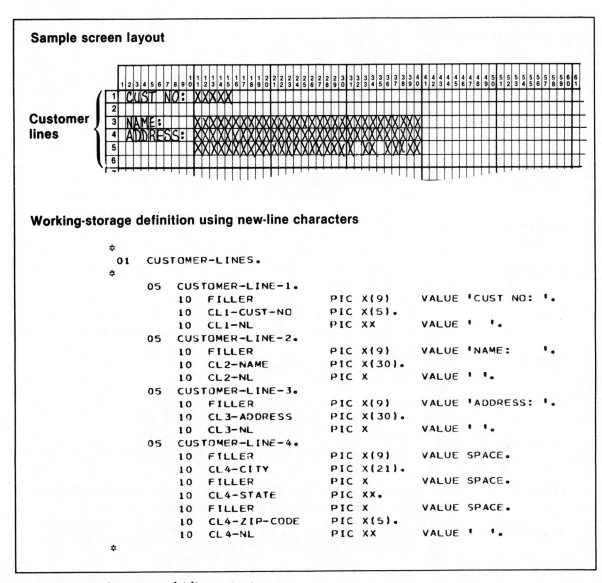

Figure 6-9 Defining a multi-line output area

Frankly, I think it's easier to code the new-line characters directly in your program. But if your text editor doesn't provide a good hexadecimal editing facility, you may want to use DFHBMPNL.

Incidentally, if you know about hardware printer orders for 3270 printers, don't let the new-line character confuse you. Although the new-line character and the new-line printer order have the same hexadecimal value and similar functions, they're not the same. The new-line character I've just described is strictly a BMS facility: it tells BMS to format output data so that a line ending will fall wherever you place it. In contrast, a new-line printer order is a hardware facility: it tells a 3270 printer to begin a new line. In the next topic, you'll learn that for printer output, BMS may or may not use new-line printer orders for line endings. But the BMS new-line character works for printer or display terminals and has nothing to do with the new-line printer order.

The ACCUM and PAGING options   You code the ACCUM and PAGING options on a SEND TEXT command to indicate that it's being used to build a logical message. Quite simply, ACCUM means that output from one or more SEND TEXT commands is accumulated in a page buffer rather than sent directly to the terminal. If you code the PAGING option, the message is created with paging disposition; that is, each page of the message is written to temporary storage. When the program ends, the terminal operator can display individual pages of the message using the message retrieval commands I described in the last topic. If you omit PAGING, the message is created with terminal disposition; as a result, it's written directly to the terminal.

The HEADER and TRAILER options   When you use the SEND TEXT command to build a logical message, BMS automatically formats header and trailer lines if you specify HEADER, TRAILER, or both. Simply put, the HEADER option identifies data that BMS places at the top of each page, and the TRAILER option identifies data that BMS places at the bottom of each page. When you use these options, you don't have to worry about counting the number of output lines to determine where to place header and trailer data. BMS handles that *overflow processing* for you.

To illustrate how overflow processing works, figure 6-10 shows the processing BMS does for a SEND TEXT command. First, BMS compares the number of output lines in your FROM area with the number of lines remaining on the page, allowing for the size of your trailer data. If there's enough room remaining on the page, BMS adds the FROM data to it and returns. However, if the FROM data won't fit, BMS adds the trailer data, writes the page to temporary storage, clears the page, and then adds the header data and the FROM data to the new page.

For BMS overflow processing to work, each header and trailer area must begin with a four-byte prefix that contains control

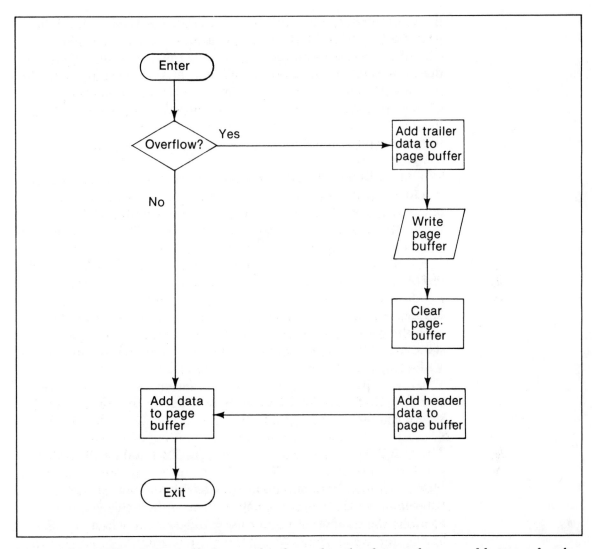

Figure 6-10 BMS automatically formats header and trailer data at the top and bottom of each page

information. In figure 6-7, the header area's prefix is HA-PREFIX and the trailer area's is TA-PREFIX.

As you can see in figure 6-7, HA-PREFIX contains three fields. The first is a two-byte length field (PIC S9(4) COMP) that defines the length of the header or trailer area, *not* including the four-byte prefix. The second is a one-byte field that's used for automatic page numbering. I'll explain how you use it in a moment. The third is a one-byte FILLER item that's reserved for use by BMS. Because page numbering isn't required in TA-PREFIX, I defined it with just two fields: the length field and a two-byte FILLER item.

After the four-byte prefix, you code the header or trailer data—as many bytes as you specify in the prefix's length field. To indicate line endings in a header or trailer, you use new-line characters just as you do in the FROM area.

Automatic page numbering   If you specify a non-blank value in the page-numbering field (byte 3) of a header or trailer prefix, BMS automatically numbers output pages for you. When an overflow situation occurs, BMS scans the header or trailer data until it finds one or more occurrences of the character you specify in byte 3 of the prefix. Then, it replaces those characters with the current page number.

In figure 6-7, I specified an asterisk (*) in the VALUE clause of HA-PAGE-CODE. Then, in the data portion of the header area, I coded three consecutive asterisks to indicate where the page numbers should go. As a result, BMS replaces those three asterisks with the page number. You can use any character that's part of the standard COBOL character set for a page code, other than HIGH-VALUE. And you can use up to five bytes for the page number. When you specify a page code in a header or trailer area, make sure that character doesn't appear anywhere in that area other than where you want the page number.

The SEND TEXT commands in modules 2200 and 3000   Now that you know how the SEND TEXT command works, you should have little trouble understanding modules 2200 and 3000 in figure 6-7. After module 2200 moves inventory data to the fields of INVENTORY-LINE, it issues this SEND TEXT command:

```
EXEC CICS
    SEND TEXT FROM(INVENTORY-LINE)
              LENGTH(51)
              ACCUM
              PAGING
              ERASE
              HEADER(HEADER-AREA)
              TRAILER(TRAILER-AREA)
    END-EXEC.
```

This command adds an inventory line to the logical message. If the

inventory line won't fit on the current page, the trailer data in
TRAILER-AREA is added to the bottom of the page, the page is
written to temporary storage, the header information in HEADER-
AREA is added to the top of the next page, and the inventory line
is added as the first detail line of that page. Because the prefix in
HEADER-AREA specifies page numbering, BMS automatically
numbers each page.

The SEND TEXT command in module 3000 is similar to the
one in module 2200, but instead of sending an inventory line, it
sends a total line. And I omit the HEADER and TRAILER options
so the final total line always appears on the same page as the last
detail line. There's always enough room on that page for the total
line, because the SEND TEXT command in module 2200 reserves
two lines for a trailer area.

The SEND PAGE command

When you use the SEND TEXT command to build a logical
message, data is accumulated in the page buffer. That data isn't
written to temporary storage until the buffer is filled. To ensure
that the last page of data is written to temporary storage even if it's
not complete, you should always code a SEND PAGE command
after the last SEND TEXT command in your program. (The
program in figure 6-7 issues a SEND PAGE command from module
0000 just before it ends.)

Figure 6-11 gives the format of the SEND PAGE command.
You normally code it like this:

```
EXEC CICS
    SEND PAGE
        OPERPURGE
END-EXEC.
```

The OPERPURGE option tells BMS that an operator must
explicitly purge the message by entering a termination command
(like T/B). If you omit the OPERPURGE option, BMS purges the
message as soon as the operator enters anything that's not a valid
page retrieval command. Since it's easy for an operator to make a
keying mistake, I recommend you always code OPERPURGE so the
operator doesn't accidentally purge your message.

The SEND PAGE command

```
EXEC CICS
     SEND PAGE
          [OPERPURGE]
END-EXEC
```

Explanation

OPERPURGE   Specifies that the operator must issue a message termination
                 command to delete the logical message. If you omit
                 OPERPURGE, the message is automatically deleted when the
                 operator enters anything that's not a page-retrieval command.

Figure 6-11   The SEND PAGE command

THE INVENTORY-LISTING PROGRAM: SEND MAP VERSION

Now that you know how to use the SEND TEXT command to create a logical message, I'll present another version of the inventory-listing program, this time using the SEND MAP command. To use the SEND MAP technique, you must do two things. First, you must create a BMS mapset that defines the maps that make up your logical message. You do that using the same BMS macro instructions you use for a non-message building program, with additional parameters on the DFHMDI macro. Second, you code your application program using the SEND MAP command to build the logical message and the SEND PAGE command to complete it.

The mapset: DFHMDI parameters for message building

Figure 6-12 shows the mapset I created for the inventory-listing program. (The screen layout is in figure 6-5.) If you study this mapset for a moment, you'll see that it consists of four maps, each defined by a DFHMDI macro instruction. There's one map for the report's five-line header, one for the detail line, one for the two-line trailer, and one for the final total line.

```
          PRINT NOGEN
LSTSET1   DFHMSD TYPE=&SYSPARM,                                          X
                 LANG=COBOL,                                             X
                 MODE=INOUT,                                             X
                 TERM=3270-2,                                            X
                 CTRL=FREEKB,                                            X
                 STORAGE=AUTO,                                           X
                 TIOAPFX=YES
*****************************************************************************
*****************************************************************************
LSTMAP1   DFHMDI SIZE=(5,80),                                           X
                 JUSTIFY=FIRST,                                          X
                 HEADER=YES
*****************************************************************************
          DFHMDF POS=(1,17),                                            X
                 LENGTH=17,                                              X
                 ATTRB=PROT,                                             X
                 INITIAL='INVENTORY LISTING'
          DFHMDF POS=(1,42),                                            X
                 LENGTH=5,                                               X
                 ATTRB=PROT,                                             X
                 INITIAL='PAGE:'
PAGENO    DFHMDF POS=(1,48),                                            X
                 LENGTH=3,                                               X
                 ATTRB=PROT,                                             X
                 PICOUT='ZZ9'
          DFHMDF POS=(3,1),                                             X
                 LENGTH=19,                                              X
                 ATTRB=PROT,                                             X
                 INITIAL='ITEM       DESCRIPTION'
          DFHMDF POS=(3,37),                                            X
                 LENGTH=12,                                              X
                 ATTRB=PROT,                                             X
                 INITIAL='UNIT       QTY'
          DFHMDF POS=(4,2),                                             X
                 LENGTH=3,                                               X
                 ATTRB=PROT,                                             X
                 INITIAL='NO.'
          DFHMDF POS=(4,36),                                            X
                 LENGTH=15,                                              X
                 ATTRB=PROT,                                             X
                 INITIAL='PRICE     ON HAND'
*****************************************************************************
*****************************************************************************
LSTMAP2   DFHMDI SIZE=(1,80),                                           X
                 LINE=NEXT,                                              X
                 COLUMN=1
*****************************************************************************
ITEMNO    DFHMDF POS=(1,1),                                             X
                 LENGTH=5,                                               X
                 ATTRB=PROT
```

Figure 6-12   Mapset listing for the inventory-listing program (SEND MAP) (part 1 of 2)

```
DESCR     DFHMDF POS=(1,9),                                              X
                 LENGTH=20,                                              X
                 ATTRB=PROT
UPRICE    DFHMDF POS=(1,32),                                             X
                 LENGTH=9,                                               X
                 ATTRB=PROT,                                             X
                 PICOUT='ZZ,ZZ9.99'
ONHAND    DFHMDF POS=(1,45),                                             X
                 LENGTH=6,                                               X
                 ATTRB=PROT,                                             X
                 PICOUT='ZZ,ZZ9'
*****************************************************************************
*****************************************************************************
LSTMAP3   DFHMDI SIZE=(2,80),                                            X
                 JUSTIFY=LAST,                                           X
                 TRAILER=YES
*****************************************************************************
          DFHMDF POS=(2,1),                                             X
                 LENGTH=25,                                             X
                 ATTRB=PROT,                                            X
                 INITIAL='CONTINUED ON NEXT PAGE...'
*****************************************************************************
*****************************************************************************
LSTMAP4   DFHMDI SIZE=(2,80),                                           X
                 LINE=NEXT,                                             X
                 COLUMN=1,                                              X
                 TRAILER=YES
*****************************************************************************
COUNT     DFHMDF POS=(2,1),                                            X
                 LENGTH=6,                                             X
                 ATTRB=PROT,                                           X
                 PICOUT='ZZ,ZZ9'
          DFHMDF POS=(2,8),                                            X
                 LENGTH=29,                                            X
                 ATTRB=PROT,                                           X
                 INITIAL='RECORDS IN THE INVENTORY FILE'
*****************************************************************************
          DFHMSD TYPE=FINAL
          END
```

Figure 6-12   Mapset listing for the inventory-listing program (SEND MAP) (part 2 of 2)

The DFHMDI macros shaded in figure 6-12 present some new elements. Since none of the other macro instructions in this mapset require new coding elements, I'll concentrate on just the DFHMDI macro instruction.

Figure 6-13 shows the format of the DFHMDI macro and the parameters you code on it to produce a logical message. The label on the DFHMDI macro instruction is the name of the map (it must be unique within a mapset). If your installation has standards for forming map names, by all means follow them. In figure 6-12, I

The DFHMDI macro

```
map-name   DFHMDI      SIZE=(lines,columns),

                       [LINE= {line-number},]
                              {NEXT       }

                       [COLUMN=column-number,]

                       [JUSTIFY= {FIRST},]
                                 {LAST }

                       [{HEADER=YES  }]
                        {TRAILER=YES }
```

Explanation

SIZE	Specifies the size of the map in lines and columns.
LINE	Specifies the position of the first line of the map. If you code a line-number, the map is positioned at the line you specify. If you code LINE = NEXT, the map is positioned starting at the next available line.
COLUMN	Specifies the starting column number for the map.
JUSTIFY	Specifies that the map should be aligned with one of the page margins. If you code JUSTIFY = FIRST, the map is placed at the top of a new page. If you code JUSTIFY = LAST, the map is placed at the bottom of the current page. If you use JUSTIFY, do not use LINE or COLUMN.
HEADER	If you code HEADER = YES, the map is treated as a header map.
TRAILER	If you code TRAILER = YES, the map is treated as a trailer map.

Figure 6-13   The DFHMDI macro

simply numbered the maps: LSTMAP1, LSTMAP2, LSTMAP3, and LSTMAP4.

The SIZE parameter   The SIZE parameter tells BMS the number of lines and columns in the map. The number of lines you specify depends on the number of lines required by your header, detail, or trailer area. For example, the header area in figure 6-5 requires five lines (lines 2 and 5 are blank). As a result, I specify SIZE = (5,80) in the DFHMDI macro for LSTMAP1 in figure 6-12.

The LINE, COLUMN, and JUSTIFY parameters You use the next three parameters—LINE, COLUMN, and JUSTIFY—to specify the starting position within the current page for each map. For a non-message building program, you usually code a specific line number in the LINE parameter. Although you can do that in a mapset for a message building application, it's uncommon. You're more likely to use LINE = NEXT, JUSTIFY = FIRST, or JUSTIFY = LAST to position a map that's part of a logical message.

If you code LINE = NEXT, your map is positioned on the next line of the page. You usually code LINE = NEXT for a detail map. That way, detail maps are positioned on successive lines. In figure 6-12, I specified LINE = NEXT for the inventory detail map (LSTMAP2). I also coded LINE = NEXT for the final total map so it will follow the last detail map.

If you code JUSTIFY = FIRST, the map is placed at the beginning of the next page. You usually code JUSTIFY = FIRST for a header map, as I did for LSTMAP1 in figure 6-12. The effect of JUSTIFY = FIRST is similar to coding LINE = 1 and COLUMN = 1. The difference is that when you code JUSTIFY = FIRST, data in the page buffer is automatically written to temporary storage before any new data is added. In contrast, the combination LINE = 1 and COLUMN = 1 doesn't cause the page buffer to be automatically written to temporary storage. So always specify JUSTIFY = FIRST rather than LINE = 1 and COLUMN = 1 on your header maps.

As you might expect, JUSTIFY = LAST has the opposite effect of JUSTIFY = FIRST: it causes the map to be positioned at the bottom of the current page. Normally, you'll code JUSTIFY = LAST for trailer maps. In figure 6-12, I specified JUSTIFY = LAST for LSTMAP3.

Don't let the vertical orientation of the JUSTIFY parameter confuse you. If you're like me, you normally think of justification in horizontal terms—that is, left or right justification. Although you can specify other values for the JUSTIFY parameter, you're most likely to use the vertical justification provided by JUSTIFY = FIRST and JUSTIFY = LAST.

Within a map, fields you define with a DFHMDF macro are positioned relative to the beginning of the map, without regard for how the map is positioned within the page. For example, suppose you define a field like this:

```
FIELD1          DFHMDF POS=(2,25),
                       LENGTH=5,
                       ATTRB=PROT
```

Then, if you specify JUSTIFY = FIRST in the DFHMDI macro, FIELD1 is displayed at column 25 of line 2. But if you specify LINE = NEXT and the next line is line 10, FIELD1 is displayed at column 25 of line 11; that's position (2,25) relative to the start of the map.

The HEADER and TRAILER parameters   You use the HEADER and TRAILER parameters for header and trailer maps. For a header map, code HEADER = YES. And for a trailer map, code TRAILER = YES.

The HEADER and TRAILER parameters have nothing to do with map positioning. In other words, HEADER = YES doesn't mean that the map is automatically placed at the top of a new page. Nor does TRAILER = YES cause a map to be placed at the bottom of a page. It's the JUSTIFY parameter that controls positioning for header and trailer maps. The purpose of the HEADER and TRAILER parameters is to control overflow processing.

You'll learn the details of SEND MAP overflow processing in a moment. For now, though, I want you to understand two things. First, each time your program sends a detail map (one that doesn't specify HEADER = YES or TRAILER = YES), BMS makes sure there's enough room on the current page for both the map that's being sent and the largest trailer map (TRAILER = YES) in the mapset. If there is, the detail map is added to the page, but if there isn't, an overflow situation occurs.

When an overflow occurs, the detail map isn't added to the page. Instead, BMS raises the OVERFLOW condition, which your program can detect if it has already issued an appropriate HANDLE CONDITION command. It's then up to your program to send trailer and header maps to complete the current page and begin a new one; BMS doesn't automatically send those lines like it does when you use the SEND TEXT command. Then, after the new page has been started, your program must reissue the SEND MAP command for the detail line.

The second point I want you to understand is that the OVERFLOW condition is never raised when you send a header or trailer map. So once OVERFLOW occurs, you can send as many header or trailer maps as you wish without worrying about OVERFLOW occurring again. BMS begins checking again for page overflow as soon as you send a map that doesn't specify HEADER = YES or TRAILER = YES.

Incidentally, you don't have to code a trailer map at all if your program doesn't require a trailer area. In that case, the size of the trailer area is zero, so the OVERFLOW condition isn't raised until detail lines reach the bottom of the page.

The symbolic map

Figure 6-14 shows the symbolic map I created for the inventory-listing mapset. There's nothing unusual about this symbolic map. Notice that there's no 01-level entry for LSTMAP3. That's because the trailer map doesn't contain data that's sent from the application program.

The program: SEND MAP options for message building

Figures 6-15 and 6-16 present the SEND MAP version of the inventory-listing program. The structure chart, shown in figure 6-15, is similar to the structure chart for the SEND TEXT version presented earlier in this topic. The only difference is that I provided modules to send header and trailer information, since that's *not* done automatically when you use the SEND MAP command. Notice that module 2230 is invoked from module 0000 at the start of the program. That way, the header map for the first page of the logical message is sent before any detail maps are sent.

Figure 6-16 gives the source listing for the inventory-listing program. Because most of this program is the same as the SEND TEXT version, I'll focus on module 2200 and its subordinates and on module 3000. Those are the modules that contain the program's message building functions.

This program uses four SEND MAP commands: one for each map in the program's mapset. The SEND MAP command in module 2210 sends an inventory detail map, the ones in modules 2220 and 2230 send trailer and header maps, and the one in module 3000 sends the total map.

```
   01    INVENTORY-LISTING-MAP-1.
*
         05   FILLER                          PIC X(12).
*
         05   ILM1-L-PAGE-NO                  PIC S9(4)      COMP.
         05   ILM1-A-PAGE-NO                  PIC X.
         05   ILM1-D-PAGE-NO                  PIC ZZ9.
*
   01    INVENTORY-LISTING-MAP-2.
*
         05   FILLER                          PIC X(12).
*
         05   ILM2-L-ITEM-NUMBER              PIC S9(4)    COMP.
         05   ILM2-A-ITEM-NUMBER              PIC X.
         05   ILM2-D-ITEM-NUMBER              PIC 99999.
*
         05   ILM2-L-ITEM-DESCRIPTION PIC S9(4)     COMP.
         05   ILM2-A-ITEM-DESCRIPTION PIC X.
         05   ILM2-D-ITEM-DESCRIPTION PIC X(20).
*
         05   ILM2-L-UNIT-PRICE               PIC S9(4)     COMP.
         05   ILM2-A-UNIT-PRICE               PIC X.
         05   ILM2-D-UNIT-PRICE               PIC ZZ,ZZ9.99.
*
         05   ILM2-L-ON-HAND-QUANTITY PIC S9(4)     COMP.
         05   ILM2-A-ON-HAND-QUANTITY PIC X.
         05   ILM2-D-ON-HAND-QUANTITY PIC ZZ,ZZ9.
*
   01    INVENTORY-LISTING-MAP-4.
*
         05   FILLER                          PIC X(12).
*
         05   ILM4-L-RECORD-COUNT             PIC S9(4)     COMP.
         05   ILM4-A-RECORD-COUNT             PIC X.
         05   ILM4-D-RECORD-COUNT             PIC ZZ,ZZ9.
```

Figure 6-14   Programmer-generated symbolic map for the inventory-listing program (SEND MAP)

Figure 6-17 gives the format of the SEND MAP command. It's similar to the format given in figure 6-14 of *Part 1: An introductory course*. But I've added two options (ACCUM and PAGING) that you code to build messages. And I've dropped two (ERASEAUP and CURSOR) because they aren't used for message building.

The ACCUM and PAGING options   You use the ACCUM and PAGING options together to indicate that a SEND MAP command is used to build a logical message. ACCUM means that data isn't sent immediately to the terminal; instead, it's accumulated in the

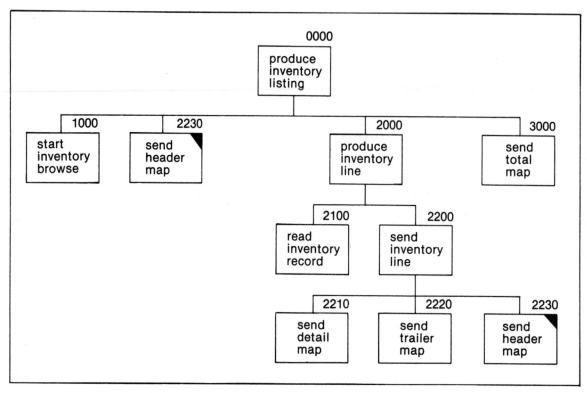

Figure 6-15   Structure chart for the inventory-listing program (SEND MAP)

page buffer until an entire page has been built. And PAGING means that when the page buffer is full, it's written to temporary storage rather than sent to the terminal. So the combined effect of ACCUM and PAGING is that pages of a logical message are built and stored in temporary storage.

Overflow processing   As I've already mentioned, the SEND MAP command does *not* automatically format headers and trailers as the SEND TEXT command does. Instead, it raises the OVERFLOW condition whenever a map won't fit in the current page, allowing for the largest trailer map in the mapset.

By issuing a HANDLE CONDITION command for the OVERFLOW condition, your program can detect page overflow and invoke an *overflow routine* to send trailer and header maps. As you can see in figure 6-16, I issue a HANDLE CONDITION OVERFLOW command in module 0000 of the inventory-listing program. The code to process the overflow condition is in module 2200 and its subordinates.

```
   IDENTIFICATION DIVISION.
*
 PROGRAM-ID.   INVLST3.
*
 ENVIRONMENT DIVISION.
*
 DATA DIVISION.
*
 WORKING-STORAGE SECTION.
*
 01   SWITCHES.
*
     05   INVMAST-EOF-SW          PIC X          VALUE 'N'.
          88   INVMAST-EOF                       VALUE 'Y'.
     05   PAGE-OVERFLOW-SW        PIC X          VALUE 'N'.
          88   PAGE-OVERFLOW                     VALUE 'Y'.
*
 01   WORK-FIELDS.
*
     05   RECORD-COUNT            PIC S9(5)      VALUE ZERO  COMP-3.
     05   PAGE-NO                 PIC S9(3)      VALUE +1    COMP-3.
*
 COPY LSTSET1.
*
 01   INVENTORY-MASTER-RECORD.
*
     05   IM-ITEM-NUMBER          PIC X(5).
     05   IM-ITEM-DESCRIPTION     PIC X(20).
     05   IM-UNIT-PRICE           PIC S9(5)V99              COMP-3.
     05   IM-ON-HAND-QUANTITY     PIC S9(5)                 COMP-3.
*
 PROCEDURE DIVISION.
*
 0000-PRODUCE-INVENTORY-LISTING SECTION.
*
     MOVE LOW-VALUE TO INVENTORY-LISTING-MAP-1
                       INVENTORY-LISTING-MAP-2
                       INVENTORY-LISTING-MAP-4.
     PERFORM 1000-START-INVENTORY-BROWSE.
     EXEC CICS
         HANDLE CONDITION ENDFILE(2100-ENDFILE)
                          OVERFLOW(2210-OVERFLOW)
     END-EXEC.
     PERFORM 2230-SEND-HEADER-MAP.
     PERFORM 2000-PRODUCE-INVENTORY-LINE
         UNTIL INVMAST-EOF.
     PERFORM 3000-SEND-TOTAL-MAP.
     EXEC CICS
         SEND PAGE
                 OPERPURGE
     END-EXEC.
     EXEC CICS
         RETURN
     END-EXEC.
```

Figure 6-16   Source listing for the inventory-listing program (SEND MAP) (part 1 of 4)

```
*
 1000-START-INVENTORY-BROWSE SECTION.
*
     EXEC CICS
         HANDLE CONDITION NOTFND(1000-NOTFND)
     END-EXEC.
     MOVE ZERO TO IM-ITEM-NUMBER.
     EXEC CICS
         STARTBR DATASET('INVMAST')
                 RIDFLD(IM-ITEM-NUMBER)
     END-EXEC.
     GO TO 1000-EXIT.
*
 1000-NOTFND.
*
     MOVE 'Y' TO INVMAST-EOF-SW.
*
 1000-EXIT.
*
     EXIT.
*
 2000-PRODUCE-INVENTORY-LINE SECTION.
*
     PERFORM 2100-READ-INVENTORY-RECORD.
     IF NOT INVMAST-EOF
         PERFORM 2200-SEND-INVENTORY-LINE.
*
 2100-READ-INVENTORY-RECORD SECTION.
*
     EXEC CICS
         READNEXT DATASET('INVMAST')
                  INTO(INVENTORY-MASTER-RECORD)
                  RIDFLD(IM-ITEM-NUMBER)
     END-EXEC.
     ADD 1 TO RECORD-COUNT.
     GO TO 2100-EXIT.
*
 2100-ENDFILE.
*
     MOVE 'Y' TO INVMAST-EOF-SW.
*
 2100-EXIT.
*
     EXIT.
*
 2200-SEND-INVENTORY-LINE SECTION.
*
     MOVE IM-ITEM-NUMBER      TO ILM2-D-ITEM-NUMBER.
     MOVE IM-ITEM-DESCRIPTION TO ILM2-D-ITEM-DESCRIPTION.
     MOVE IM-UNIT-PRICE       TO ILM2-D-UNIT-PRICE.
     MOVE IM-ON-HAND-QUANTITY TO ILM2-D-ON-HAND-QUANTITY.
```

Figure 6-16   Source listing for the inventory-listing program (SEND MAP) (part 2 of 4)

```
       PERFORM 2210-SEND-DETAIL-MAP.
       IF PAGE-OVERFLOW
           PERFORM 2220-SEND-TRAILER-MAP
           PERFORM 2230-SEND-HEADER-MAP
           PERFORM 2210-SEND-DETAIL-MAP
           MOVE 'N' TO PAGE-OVERFLOW-SW.

2210-SEND-DETAIL-MAP SECTION.

    EXEC CICS
        SEND MAP('LSTMAP2')
             MAPSET('LSTSET1')
             FROM(INVENTORY-LISTING-MAP-2)
             ACCUM
             PAGING
             ERASE
    END-EXEC.
    GO TO 2210-EXIT.

2210-OVERFLOW.

    MOVE 'Y' TO PAGE-OVERFLOW-SW.

2210-EXIT.

    EXIT.

2220-SEND-TRAILER-MAP SECTION.

    EXEC CICS
        SEND MAP('LSTMAP3')
             MAPSET('LSTSET1')
             MAPONLY
             ACCUM
             PAGING
             ERASE
    END-EXEC.

2230-SEND-HEADER-MAP SECTION.

    MOVE PAGE-NO TO ILM1-D-PAGE-NO.
    EXEC CICS
        SEND MAP('LSTMAP1')
             MAPSET('LSTSET1')
             FROM(INVENTORY-LISTING-MAP-1)
             ACCUM
             PAGING
             ERASE
    END-EXEC.
    ADD 1 TO PAGE-NO.
```

Figure 6-16   Source listing for the inventory-listing program (SEND MAP) (part 3 of 4)

```
3000-SEND-TOTAL-MAP SECTION.

    MOVE RECORD-COUNT TO ILM4-D-RECORD-COUNT.
    EXEC CICS
        SEND MAP('LSTMAP4')
             MAPSET('LSTSET1')
             FROM(INVENTORY-LISTING-MAP-4)
             ACCUM
             PAGING
             ERASE
    END-EXEC.
```

Figure 6-16   Source listing for the inventory-listing program (SEND MAP) (part 4 of 4)

When an OVERFLOW condition occurs, it means that just enough space remains in the page buffer for a trailer map. As a result, you should issue a SEND MAP command for the trailer map to complete the page. Then, you should start a new page by issuing a SEND MAP command for your header map. That writes the old page to temporary storage, clears the page buffer, and adds your header map. Since the detail map specified in the original SEND MAP command was never actually sent, you should issue another SEND MAP command to place the detail map on the new page.

Look now at how the program in figure 6-16 provides for overflow processing. After moving fields to the symbolic map, module 2200 performs module 2210 to send an inventory detail map (LSTMAP2). Because the DFHMDI macro for LSTMAP2 specifies LINE = NEXT, detail maps are added to successive lines of each page. When a page becomes full, control transfers to the routine for the OVERFLOW condition (2210-OVERFLOW). It sets a switch (PAGE-OVERFLOW-SW) to indicate that the OVERFLOW condition occurred. The real overflow processing happens in module 2200:

```
IF PAGE-OVERFLOW
    PERFORM 2220-SEND-TRAILER-MAP
    PERFORM 2230-SEND-HEADER-MAP
    PERFORM 2210-SEND-DETAIL-MAP
    MOVE 'N' TO PAGE-OVERFLOW-SW.
```

Here, three modules are invoked in sequence: module 2220 to send a trailer map, module 2230 to send a header map and start a new page, and module 2210 to send the detail map again, this time to the new page. Then, the program moves N to PAGE-OVERFLOW-SW so this processing won't happen again until the OVERFLOW condition is raised when the new page is filled.

The SEND MAP command

```
EXEC CICS
     SEND MAP(data-name|literal)
          MAPSET(data-name|literal)
         [FROM(data-name)]
         [MAPONLY|DATAONLY]
         [ACCUM]
         [PAGING]
         [ERASE]
END-EXEC
```

Explanation

MAP	Specifies the name of the map.
MAPSET	Specifies the name of the mapset that contains the map.
FROM	Specifies the name of the symbolic map.
MAPONLY	Specifies that only data from the physical map (that is, headings and constants) is sent. If you code MAPONLY, omit the FROM option.
DATAONLY	Specifies that only data from the symbolic map is sent. The physical map is used to map data to its correct line and column location, but data from the physical map isn't sent.
	If you omit both MAPONLY and DATAONLY, data from both the physical map and the symbolic map is sent.
ACCUM	Specifies that this SEND MAP command is used to build a logical message.
PAGING	Specifies that output pages should be written to temporary storage for later retrieval under operator control.
ERASE	Specifies that the terminal's buffer should be erased as each page of the message is sent during page retrieval.

Figure 6-17   The SEND MAP command

Modules 2220 and 2230 contain the SEND MAP commands for the trailer and header maps. Remember, though, that the OVERFLOW condition won't occur when you send a header or trailer map. So control will never transfer from module 2220 or 2230 to 2210-OVERFLOW, even though the HANDLE

CONDITION command for the OVERFLOW condition is in effect when modules 2220 and 2230 are invoked.

Module 2230 also provides the page-numbering logic for this program. In the Working-Storage Section, I provide a field named PAGE-NO whose initial value is 1. Then, in module 2230, I move PAGE-NO to the symbolic map before I send the header map. After I send the map, I add 1 to PAGE-NO.

In module 3000, a SEND MAP command sends the total map. Because the total map specifies TRAILER = YES, though, the OVERFLOW condition isn't raised even if the page is full (the OVERFLOW condition is never raised when you send a header or trailer map). As a result, the total map always appears on the same page as the last detail map—never on a page by itself. There's always enough room on the page for the total map because BMS considers its size when it determines the size of the trailer area.

DISCUSSION

Now that you've seen both versions of the inventory-listing program, take a moment to consider the difference between the two message building techniques. Apart from whether or not a mapset is required, I think you'll agree that the way overflow processing is handled is the most significant programming difference between the SEND TEXT and SEND MAP techniques.

The advantage of the SEND TEXT method is that you don't have to worry about sending headers or trailers; they're sent automatically whenever necessary. Unfortunately, that's also a disadvantage of the SEND TEXT method: it provides little control of overflow processing. Consider, for example, a logical message that requires a page total at the bottom of each page. With the SEND MAP command, you accumulate the page total as you send detail maps. Then, when overflow occurs, you move the page total field to the trailer map, send the trailer map, and reset the page total field to zero so it's ready for the next page. Because the SEND TEXT command gives no indication of when overflow occurs, however, there's no easy way to provide page totals when you use it.

Terminology

header
trailer
new-line character
overflow processing
overflow routine

Objective

Given the specifications for a message building program, code its solution using the either the SEND TEXT command or the SEND MAP command.

Topic 3   Printer output and message routing

In this topic, you'll learn how to code programs that produce printer output. You'll learn how to code special printing options in the SEND TEXT and SEND MAP commands and how to use two techniques to direct messages to a printer.

Before I go on, I want to make sure you realize that many installations do *not* use the printing features this topic presents. Instead, they use transient data queues (as I described in chapter 5) or a special printing subsystem they've developed themselves or purchased from a software vendor. If that's the case in your shop, feel free to skip this topic altogether.

3270 PRINTER CONCEPTS

To code a message building program for printer output, you need to understand the basic concepts involved when you use a 3270 printer. To begin with, all 3270 printers contain a *buffer*. As a result, data you send to a printer isn't immediately printed. Instead, it's stored in the printer's buffer and printed later. The buffer acts as intermediate storage between the host system and the printer's print mechanism. Because the host system can write data to a printer's buffer much faster than the print mechanism can print it, buffers improve the overall efficiency of a system.

There's a close relationship between a 3270 printer's buffer and the page buffer BMS uses to build pages of a logical message. When the BMS page buffer is filled, the data in it is sent to the printer's buffer. As a result, the BMS page buffer can be no larger than the printer's buffer, which is typically 1920 bytes.

In fact, the BMS page buffer size is often specified as 11 lines of 132 columns each. That way, your program can use the full width of the printer's carriage. Since standard computer forms are 66 lines long, six 11x132 page buffers correspond to one printed page, as figure 6-18 illustrates.

It's important at this point that you don't confuse message pages with printed pages. Each page of a logical message is no larger than the size of the BMS page buffer (usually 11x132 for

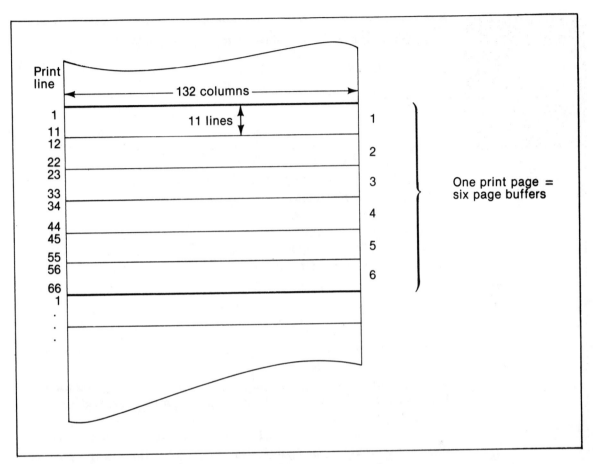

Figure 6-18   Six full 11x132 page buffers make up one printed page

printer output). In contrast, the size of a printed page varies depending on the form being used, but usually it's 66x132.

As a result, you can't use the page overflow features of message building to place headers and trailers on printed pages. That's because page overflow occurs when the page buffer becomes full, without regard to when the printed page is full. Instead, you must count lines and format your own headers and trailers. The program examples in this topic show you how to do that.

Printer orders

You can control the format of printed data by inserting special control characters called *printer orders* at appropriate locations in

Printer order	Abbreviation	Hex value
Form-feed	FF	0C
New-line	NL	15
Carriage-return	CR	0D
End-of-message	EM	19

Figure 6-19 Printer orders

the printer's buffer. Figure 6-19 shows the most commonly used printer orders and their hex values. To send a logical message to a printer, you need to understand how these printer orders work.

Form-feed   The *form-feed order* causes the printer to skip to the top of the next page. You use it to ensure that printed output is properly aligned on each page. In IBM literature, you'll often see the form-feed order abbreviated as *FF*. Don't confuse that with the hexadecimal value FF (decimal 256), though. It's just coincidental that the abbreviation FF is the same as a common hex value; the FF order's hex value is 0C.

   The FF order actually prints as a space in position 1 of the first line of the page, so the first available print position on the page is position 2 of line 1. Form-feed is the only printer order that prints as a space, though. The other printer orders I'll describe do not occupy a space on the printed page.

New-line   The *new-line* (or *NL*) *order* indicates that printing should continue in the first position of the next print line. Normally, you use an NL order to mark the end of a print line. Don't confuse the new-line printer order with the BMS new-line character. You use the BMS new-line character when you build a logical message. Then, depending on how you code the commands to build the message, BMS may or may not use new-line printer orders to force line endings in the printer's buffer.

Carriage-return   The *carriage-return* (or *CR*) *order* is similar to the NL order, except that the paper doesn't advance to the next print line. Instead, the print mechanism returns to position 1 of the current line. One use of the CR order is to overprint a line. Another use is to reclaim the space printed by the FF order. If you follow an FF order with a CR order, the print mechanism returns to position 1 of line 1.

End-of-message   The *end-of-message* (or *EM*) *order* is used to mark the end of each page of data that's transmitted to the printer. Depending on how you code your message building commands, BMS may or may not add an EM order to the end of each page of your logical message. Either way, you don't need to worry about EM orders: BMS takes care of them for you.

HOW TO SEND A MESSAGE DIRECTLY TO A PRINTER

One way to send a logical message to a printer is to attach the message building task directly to the printer. Then, the pages of your message are sent directly to the printer's buffer as they're completed. To attach a task to a printer, you use an interval control START command.

In chapter 9, I'll describe interval control and the START command in detail. For now, I just want you to know that a START command initiates a task much the same way as entering a transaction identifier at a display terminal does. When you enter a trans-id at a display terminal, a task is initiated and attached to that terminal. Then, any terminal output from the task is directed to the terminal that initiated the task. In contrast, a START command initiates a task that's attached to whatever terminal you specify in the command. If you specify a printer terminal in a START command, the task is attached to that printer. Then, terminal output from the task is sent to the printer.

It's important to realize that the message building program itself doesn't issue the START command. Typically, a menu program issues a START command to initiate a message building program in response to an operator's selection. Because the message building program runs as a separate task that isn't attached to the operator's terminal, the operator can proceed with other work while the message building program executes.

Printer options of SEND MAP and SEND TEXT

BMS provides several options that affect the way a logical message is sent to a printer. I'll describe just two of them here: PRINT and

NLEOM. The others aren't often used. You can code both PRINT and NLEOM on a SEND TEXT or a SEND MAP command. There's nothing complex about the way you code these options, so I won't include another syntax diagram for the SEND TEXT or SEND MAP command. Instead, figure 6-20 shows you how to code the PRINT and NLEOM options.

The PRINT option   The PRINT option tells BMS to activate the printer's printing mechanism so the data you send will be printed. If you omit the PRINT option, data will be sent to the printer's buffer, but not printed. So always code PRINT on each SEND TEXT or SEND MAP command you use to build a message that's intended for a printer.

The NLEOM option   The NLEOM option tells BMS to use new-line and end-of-message printer orders in the data it sends to the printer. Since that can save transmission time, I recommend you always specify NLEOM. However, you should know that BMS always sends the number of lines indicated in the page-buffer size specification in the Terminal Control Table. In other words, if the TCT says the page buffer is 11x132, BMS always sends 11 lines at a time to the printer, even if the message page actually consists of fewer than 11 lines. Normally, that's not a problem. However, it can occasionally cause page-alignment problems when you're building a message using maps and the SEND MAP command and the length of the printed page is not an even multiple of 11 lines.

A sample program

So far in this book, you've seen three versions of a program that lists the records of an inventory file. In chapter 5, you saw a program that directed the report to a printer via a transient data destination. Then, in the last topic, you saw two versions of the program that send a logical message to a display terminal, one using the SEND TEXT command, the other using the SEND MAP command. Now, I'll present a fourth version of the inventory-listing program. This time, a logical message is created and sent directly to a printer. For this program to work, it must be invoked by an interval control START command (probably issued by a menu program as a result of an operator selection) that attaches the program directly to a printer terminal.

```
A SEND TEXT command with printer options

EXEC CICS
    SEND TEXT FROM(INVENTORY-LINE)
              LENGTH(51)
              ACCUM
              ERASE
              PRINT
              NLEOM
END-EXEC

A SEND MAP command with printer options

EXEC CICS
    SEND MAP('LSTMAP2')
         MAPSET('LSTSET1')
         ACCUM
         ERASE
         PRINT
         NLEOM
END-EXEC
```

Figure 6-20   You can code printer options on a SEND TEXT command or a SEND MAP command

Figure 6-21 gives the print chart for this program. The structure chart is shown in figure 6-22, and figure 6-23 gives the complete program listing. Since you've already seen three versions of this program, you should be familiar with its operation, so I'll just point out the highlights.

Notice that the SEND TEXT commands don't specify the HEADER and TRAILER options. That's because, as I've already mentioned, overflow processing doesn't work as you'd expect for direct printer output. Instead of detecting an overflow situation when a printed page is full, BMS detects overflow when the page buffer is full. If I had used the HEADER and TRAILER options in this program, headers and trailers would print every 11 lines, instead of at the top and bottom of each 66-line page.

Rather than use BMS overflow processing, I count lines as they're added to the message. When enough lines have been added, I issue a SEND TEXT command to send header lines. At the start of the header line definition in the Working-Storage Section, I code

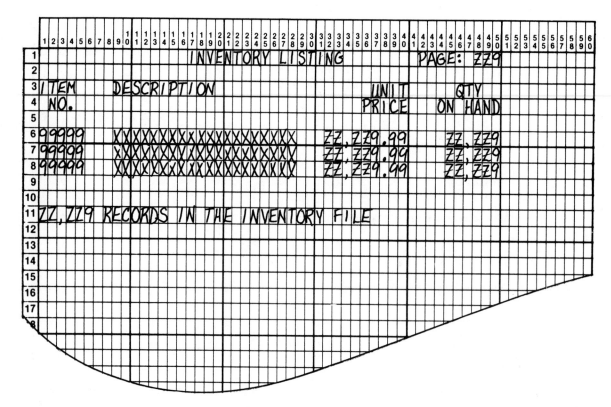

Figure 6-21 Print chart for the inventory-listing programs

two printer orders: a form-feed followed by a carriage-return. That combination causes the printer to (1) skip to the first line of the next page and (2) position the print mechanism at the first column. As a result, each page is properly aligned.

The SEND TEXT command for the inventory detail line is this:

```
EXEC CICS
    SEND TEXT FROM(INVENTORY-LINE)
              LENGTH(51)
              ACCUM
              ERASE
              PRINT
              NLEOM
END-EXEC.
```

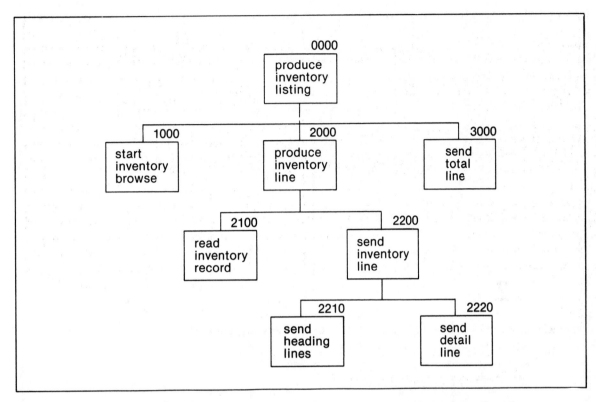

Figure 6-22   Structure chart for the inventory-listing program (SEND TEXT, printer)

Notice here that I omit the PAGING option. That way, the message is built with terminal disposition so it's sent directly to the printer instead of stored in temporary storage. The ACCUM option is still necessary, though, so an entire page buffer is accumulated before data is sent to the printer. The PRINT option causes the printer to print the data that's sent, and the NLEOM option tells BMS to format data using new-line and end-of-message printer orders.

When you build a logical message for a printer, you must still use a SEND PAGE command to force out the last page of the message. Note, however, that I omitted the OPERPURGE option from the SEND PAGE command in module 0000. That option isn't necessary; because the message is never placed in temporary storage, there's no need to delete it.

```
      IDENTIFICATION DIVISION.
 *
      PROGRAM-ID.   INVLST4.
 *
      ENVIRONMENT DIVISION.
 *
      DATA DIVISION.
 *
      WORKING-STORAGE SECTION.
 *
      01   SWITCHES.
 *
           05   INVMAST-EOF-SW    PIC X          VALUE 'N'.
                88   INVMAST-EOF                 VALUE 'Y'.
 *
      01   PRINT-FIELDS.
 *
           05   LINE-COUNT        PIC S999    VALUE +50      COMP-3.
           05   LINES-ON-PAGE     PIC S999    VALUE +50      COMP-3.
           05   PAGE-NO           PIC S999    VALUE +1       COMP-3.
 *
      01   WORK-FIELDS.
 *
           05   RECORD-COUNT      PIC S9(5)   VALUE ZERO   COMP-3.
 *
      01   HEADER-AREA.
 *
           05   HEADER-LINE-1.
                10   HA1-FF-CR    PIC XX      VALUE ' '.
                10   FILLER       PIC X(20)   VALUE '              INVE'.
                10   FILLER       PIC X(20)   VALUE 'NTORY LISTING     '.
                10   FILLER       PIC X(7)    VALUE ' PAGE: '.
                10   HA1-PAGE-NO  PIC ZZ9.
                10   HA1-NL       PIC XX      VALUE ' '.
           05   HEADER-LINE-2.
                10   FILLER       PIC X(20)   VALUE 'ITEM     DESCRIPTION '.
                10   FILLER       PIC X(20)   VALUE '                UNIT'.
                10   FILLER       PIC X(8)    VALUE '     QTY'.
                10   HA2-NL       PIC X       VALUE ' '.
           05   HEADER-LINE-3.
                10   FILLER       PIC X(20)   VALUE ' NO.              '.
                10   FILLER       PIC X(20)   VALUE '            PRICE'.
                10   FILLER       PIC X(10)   VALUE '   OH HAND'.
                10   HA3-NL       PIC X(2)    VALUE ' '.
 *
      01   INVENTORY-LINE.
 *
           05   IL-ITEM-NUMBER        PIC 9(5).
           05   FILLER                PIC X(3)        VALUE SPACE.
           05   IL-ITEM-DESCRIPTION   PIC X(20).
           05   FILLER                PIC X(3)        VALUE SPACE.
           05   IL-UNIT-PRICE         PIC ZZ,ZZ9.99.
           05   FILLER                PIC X(4)        VALUE SPACE.
           05   IL-ON-HAND-QUANTITY   PIC ZZ,ZZ9.
           05   IL-NL                 PIC X           VALUE ' '.
```

Figure 6-23   Source listing for the inventory-listing program (SEND TEXT, printer) (part 1 of 4)

```
✿
 01   TOTAL-LINE.
✿
     05   TL-NL              PIC X        VALUE ' '.
     05   TL-RECORD-COUNT    PIC ZZ,ZZ9.
     05   FILLER             PIC X(20)    VALUE ' RECORDS IN THE INVE'.
     05   FILLER             PIC X(10)    VALUE 'NTORY FILE'.
✿
 01   INVENTORY-MASTER-RECORD.
✿
     05   IM-ITEM-NUMBER         PIC X(5).
     05   IM-ITEM-DESCRIPTION    PIC X(20).
     05   IM-UNIT-PRICE          PIC S9(5)V99      COMP-3.
     05   IM-ON-HAND-QUANTITY    PIC S9(5)         COMP-3.
✿
 PROCEDURE DIVISION.
✿
 0000-PRODUCE-INVENTORY-LISTING SECTION.
✿
     PERFORM 1000-START-INVENTORY-BROWSE.
     EXEC CICS
         HANDLE CONDITION ENDFILE(2100-ENDFILE)
     END-EXEC.
     PERFORM 2000-PRODUCE-INVENTORY-LINE
         UNTIL INVMAST-EOF.
     PERFORM 3000-SEND-TOTAL-LINE.
     EXEC CICS
         SEND PAGE
     END-EXEC.
     EXEC CICS
         RETURN
     END-EXEC.
✿
 1000-START-INVENTORY-BROWSE SECTION.
✿
     EXEC CICS
         HANDLE CONDITION NOTFND(1000-NOTFND)
     END-EXEC.
     MOVE ZERO TO IM-ITEM-NUMBER.
     EXEC CICS
         STARTBR DATASET('INVMAST')
                 RIDFLD(IM-ITEM-NUMBER)
     END-EXEC.
     GO TO 1000-EXIT.
✿
 1000-NOTFND.
✿
     MOVE 'Y' TO INVMAST-EOF-SW.
✿
 1000-EXIT.
✿
     EXIT.
✿
```

Figure 6-23   Source listing for the inventory-listing program (SEND TEXT, printer) (part 2 of 4)

```
2000-PRODUCE-INVENTORY-LINE SECTION.
*
    PERFORM 2100-READ-INVENTORY-RECORD.
    IF NOT INVMAST-EOF
        PERFORM 2200-SEND-INVENTORY-LINE.
*
2100-READ-INVENTORY-RECORD SECTION.
*
    EXEC CICS
        READNEXT DATASET('INVMAST')
                 INTO(INVENTORY-MASTER-RECORD)
                 RIDFLD(IM-ITEM-NUMBER)
    END-EXEC.
    ADD 1 TO RECORD-COUNT.
    GO TO 2100-EXIT.
*
2100-ENDFILE.
*
    MOVE 'Y' TO INVMAST-EOF-SW.
*
2100-EXIT.
*
    EXIT.
*
2200-SEND-INVENTORY-LINE SECTION.
*
    IF LINE-COUNT = LINES-ON-PAGE
        PERFORM 2210-SEND-HEADING-LINES.
    PERFORM 2220-SEND-DETAIL-LINE.
*
2210-SEND-HEADING-LINES SECTION.
*
    MOVE PAGE-NO TO HA1-PAGE-NO.
    EXEC CICS
        SEND TEXT FROM(HEADER-AREA)
                  LENGTH(155)
                  ACCUM
                  ERASE
                  PRINT
                  NLEOM
    END-EXEC.
    MOVE ZERO TO LINE-COUNT.
    ADD 1 TO PAGE-NO.
*
2220-SEND-DETAIL-LINE SECTION.
*
    MOVE IM-ITEM-NUMBER      TO IL-ITEM-NUMBER.
    MOVE IM-ITEM-DESCRIPTION TO IL-ITEM-DESCRIPTION.
    MOVE IM-UNIT-PRICE       TO IL-UNIT-PRICE.
    MOVE IM-ON-HAND-QUANTITY TO IL-ON-HAND-QUANTITY.
```

Figure 6-23   Source listing for the inventory-listing program (SEND TEXT, printer) (part 3 of 4)

```
      EXEC CICS
          SEND TEXT FPOM(INVENTORY-LINE)
                    LENGTH(51)
                    ACCUM
                    ERASE
                    PRINT
                    NLEOM
      END-EXEC.
        ADD 1 TO LINE-COUNT.
   *
    3000-SEND-TOTAL-LINE SECTION.
   *
        MOVE RECORD-COUNT TO TL-RECORD-COUNT.
      EXEC CICS
          SEND TEXT FROM(TOTAL-LINE)
                    LENGTH(37)
                    ACCUM
                    ERASE
                    PRINT
                    NLEOM
      END-EXEC.
```

Figure 6-23   Source listing for the inventory-listing program (SEND TEXT, printer) (part 4 of 4)

MESSAGE ROUTING

A second way to direct output to a printer is to use a BMS feature called *message routing*. Quite simply, message routing lets you direct a logical message to a terminal other than the one your program is attached to. Using message routing, an operator can invoke a program that routes a message to a printer. It's not necessary to use an interval control START command to attach the message building task to the printer.

Although you can use message routing to direct a logical message to another display terminal, it's more common to route a message to one or more printers. To do that, you use the SEND TEXT and SEND MAP printer options you've already learned: PRINT and NLEOM. Since the routed message must be stored in temporary storage before it's routed to other terminals, you must also specify the PAGING option on the SEND TEXT or SEND MAP commands that build the message. And, you must issue a ROUTE command to tell BMS what terminals will receive the message.

```
The ROUTE command

EXEC CICS
     ROUTE LIST(data-name)
          [{INTERVAL(hhmmss)}]
          [{TIME(hhmmss)   }]
          [NLEOM]
END-EXEC


Explanation

LIST                    Specifies a list of terminals to which the logical message
                        should be routed.

INTERVAL                Specifies a time interval that must elapse before the message
                        is delivered.

TIME                    Specifies that the message should be delivered at the
                        specified time of day.

NLEOM                   Specifies that BMS should use NL and EM print orders as it
                        builds the logical message.
```

Figure 6-24   The ROUTE command

The ROUTE command

Figure 6-24 gives the format of the ROUTE command. Its options
name the terminals where a logical message is sent (LIST) and
indicate when the message should be delivered (INTERVAL or
TIME). Note also that the NLEOM option is required on a ROUTE
command if you want the message to include new-line and end-of-
message printer orders.

The LIST option   The LIST option specifies the data name for a
working-storage table called a *route list*. The route list identifies the
terminals you want your message routed to. It consists of one or
more 16-byte entries, each identifying one terminal. The entire list
is ended by a binary half-word field (PIC S9(4) COMP) initialized
to -1.

   The format of each route list entry is simple: the first four
bytes supply the terminal-id of the terminal to which your message
is routed; the other 12 bytes are FILLER data initialized to spaces.
Actually, you can put other identifying information in the FILLER

```
   01   ROUTE-LIST.
 *
       05   LIST-ENTRY-1.
            10   LE1-TERMINAL-ID          PIC X(4)      VALUE 'L1P1'.
            10   FILLER                   PIC X(12)     VALUE SPACE.
       05   LIST-ENTRY-2.
            10   LE2-TERMINAL-ID          PIC X(4)      VALUE 'L2P5'.
            10   FILLER                   PIC X(12)     VALUE SPACE.
       05   FILLER                        PIC S9(4)     VALUE -1       COMP.
```

Figure 6-25   COBOL coding for a two-entry route list

area, but it's only used when you're sending messages to specific
terminal operators or unusual devices. For routing a message to a
3270 printer, you don't need to use those fields.

Figure 6-25 shows a route list that sets up two routed printers:
one named L1P1, the other named L2P5. Here, you can clearly see
the structure of the route list: each 16-byte entry consists of a four-
byte terminal-id followed by 12 bytes of FILLER, and the entire
list is ended by a binary half-word field initialized to − 1.

The INTERVAL and TIME options   You use the ROUTE
command's INTERVAL and TIME options to indicate when a
message should be delivered. INTERVAL says to deliver the
message after a certain period of time has passed, and TIME says to
deliver the message at a specific time of day.

You specify the time or interval value in the form hhmmss,
where hh is hours, mm is minutes, and ss is seconds. So, to deliver
a message in twenty minutes, you code this ROUTE command:

```
EXEC CICS
    ROUTE LIST(ROUTE-LIST)
          INTERVAL(002000)
END-EXEC
```

And to deliver a message at 5:30 p.m., you code this ROUTE
command:

```
EXEC CICS
    ROUTE LIST(ROUTE-LIST)
          TIME(173000)
END-EXEC
```

Note that you specify the time using a 24-hour clock, so 5:30 p.m. is 173000 rather than 053000.

If you omit the INTERVAL or TIME option, or specify INTERVAL(0), the message is delivered as soon as the printer is ready for it. If yours is the only message that's been sent to the printer, it's printed immediately. But if other messages have been sent before yours, your message waits its turn.

A sample program

Figure 6-26 gives a skeleton of the coding required to send the inventory-listing report to a printer using message routing. The parts of this program that are omitted are identical to the corresponding parts of figure 6-23. As you can see, I coded the PAGING option on the SEND TEXT commands. The only other difference is the ROUTE command in module 0000 and the route list defined in the Working-Storage Section.

DISCUSSION

In this topic, I've presented just a brief introduction to the BMS facilities for printer output: I didn't cover many of the print options you can use instead of NLEOM, and I didn't explain the complications involved when you use the SEND MAP command with non-standard forms. I've made this presentation brief because there are usually better ways to prepare printed reports under CICS, like transient data destinations as I described in chapter 5. In any event, if you're called upon to write a CICS program that prepares a logical message for a printer, this topic should be enough to get you started.

```
     IDENTIFICATION DIVISION.
*
  PROGRAM-ID.   INVLST5.
*
  ENVIRONMENT DIVISION.
*
  DATA DIVISION.
*
  WORKING-STORAGE SECTION.
*
        •
        •
        •
*
 01   ROUTE-LIST.
*
      05   LIST-ENTRY-1.
           10   LE1-TERMINAL-ID   PIC X(4)      VALUE 'L86P'.
           10   FILLER            PIC X(12)     VALUE SPACE.
      05   FILLER                 PIC S9(4)     VALUE -1      COMP.
*
  PROCEDURE DIVISION.
*
  0000-PRODUCE-INVENTORY-LISTING SECTION.
*
      PERFORM 1000-START-INVENTORY-BROWSE.
      EXEC CICS
           HANDLE CONDITION ENDFILE(2100-ENDFILE)
      END-EXEC.
      EXEC CICS
           ROUTE LIST(ROUTE-LIST)
                 NLEOM
      END-EXEC.
      PERFORM 2000-PRODUCE-INVENTORY-LINE
           UNTIL INVMAST-EOF.
      PERFORM 3000-SEND-TOTAL-LINE.
      EXEC CICS
           SEND PAGE
      END-EXEC.
      EXEC CICS
           RETURN
      END-EXEC.
*
        •
        •
        •
*
  2000-PRODUCE-INVENTORY-LINE SECTION.
*
      PERFORM 2100-READ-INVENTORY-RECORD.
      IF NOT INVMAST-EOF
           PERFORM 2200-SEND-INVENTORY-LINE.
*
```

Figure 6-26 Partial source listing for the inventory-listing program (ROUTE) (part 1 of 2)

```
        .
        .
        .
*
 2200-SEND-INVENTORY-LINE SECTION.
*
     IF LINE-COUNT = LINES-ON-PAGE
         PERFORM 2210-SEND-HEADING-LINES.
     PERFORM 2220-SEND-DETAIL-LINE.
*
 2210-SEND-HEADING-LINES SECTION.
*
     MOVE PAGE-NO TO HA1-PAGE-NO.
     EXEC CICS
         SEND TEXT FROM(HEADER-AREA)
                   LENGTH(155)
                   ACCUM
                   PAGING
                   ERASE
                   PRINT
                   NLEOM
     END-EXEC.
     MOVE ZERO TO LINE-COUNT.
     ADD 1 TO PAGE-NO.
*
 2220-SEND-DETAIL-LINE SECTION.
*
     MOVE IM-ITEM-NUMBER       TO  IL-ITEM-NUMBER.
     MOVE IM-ITEM-DESCRIPTION TO IL-ITEM-DESCRIPTION.
     MOVE IM-UNIT-PRICE        TO  IL-UNIT-PRICE.
     MOVE IM-ON-HAND-QUANTITY TO IL-ON-HAND-QUANTITY.
     EXEC CICS
         SEND TEXT FROM(INVENTORY-LINE)
                   LENGTH(51)
                   ACCUM
                   PAGING
                   ERASE
                   PRINT
                   NLEOM
     END-EXEC.
     ADD 1 TO LINE-COUNT.
*
 3000-SEND-TOTAL-LINE SECTION.
*
     MOVE RECORD-COUNT TO TL-RECORD-COUNT.
     EXEC CICS
         SEND TEXT FROM(TOTAL-LINE)
                   LENGTH(37)
                   ACCUM
                   PAGING
                   ERASE
                   PRINT
                   NLEOM
     END-EXEC.
```

Figure 6-26 Partial source listing for the inventory-listing program (ROUTE) (part 2 of 2)

Terminology

buffer
printer order
form-feed order
FF order
new-line order
NL order
carriage-return order
CR order
end-of-message order
EM order
message routing
route list

Objective

Given a programming problem that requires you to print a logical
message, code an acceptable program for its solution. You may
either attach the message building task directly to the printer or use
message routing.

Chapter 7

How to use color
and extended highlighting

In this chapter, I'll show you how to use BMS to control the color display and extended highlighting features available on some 3270 display stations. Since most 3270s provide only the basic display capabilities you already know about, your installation may not have any terminals with these advanced display features. If so, you can skip this chapter. On the other hand, if your installation does use 3270s that support color or extended highlighting, you need to read this chapter to learn what those features are and how to control them.

ADVANCED DISPLAY CAPABILITIES
OF 3270 TERMINALS

A variety of advanced display features are available as options on some 3270 models. Typically, they're used in data-entry and inquiry applications to draw attention to important screen fields. Of the features that are available, color display and extended highlighting are the most common.

Color display

There are two ways a 3270 terminal can be configured with color capability. Inexpensive *base color terminals* provide limited support for four display colors. More expensive *extended color terminals* provide full support for seven display colors.

Base color   Base color terminals provide color display capability at a low cost. In fact, a base color terminal costs just a few hundred dollars more than a monochrome terminal. And you can attach a base color terminal to your system without making programming modifications.

Rather than display green characters against a dark background, a base color terminal displays characters in four colors: white, green, blue, and red. Color is selected on a field-by-field basis. So one field might be displayed in white, while an adjacent field is red. However, within a field, individual characters are always the same color.

Figure 7-1 shows how a base color terminal determines what color to use for a field. As you can see, the terminal examines the settings of the protection and intensity attributes in each field's attribute byte. For example, any field whose attribute byte indicates protected and normal intensity is displayed blue; protected bright fields are displayed white, and so on.

In *Part 1: An introductory course*, I recommended that screen captions, error messages, and operator instructions should be protected and bright, data-entry fields should be unprotected and normal intensity, data-entry fields flagged as errors should be unprotected and bright, and display-only fields displayed by your program, like inquiry results, should be protected with normal intensity. Using this scheme, captions, messages, and instructions display in white on a base color terminal. Data-entry fields are green, but turn red when they're flagged as errors. And display-only fields are blue.

Although base-color terminals provide color capability at a reasonable cost, it's debatable whether they increase productivity in the data-entry department. In any event, since they use basic attributes to determine display color, they have no effect on how you write your CICS programs.

Extended color   Extended color lets you specify that a field should be displayed in one of seven colors: blue, red, pink, green, turquoise, yellow, or neutral (that's white on most terminals).

Protection attribute	Intensity attribute	Resulting color
Protected	Normal	Blue
Protected	Bright	White
Unprotected	Normal	Green
Unprotected	Bright	Red

Figure 7-1 How color is determined for a base-color terminal

Typically, you use extended color to draw attention to specific fields. In addition, color is often used to show relationships among fields that might otherwise appear unrelated. For example, in an inquiry application, all data from one file might be blue, while data from another file might be turquoise.

Extended color is controlled on a field-by-field basis by special *extended attribute bytes*. There are two ways you can provide for these extended attribute bytes in your CICS programs. The first, and simplest, is to modify your mapsets so they indicate what color each field should have. When you use this technique, you don't have to change any of your application programs. However, when you specify colors like this, your application programs have no control over them.

The second way to support extended colors is to provide for them in both your mapsets and your application programs. When you use this technique, your application program can change the extended attributes of a field.

Extended highlighting

Extended highlighting, available on both monochrome and color terminals, lets you draw attention to a field by *underlining* it, causing it to *blink*, or displaying it in *reverse-video*—that is, dark characters against a light background, instead of the other way around. These forms of highlighting, along with the standard intensity attribute, are used most commonly to draw attention to a field, such as an error message. You control extended highlighting just as you do extended color: by providing support for extended attribute bytes in the mapset alone or in both the mapset and the program.

BMS MAPSETS FOR COLOR
AND EXTENDED HIGHLIGHTING

When you create a mapset, you use additional parameters in the DFHMSD and DFHMDF macros for extended attributes. In the DFHMSD macro, you specify whether extended attributes are included in the mapset only, are included in both the mapset and the application program, or aren't used at all. And in DFHMDF macros, you indicate what extended attributes are used for each field in the mapset.

The DFHMSD macro

Figure 7-2 gives an expanded format of the DFHMSD macro. All of the parameters except the last are the same as for any BMS mapset, so I won't explain them. The EXTATT parameter indicates the level of support to be provided for extended attributes.

If you code EXTATT = NO, or omit the EXTATT parameter, no support for extended attributes is provided. If you code EXTATT = YES or EXTATT = MAPONLY, extended attribute support is provided.

EXTATT = MAPONLY means that extended attributes are generated only in the physical mapset; the symbolic map is the same as if extended attributes weren't provided. As a result, if you code EXTATT = MAPONLY, you can specify extended attributes in your mapset, but you can't modify them in your application program.

In contrast, EXTATT = YES provides support for extended attributes in both the physical map *and* the symbolic map. So not only can you specify extended attributes in the mapset, but your application program can also change them dynamically. EXTATT = YES adds additional fields to the symbolic map. So if you create your own symbolic maps, you'll have to provide for those fields. I'll show you how to do that in a moment.

The DFHMDF macro

In a DFHMDF macro, you can specify whether a field has extended highlighting or color by coding the HILIGHT or COLOR parameter. An expanded format of the DFHMDF macro is given in figure 7-3. I'll cover just the last two parameters here, since the

---

The DFHMSD macro

```
mapset-name    DFHMSD    TYPE= ⎧&SYSPARM⎫
                               ⎨ DSECT  ⎬ ,
                               ⎩ MAP    ⎭

                         LANG= ⎧COBOL⎫
                               ⎨ ASM ⎬ ,
                               ⎩ PLI ⎭

                         MODE= ⎧ IN  ⎫
                               ⎨ OUT ⎬ ,
                               ⎩INOUT⎭

                         TERM=terminal-type,

                         CTRL=(control-option,control-option...),

                         STORAGE=AUTO,

                         TIOAPFX= ⎧YES⎫ ,
                                  ⎩NO ⎭

                         EXTATT= ⎧ NO    ⎫
                                 ⎨ YES   ⎬
                                 ⎩MAPONLY⎭
```

Explanation

EXTATT   Indicates whether the mapset should provide for extended attributes. If you code EXTATT = NO, or omit EXTATT, extended attributes are not provided for. If you code EXTATT = YES, extended attributes are provided for in the physical map, and the symbolic map is adjusted so that you can change extended attributes dynamically. If you code EXTATT = MAPONLY, the extended attribute specifications in your mapset are processed, but the symbolic map doesn't provide for extended attributes.

Note: All other parameters are the same as when extended attributes are not used.

Figure 7-2   The DFHMSD macro instruction for extended attributes

first six work the same way they do for a field without extended attributes.

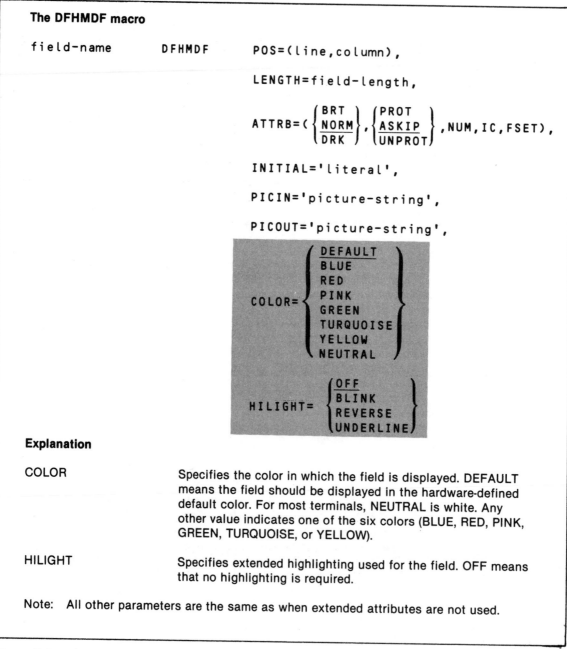

Figure 7-3   The DFHMDF macro instruction for extended attributes

The COLOR parameter   You use the COLOR parameter when you want to provide extended color support for a field. For example, to display a field in red, you specify COLOR = RED in

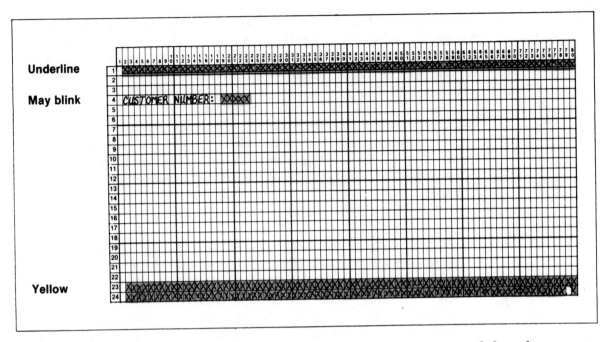

Figure 7-4   Screen layout for a customer-maintenance program that uses extended attributes

the DFHMDF macro for the field. If you specify
COLOR = DEFAULT, or omit the COLOR parameter, the field is
displayed in its base color; that depends on its intensity and
protection attributes.

The HILIGHT parameter   You use the HILIGHT parameter to
specify extended highlighting attributes (underlining, reverse-video,
or blinking) for a field. For example, to cause a field to be
underlined, you code HILIGHT = UNDERLINE on the field's
DFHMDF macro. If you code HILIGHT = OFF or omit the
HILIGHT parameter, extended highlighting isn't provided for the
field.

A sample BMS mapset

Figure 7-4 gives the screen layout for the first screen of a customer-
maintenance program that will be run on a terminal that supports
both extended color and extended highlighting. To make the screen
easier for the operator to use, the program uses several extended
display features. First, the entire heading line is underlined to

separate it from the data area. Second, the customer number data-entry field blinks if it's entered in error. And third, the message area (lines 23 and 24) is displayed in yellow to draw attention to it. Although this screen doesn't use extended display features as much as some, it illustrates the programming requirements you need to know for extended color and highlighting.

Figure 7-5 gives the BMS map definition for this screen. The shading in figure 7-5 shows the coding for extended attributes. As you can see, the DFHMSD macro specifies EXTATT = YES so extended display support will be provided in both the physical mapset and in the symbolic map.

For the TITLE field, I specified HILIGHT = UNDERLINE, and for both the MESSAG1 and ERROR1 fields, I specified COLOR = YELLOW. Notice that I didn't specify the HILIGHT parameter for the NUMBER1 field, even though the field is supposed to blink if it's entered in error. Because I specified EXTATT = YES in the DFHMSD macro for the mapset, the symbolic map contains fields for the extended attributes. So the program can change the display attributes for the NUMBER1 field when an error is detected.

Extended attributes and the symbolic map

Figure 7-6 gives the symbolic mapset generated by BMS for the mapset in figure 7-5. To support extended attributes, BMS adds four one-byte fields to the symbolic map for each named field in the mapset. In figure 7-6, I've shaded the fields that were added for the NUMBER1 field. (The four-byte FILLER subordinate to MNTMAP1I occupies the same storage locations as the four one-byte fields subordinate to MNTMAP1O.)

Each of the four extended attribute byte fields controls one of the extended display features, as indicated by the field-name suffixes. So NUMBER1C controls the field's color (C = color), while NUMBER1H controls the field's highlighting (H = highlighting). The other two suffixes, P and V, are used for programmed-symbols and field-validation, two advanced display features I'm not covering in this book.

If you create your own symbolic maps rather than use the ones BMS generates, you must provide for extended attributes if you coded EXTATT = YES on the DFHMSD macro for the mapset. To illustrate, consider figure 7-7, the programmer-generated symbolic map for the mapset in figure 7-5. Here, I code four fields for the extended attributes of each display field. Again, two of them are

```
          PRINT NOGEN
MNTSET2   DFHMSD TYPE=&SYSPARM,                                              X
                 LANG=COBOL,                                                 X
                 MODE=INOUT,                                                 X
                 TERM=3270-2,                                                X
                 CTRL=FREEKB,                                                X
                 STORAGE=AUTO,                                               X
                 TIOAPFX=YES,                                                X
                 EXTATT=YES
**************************************************************************************
**************************************************************************************
MNTMAP1   DFHMDI SIZE=(24,80),                                              X
                 LINE=1,                                                     X
                 COLUMN=1
**************************************************************************************
TITLE     DFHMDF POS=(1,1),                                                 X
                 LENGTH=79,                                                  X
                 ATTRB=(BRT,PROT),                                           X
                 HILIGHT=UNDERLINE
**************************************************************************************
          DFHMDF POS=(4,1),                                                 X
                 LENGTH=16,                                                  X
                 ATTRB=(BRT,PROT),                                           X
                 INITIAL='CUSTOMER NUMBER:'
NUMBER1   DFHMDF POS=(4,18),                                                X
                 LENGTH=5,                                                   X
                 ATTRB=(UNPROT,IC)
          DFHMDF POS=(4,24),                                                X
                 LENGTH=1,                                                   X
                 ATTRB=ASKIP
**************************************************************************************
MESSAG1   DFHMDF POS=(23,1),                                               X
                 LENGTH=79,                                                  X
                 ATTRB=(BRT,PROT),                                           X
                 COLOR=YELLOW
ERROR1    DFHMDF POS=(24,1),                                                X
                 LENGTH=77,                                                  X
                 ATTRB=(BRT,PROT),                                           X
                 COLOR=YELLOW
DUMMY1    DFHMDF POS=(24,79),                                               X
                 LENGTH=1,                                                   X
                 ATTRB=(DRK,PROT,FSET),                                      X
                 INITIAL=' '
**************************************************************************************
```

Figure 7-5 Partial mapset listing for a customer-maintenance program that uses extended
attributes

for features I don't cover in this book. The others use C and H to
indicate color and highlighting. So KM-C-CUSTOMER-NUMBER
is the attribute field for color, while KM-H-CUSTOMER-NUMBER
is for highlighting.

```
01   MNTMAP1I.
     02   FILLER PIC X(12).
     02   TITLEL     COMP  PIC  S9(4).
     02   TITLEF     PICTURE X.
     02   FILLER REDEFINES TITLEF.
        03 TITLEA     PICTURE X.
     02   FILLER    PICTURE X(4).
     02   TITLEI  PIC X(79).
     02   NUMBER1L    COMP  PIC  S9(4).
     02   NUMBER1F    PICTURE X.
     02   FILLER REDEFINES NUMBER1F.
        03 NUMBER1A    PICTURE X.
     02   FILLER    PICTURE X(4).
     02   NUMBER1I  PIC X(5).
     02   MESSAG1L    COMP  PIC  S9(4).
     02   MESSAG1F    PICTURE X.
     02   FILLER REDEFINES MESSAG1F.
        03 MESSAG1A    PICTURE X.
     02   FILLER    PICTURE X(4).
     02   MESSAG1I  PIC X(79).
     02   ERROR1L    COMP  PIC  S9(4).
     02   ERROR1F    PICTURE X.
     02   FILLER REDEFINES ERROR1F.
        03 ERROR1A    PICTURE X.
     02   FILLER    PICTURE X(4).
     02   ERROR1I  PIC X(77).
     02   DUMMY1L    COMP  PIC  S9(4).
     02   DUMMY1F    PICTURE X.
     02   FILLER REDEFINES DUMMY1F.
        03 DUMMY1A    PICTURE X.
     02   FILLER    PICTURE X(4).
     02   DUMMY1I  PIC X(1).
```

Figure 7-6   BMS-generated symbolic map for a customer-maintenance program that uses extended attributes (part 1 of 2)

Remember when you code your symbolic maps that you must supply the four extended attribute fields in the right sequence (C, P, H, and V). And you must provide them for *all* of the named fields in the mapset, even though you may not use extended attributes for all of them. If you code them in a different order or omit one or more of them, errors will result.

HOW TO MODIFY EXTENDED ATTRIBUTES

In your application program, it's easy to change a field's extended attributes. All you do is move the correct attribute value to the

```
01   MNTMAP1O REDEFINES MNTMAP1I.
     02   FILLER PIC X(12).
     02   FILLER PICTURE X(3).
     02   TITLEC       PICTURE X.
     02   TITLEP       PICTURE X.
     02   TITLEH       PICTURE X.
     02   TITLEV       PICTURE X.
     02   TITLEO  PIC X(79).
     02   FILLER PICTURE X(3).
     02   NUMBER1C     PICTURE X.
     02   NUMBER1P     PICTURE X.
     02   NUMBER1H     PICTURE X.
     02   NUMBER1V     PICTURE X.
     02   NUMBER1O  PIC X(5).
     02   FILLER PICTURE X(3).
     02   MESSAG1C     PICTURE X.
     02   MESSAG1P     PICTURE X.
     02   MESSAG1H     PICTURE X.
     02   MESSAG1V     PICTURE X.
     02   MESSAG1O  PIC X(79).
     02   FILLER PICTURE X(3).
     02   ERROR1C      PICTURE X.
     02   ERROR1P      PICTURE X.
     02   ERROR1H      PICTURE X.
     02   ERROR1V      PICTURE X.
     02   ERROR1O  PIC X(77).
     02   FILLER PICTURE X(3).
     02   DUMMY1C      PICTURE X.
     02   DUMMY1P      PICTURE X.
     02   DUMMY1H      PICTURE X.
     02   DUMMY1V      PICTURE X.
     02   DUMMY1O  PIC X(1).
```

Figure 7-6 BMS-generated symbolic map for a customer-maintenance program that uses
extended attributes (part 2 of 2)

corresponding attribute field *before* you issue a SEND MAP
command for the map. So, changing an extended attribute byte is
similar to changing a standard attribute byte.

How do you determine what value to move to an extended
attribute byte? The best way is to use a standard COPY book to
include attribute byte definitions in your program. As you know,
IBM supplies a standard COPY member named DFHBMSCA that
defines many attribute characters. The shading in figure 7-8 shows
the ones that apply to color and extended highlighting. Personally,
I prefer to use the COPY book in figure 7-9. The field names are
more meaningful, and it provides just the attribute definitions I
need for color and extended highlighting.

```
 01    KEY-MAP.
 *
       05   FILLER                    PIC X(12).
 *
       05   KM-L-TITLE                PIC S9(4)      COMP.
       05   KM-A-TITLE                PIC X.
       05   KM-C-TITLE                PIC X.
       05   KM-P-TITLE                PIC X.
       05   KM-H-TITLE                PIC X.
       05   KM-V-TITLE                PIC X.
       05   KM-D-TITLE                PIC X(79).
 *
       05   KM-L-CUSTOMER-NUMBER      PIC S9(4)      COMP.
       05   KM-A-CUSTOMER-NUMBER      PIC X.
       05   KM-C-CUSTOMER-NUMBER      PIC X.
       05   KM-P-CUSTOMER-NUMBER      PIC X.
       05   KM-H-CUSTOMER-NUMBER      PIC X.
       05   KM-V-CUSTOMER-NUMBER      PIC X.
       05   KM-D-CUSTOMER-NUMBER      PIC X(5).
 *
       05   KM-L-OPERATOR-MESSAGE     PIC S9(4)      COMP.
       05   KM-A-OPERATOR-MESSAGE     PIC X.
       05   KM-C-OPERATOR-MESSAGE     PIC X.
       05   KM-P-OPERATOR-MESSAGE     PIC X.
       05   KM-H-OPERATOR-MESSAGE     PIC X.
       05   KM-V-OPERATOR-MESSAGE     PIC X.
       05   KM-D-OPERATOR-MESSAGE     PIC X(79).
 *
       05   KM-L-ERROR-MESSAGE        PIC S9(4)      COMP.
       05   KM-A-ERROR-MESSAGE        PIC X.
       05   KM-C-ERROR-MESSAGE        PIC X.
       05   KM-P-ERROR-MESSAGE        PIC X.
       05   KM-H-ERROR-MESSAGE        PIC X.
       05   KM-V-ERROR-MESSAGE        PIC X.
       05   KM-D-ERROR-MESSAGE        PIC X(5).
 *
       05   KM-L-DUMMY                PIC S9(4)      COMP.
       05   KM-A-DUMMY                PIC X.
       05   KM-C-DUMMY                PIC X.
       05   KM-P-DUMMY                PIC X.
       05   KM-H-DUMMY                PIC X.
       05   KM-V-DUMMY                PIC X.
       05   KM-D-DUMMY                PIC X.
 *
```

Figure 7-7   Programmer-generated symbolic map for a customer-maintenance program that uses extended attributes

Using the COPY book shown in figure 7-9, you could cause a field to blink like this:

```
MOVE EAC-H-BLINK TO KM-H-CUSTOMER-NUMBER
```

```
01        DFHBMSCA.
  02      DFHBMPEM    PICTURE X     VALUE  IS   ' '.
  02      DFHBMPNL    PICTURE X     VALUE  IS   ' '.
  02      DFHBMASK    PICTURE X     VALUE  IS   '0'.
  02      DFHBMUNP    PICTURE X     VALUE  IS   ' '.
  02      DFHBMUNN    PICTURE X     VALUE  IS   'Ɛ'.
  02      DFHBMPRO    PICTURE X     VALUE  IS   '-'.
  02      DFHBMBRY    PICTURE X     VALUE  IS   'H'.
  02      DFHBMDAR    PICTURE X     VALUE  IS   '<'.
  02      DFHBMFSE    PICTURE X     VALUE  IS   'A'.
  02      DFHBMPRF    PICTURE X     VALUE  IS   '/'.
  02      DFHBMASF    PICTURE X     VALUE  IS   '1'.
  02      DFHBMASB    PICTURE X     VALUE  IS   '8'.
  02      DFHSA       PICTURE X     VALUE  IS   ' '.
  02      DFHCOLOR    PICTURE X     VALUE  IS   ' '.
  02      DFHPS       PICTURE X     VALUE  IS   ' '.
  02      DFHHLT      PICTURE X     VALUE  IS   ' '.
  02      DFH3270     PICTURE X     VALUE  IS   ' '.
  02      DFHVAL      PICTURE X     VALUE  IS   'A'.
  02      DFHALL      PICTURE X     VALUE  IS   ' '.
  02      DFHERROR    PICTURE X     VALUE  IS   ' '.
  02      DFHDFT      PICTURE X     VALUE  IS   ' '.
  02      DFHDFCOL    PICTURE X     VALUE  IS   ' '.
  02      DFHBLUE     PICTURE X     VALUE  IS   '1'.
  02      DFHRED      PICTURE X     VALUE  IS   '2'.
  02      DFHPINK     PICTURE X     VALUE  IS   '3'.
  02      DFHGREEN    PICTURE X     VALUE  IS   '4'.
  02      DFHTURQ     PICTURE X     VALUE  IS   '5'.
  02      DFHYELLO    PICTURE X     VALUE  IS   '6'.
  02      DFHNEUTR    PICTURE X     VALUE  IS   '7'.
  02      DFHBASE     PICTURE X     VALUE  IS   ' '.
  02      DFHDFHI     PICTURE X     VALUE  IS   ' '.
  02      DFHBLINK    PICTURE X     VALUE  IS   '1'.
  02      DFHREVRS    PICTURE X     VALUE  IS   '2'.
  02      DFHUNDLN    PICTURE X     VALUE  IS   '4'.
  02      DFHMFIL     PICTURE X     VALUE  IS   ' '.
  02      DFHMENT     PICTURE X     VALUE  IS   ' '.
  02      DFHMFE      PICTURE X     VALUE  IS   ' '.
```

Figure 7-8   The IBM-supplied COPY member DFHBMSCA

And this statement:

```
MOVE EAC-H-OFF TO KM-H-CUSTOMER-NUMBER
```

cancels the blinking attribute.

Similarly, you can change a field's extended color like this:

```
MOVE EAC-C-TURQUOISE TO KM-C-CUSTOMER-NUMBER
```

```
 01   EXTENDED-ATTRIBUTE-CHARACTERS.
*
      05   EAC-H-OFF                      PIC X       VALUE HIGH-VALUE.
      05   EAC-H-BLINK                    PIC X       VALUE '1'.
      05   EAC-H-REVERSE-VIDEO            PIC X       VALUE '2'.
      05   EAC-H-UNDERSCORE               PIC X       VALUE '4'.
*
      05   EAC-C-DEFAULT                  PIC X       VALUE HIGH-VALUE.
      05   EAC-C-BLUE                     PIC X       VALUE '1'.
      05   EAC-C-RED                      PIC X       VALUE '2'.
      05   EAC-C-PINK                     PIC X       VALUE '3'.
      05   EAC-C-GREEN                    PIC X       VALUE '4'.
      05   EAC-C-TURQUOISE                PIC X       VALUE '5'.
      05   EAC-C-YELLOW                   PIC X       VALUE '6'.
      05   EAC-C-NEUTRAL                  PIC X       VALUE '7'.
```

Figure 7-9   An improved COPY member containing extended attribute byte definitions

To return a field to its base color, code this:

```
MOVE EAC-C-DEFAULT TO KM-C-CUSTOMER-NUMBER
```

In short, your program has complete control over a field's color and extended highlighting.

Like standard attribute settings, the extended attributes don't actually take effect until you issue a SEND MAP command. And the MAPONLY and DATAONLY options work the same way they do for standard attributes: if you specify DATAONLY, extended attributes in your symbolic map are sent to the screen. If you specify MAPONLY, the extended attributes you specify in the physical map are used.

DISCUSSION

As I mentioned at the start of this chapter, color and extended highlighting aren't available on most terminals. Even if some of the terminals at your installation do support these features, you should be careful about how you use them. It's tempting to use every feature available on your terminals, whether or not they contribute to the efficiency of your programs and operators. As a result, if your shop does have terminals that support color and extended highlighting, it probably also has standards that govern their use. If so, you should find out what they are and follow them.

Terminology

base color terminal
extended color terminal
extended attribute byte
extended highlighting
underline
blink
reverse-video

Objectives

1. Explain the difference between a base color terminal and an extended color terminal.

2. Given a programming problem that requires color and/or extended highlighting, create a BMS mapset that provides the required capability.

3. Explain how to modify extended attributes in an application program.

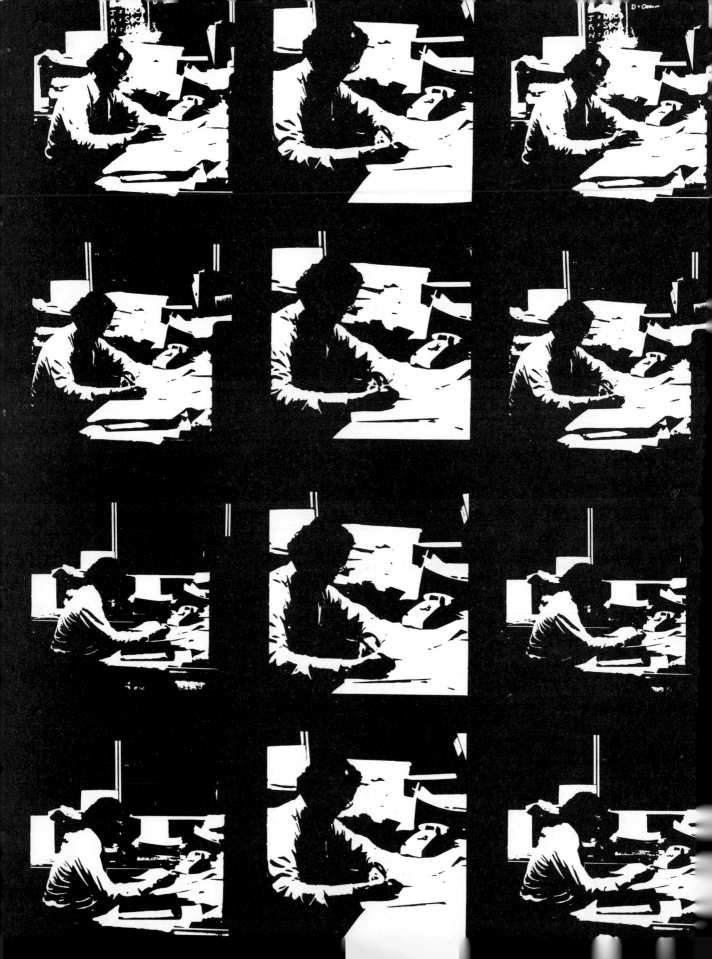

Chapter 8

Terminal control

In *Part 1: An introductory course* and in chapters 6 and 7 of this book, you learned how to use Basic Mapping Support (BMS) facilities to communicate with 3270 terminals. As you know, BMS is actually an interface between your application program and the CICS *terminal control module*, which handles all terminal I/O. In this chapter, you'll learn how to use terminal control commands to process terminal input and output directly, without using BMS as an interface.

Before I go on, a word of caution is in order. The programming requirements for terminal control are complicated. It's unreasonable to use terminal control for a full-screen interactive program; that's what BMS is for. Even so, there are times when it's appropriate to use terminal control directly for simple programs. But because terminal control programming is so complicated, I'll present just a small subset of it in this chapter.

To illustrate how terminal control works, this chapter presents two programming examples. The first is a simple inquiry program that accepts terminal input from an operator and displays the results of the inquiry on the terminal's screen. The second is a more complicated program: it retrieves records stored in a transient data queue and prints them on a 3270 printer. (In chapter 5, you saw a program that writes records to that queue.)

The operator enters a transaction identifier and a customer number:

```
INQ3 01050
```

Figure 8-1   Operation of the customer-inquiry program (part 1 of 2)

A CUSTOMER-INQUIRY PROGRAM

In *Part 1: An introductory course,* I described two broad types of CICS applications: *menu-driven applications* and *command-driven applications.* A menu-driven application is one in which the operator invokes programs by selecting options presented by a *menu program.* I presented a simple menu program in *Part 1.* In a command-driven system, an operator invokes programs directly by entering a transaction identifier. In addition, a command-driven system may allow an operator to enter data along with the trans-id that invokes the program.

Figure 8-1 shows the operation of a simple command-driven inquiry program. In part 1, the operator enters this line:

```
INQ3 01050
```

Here, the trans-id is INQ3. The data that follows the trans-id, 01050, is a customer number. In part 2, you can see that the

The program retrieves the customer's record and displays it:

```
  CUSTOMER: 01050      BARRY'S HARDWARE STORE
                       2101 N. FIRST STREET
                       FRESNO              CA 93726
```

Figure 8-1   Operation of the customer-inquiry program (part 2 of 2)

program retrieves the record for customer 01050 and displays it. Then, the program ends.

To display data for another customer, the operator must clear the screen and enter another command line. As a result, this program is *not* pseudo-conversational: the operator must explicitly invoke the program to display each customer's record.

Figure 8-2 shows the structure chart for this customer-inquiry program. As you can see, the program has a simple structure. Module 0000 is the main control module. It first invokes module 1000 to receive the data entered by the operator—that is, the command line that contains the customer number. Then, module 0000 invokes module 2000 to read the customer's record. Assuming the customer record is found, module 0000 invokes module 3000 to send the customer's data to the terminal. If the record isn't found, module 4000 is invoked to display an error message.

Figure 8-3 gives the complete source listing for the customer-inquiry program. In a moment, I'll explain some of the coding in the Data Division. For now, I want to draw your attention to the

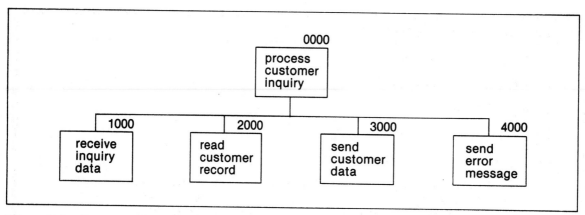

Figure 8-2 Structure chart for the customer-inquiry program

three Procedure Division commands that are shaded. The RECEIVE command (module 1000) is similar to the RECEIVE MAP command, except no BMS mapset is used. Likewise, the SEND command (modules 3000 and 4000) is like the SEND MAP and SEND TEXT commands, but no BMS facilities are involved.

The RECEIVE command

Figure 8-4 gives the format of the RECEIVE command. It's coded in module 1000 of the customer-inquiry program like this:

```
EXEC CICS
    RECEIVE INTO(COMMAND-LINE)
            LENGTH(COMMAND-LENGTH)
END-EXEC.
```

The INTO option names the area into which the input data is copied. Initially, the LENGTH field contains the length of the input area. After the RECEIVE command finishes, the length field contains the actual length of the received data. You should define the length field as a half-word binary item: PIC S9(4) COMP.

The input area contains the input exactly as it's entered by the operator, including the transaction identifier that invokes the program. So if the operator enters

```
INQ3 01050
```

```
     IDENTIFICATION DIVISION.
*
  PROGRAM-ID.   CUSTINQ3.
*
  ENVIRONMENT DIVISION.
*
  DATA DIVISION.
*
  WORKING-STORAGE SECTION.
*
  01   SWITCHES.
*
      05   VALID-DATA-SW              PIC X          VALUE 'Y'.
           88   VALID-DATA                           VALUE 'Y'.
      05   CUSTOMER-FOUND-SW          PIC X          VALUE 'Y'.
           88   CUSTOMER-FOUND                       VALUE 'Y'.
*
  01   COMMAND-LINE.
*
      05   CL-TRANS-ID                PIC X(4).
      05   FILLER                     PIC X.
      05   CL-CUSTOMER-NUMBER         PIC X(5).
*
  01   COMMAND-LENGTH                 PIC S9(4)      VALUE +10   COMP.
*
  01   CUSTOMER-MASTER-RECORD.
*
      05   CM-CUSTOMER-NUMBER         PIC X(5).
      05   CM-NAME                    PIC X(30).
      05   CM-ADDRESS                 PIC X(30).
      05   CM-CITY                    PIC X(21).
      05   CM-STATE                   PIC XX.
      05   CM-ZIP-CODE                PIC X(5).
*
  01   CUSTOMER-DATA-LINES.
*
      05   CDL-LINE-1.
           10   FILLER                PIC X(10)      VALUE 'CUSTOMER: '.
           10   CDL-CUSTOMER-NUMBER   PIC X(5).
           10   FILLER                PIC X(5)       VALUE SPACE.
           10   CDL-NAME              PIC X(30).
           10   FILLER                PIC X(30)      VALUE SPACE.
      05   CDL-LINE-2.
           10   FILLER                PIC X(20)      VALUE SPACE.
           10   CDL-ADDRESS           PIC X(30).
           10   FILLER                PIC X(30)      VALUE SPACE.
      05   CDL-LINE-3.
           10   FILLER                PIC X(20)      VALUE SPACE.
           10   CDL-CITY              PIC X(21).
           10   FILLER                PIC X          VALUE SPACE.
           10   CDL-STATE             PIC XX.
           10   FILLER                PIC X          VALUE SPACE.
           10   CDL-ZIP-CODE          PIC X(5).
           10   FILLER                PIC X(30)      VALUE SPACE.
```

Figure 8-3   Source listing for the customer-inquiry program (part 1 of 3)

```
*
 01   ERROR-LINE.
*
     05   FILLER                        PIC X          VALUE SPACE.
     05   ERROR-MESSAGE                 PIC X(79).
*
 PROCEDURE DIVISION.
*
 0000-PROCESS-CUSTOMER-INQUIRY SECTION.
*
     PERFORM 1000-RECEIVE-INQUIRY-DATA.
     IF VALID-DATA
         PERFORM 2000-READ-CUSTOMER-RECORD
         IF CUSTOMER-FOUND
             PERFORM 3000-SEND-CUSTOMER-DATA.
     IF NOT VALID-DATA
         PERFORM 4000-SEND-ERROR-MESSAGE.
     EXEC CICS
         RETURN
     END-EXEC.
*
 1000-RECEIVE-INQUIRY-DATA SECTION.
*
     EXEC CICS
         HANDLE AID ANYKEY(1000-ANYKEY)
     END-EXEC.
     EXEC CICS
         HANDLE CONDITION LENGERR(1000-LENGERR)
     END-EXEC.
     EXEC CICS
         RECEIVE INTO(COMMAND-LINE)
                 LENGTH(COMMAND-LENGTH)
     END-EXEC.
     IF CL-CUSTOMER-NUMBER = SPACE OR LOW-VALUE
         MOVE 'N' TO VALID-DATA-SW
         MOVE 'YOU MUST SUPPLY A CUSTOMER NUMBER'
             TO ERROR-MESSAGE.
     GO TO 1000-EXIT.
*
 1000-ANYKEY.
*
     MOVE 'N' TO VALID-DATA-SW.
     MOVE 'WRONG KEY PRESSED' TO ERROR-MESSAGE.
     GO TO 1000-EXIT.
*
 1000-LENGERR.
*
     MOVE 'N' TO VALID-DATA-SW.
     MOVE 'TOO MUCH DATA ENTERED' TO ERROR-MESSAGE.
*
 1000-EXIT.
*
     EXIT.
```

Figure 8-3   Source listing for the customer-inquiry program (part 2 of 3)

```
*
 2000-READ-CUSTOMER-RECORD SECTION.
*
     EXEC CICS
         HANDLE CONDITION NOTFND(2000-NOTFND)
     END-EXEC.
     EXEC CICS
         READ DATASET('CUSTMAS')
              INTO(CUSTOMER-MASTER-RECORD)
              RIDFLD(CL-CUSTOMER-NUMBER)
     END-EXEC.
     GO TO 2000-EXIT.
*
 2000-NOTFND.
*
     MOVE 'N' TO CUSTOMER-FOUND-SW
                 VALID-DATA-SW.
     MOVE 'CUSTOMER NOT FOUND' TO ERROR-MESSAGE.
*
 2000-EXIT.
*
     EXIT.
*
 3000-SEND-CUSTOMER-DATA SECTION.
*
     MOVE CM-CUSTOMER-NUMBER TO CDL-CUSTOMER-NUMBER.
     MOVE CM-NAME            TO CDL-NAME.
     MOVE CM-ADDRESS         TO CDL-ADDRESS.
     MOVE CM-CITY            TO CDL-CITY.
     MOVE CM-STATE           TO CDL-STATE.
     MOVE CM-ZIP-CODE        TO CDL-ZIP-CODE.
     EXEC CICS
         SEND FROM(CUSTOMER-DATA-LINES)
              LENGTH(240)
              ERASE
     END-EXEC.
*
 4000-SEND-ERROR-MESSAGE SECTION.
*
     EXEC CICS
         SEND FROM(ERROR-LINE)
              LENGTH(80)
     END-EXEC.
```

Figure 8-3   Source listing for the customer-inquiry program (part 3 of 3)

that's exactly what's placed in COMMAND-LINE. If you line up the fields subordinate to COMMAND-LINE with the operator's entry, you'll see that CL-CUSTOMER-NUMBER contains 01050. The program uses this field to read the correct customer record.

```
The RECEIVE command

EXEC CICS
      RECEIVE INTO(data-name)
              LENGTH(data-name)
END-EXEC


Explanation

INTO                    The area that will contain the data read from the terminal.

LENGTH                  Initially, this field must contain the length of the input area.
                        After the RECEIVE command executes, this field contains the
                        length of the data actually received. Must be a binary half-
                        word (PIC S9(4) COMP).
```

Figure 8-4   The RECEIVE command

The LENGERR condition   The LENGERR condition occurs whenever the operator enters more input data than will fit in your input area (as indicated by the LENGTH field). In the customer-inquiry program, I provide a 10-byte input area. If the operator enters more than 10 bytes, the LENGERR condition is raised when the RECEIVE command executes. If you don't provide for the LENGERR condition with a HANDLE CONDITION command, your program is terminated whenever the condition occurs. As a result, you should always issue a HANDLE CONDITION command for the LENGERR condition before you issue a RECEIVE command.

The LENGERR routine in figure 8-3 (1000-LENGERR) formats an error message and sets VALID-DATA-SW to N, so the error message will be sent by module 4000. Depending on your application's requirements, you could ignore the LENGERR condition and try to process the data that was entered. For this program, though, I consider the LENGERR condition to be an error and handle it as such.

How to detect PF keys   Like the RECEIVE MAP command, the RECEIVE command provides two methods of detecting the use of PF keys. One is to issue a HANDLE AID command before the RECEIVE command. The other is to test EIBAID, updated each time a RECEIVE command is executed. In general, I prefer to use the HANDLE AID command.

In the customer-inquiry program, I issue a HANDLE AID command that specifies ANYKEY. Then, if the operator uses a PF key rather than the enter key, the ANYKEY routine in module 1000 moves 'N' to VALID-DATA-SW and formats an error message. Incidentally, you should realize that a program that isn't pseudo-conversational doesn't need to test for the CLEAR key or the PA keys. To illustrate why, suppose an operator keys in

```
INQ3 01050
```

and presses the clear key. Since the clear key doesn't transmit any data, the trans-id (INQ3) is never processed. As a result, your program never starts.

The SEND command

Figure 8-5 shows the format of the SEND command. You use it to transmit output data to a terminal. In module 3000 of the customer-inquiry program, I code this SEND command:

```
EXEC CICS
    SEND FROM(CUSTOMER-DATA-LINES)
         LENGTH(240)
         ERASE
END-EXEC.
```

As a result, the contents of CUSTOMER-DATA-LINES, 240 bytes long, are sent to the terminal; the previous contents of the screen are erased.

If you'll look at the working-storage definition of CUSTOMER-DATA-LINES, you'll see that three 80-byte display lines are defined. Here, the display fields are separated by FILLER items that specify VALUE SPACE. Since each line is 80 characters long, the alignment is correct. Although it's possible to use control characters (called *orders*) to format output data, I recommend you don't. If your screen's format is complicated enough to require orders, you should use BMS instead. For 3270 printers, however, orders aren't that difficult to use. You'll see an example of a printer program that uses orders in a moment.

If you don't specify the ERASE option on a SEND command, the previous screen data isn't erased and the new output data is placed at the current position of the cursor. For example, suppose

---

The SEND command

```
EXEC CICS
    SEND FROM(data-name)
         LENGTH(data-name|literal)
        [CTLCHAR(data-name)]
        [ERASE]
END-EXEC
```

Explanation

FROM	The area that contains the data to be sent to the terminal.
LENGTH	The length of the FROM field. If you use a data-name, it must be a binary half-word (PIC S9(4) COMP).
CTLCHAR	Specifies a one-byte alphanumeric field that contains a write control character. Recommended value for printer terminals: 'H'.
ERASE	Specifies that the terminal's buffer should be erased.

Figure 8-5   The SEND command

the operator enters this line:

```
INQ3 99999
```

Assuming that customer 99999 doesn't exist, module 4000 is invoked to send an error message. Since the SEND command in module 4000 does *not* specify the ERASE option, the error message is positioned at the current cursor location—that is, after the data entered by the operator. So after the error message is sent, the screen looks like this:

```
INQ3 99999 CUSTOMER NOT FOUND
```

In the working-storage definition of ERROR-LINE, notice the FILLER item that defines a space in the first byte. That's included to place a space between the operator's entry and the error message.

You use the CTLCHAR option of the SEND command to supply a *write control character* (or *WCC*) that the 3270 uses to control output operations. For display devices, you can omit the

Character	Resulting printer action
blank	Skip one line before printing.
0	Skip two lines before printing.
–	Skip three lines before printing.
1	Skip to the top of the next page before printing.

Figure 8-6   ASA control characters

CTLCHAR option. Later in this chapter, you'll see how to specify
a write control character for a printer.

There are no exceptional conditions that are likely to occur
when you issue a SEND command. As a result, there's no
HANDLE CONDITION command in module 3000 or 4000.

THE TRANSIENT DATA PRINT PROGRAM

In chapter 5, you saw an inventory-listing program that directs
data to a printer by writing records to a transient data queue
named L86P. Now, I'll present a program that reads records from
the L86P queue, formats them in a 1920-byte buffer area, and
sends them to a printer. The transient data queue is defined in the
DCT (Destination Control Table) so that the print program is
started automatically as an ATI (Automatic Transaction Initiation)
task whenever a record is written to the queue. If you don't
remember how ATI works, you can review chapter 5.

Each record in the transient data queue includes a standard
ASA carriage control character in position 1 to indicate printer
spacing. Figure 8-6 shows the ASA control characters supported by
the transient data print program. (You should recognize this figure
from chapter 5.) If the program encounters a character in position
1 other than one of those shown in figure 8-6, it assumes single
spacing.

Figure 8-7 gives the structure chart for the transient data print
program, and figure 8-8 gives the program's source listing. For
efficiency reasons, the transient data print program formats as
many print lines as possible in a 1920-byte buffer area before it
issues a SEND command. Unfortunately, the processing required to

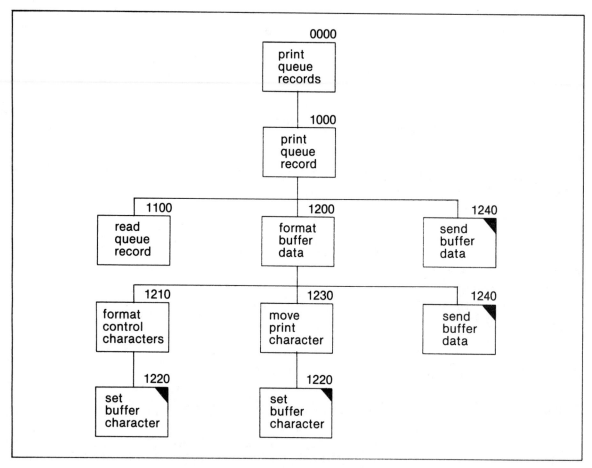

Figure 8-7 Structure chart for the transient data print program

do that can be confusing. So expect to spend more than a few moments studying the transient data print program if you want to understand it completely.

In the Working-Storage Section, there are three things I want you to notice. First, notice how I defined the transient data queue's input record:

```
01  PRINT-QUEUE-RECORD.
*
    05  PRINT-CC        PIC X.
    05  PRINT-CHAR      OCCURS 132
                        INDEXED BY PRINT-INDEX
                        PIC X.
```

```
    IDENTIFICATION DIVISION.
*
   PROGRAM-ID.   PRTASA1.
*
   ENVIRONMENT DIVISION.
*
   DATA DIVISION.
*
   WORKING-STORAGE SECTION.
*
   01   SWITCHES.
*
       05   PRINT-QUEUE-EOF-SW       PIC X         VALUE 'N'.
            88   PRINT-QUEUE-EOF                    VALUE 'Y'.
*
   01   WORK-FIELDS.
*
       05   NL-COUNT                 PIC 9.
       05   SET-CHAR                 PIC X.
*
   01   PRINT-QUEUE-RECORD.
*
       05   PRINT-CC                 PIC X.
            88   FORM-FEED                          VALUE '1'.
            88   SINGLE-SPACE                       VALUE ' '.
            88   DOUBLE-SPACE                       VALUE '0'.
            88   TRIPLE-SPACE                       VALUE '-'.
       05   PRINT-CHAR               OCCURS 132
                                     INDEXED BY PRINT-INDEX
                                     PIC X.
*
   01   PRINT-RECORD-LENGTH          PIC S9(4)   COMP.
*
   01   BUFFER-AREA.
*
       05   BUFFER-CHAR              OCCURS 1920
                                     INDEXED BY BUFFER-INDEX
                                     PIC X.
*
   01   PRINT-ORDERS.
*
       05   NL-ORDER                 PIC X         VALUE ' '.
       05   FF-ORDER                 PIC X         VALUE ' '.
       05   CR-ORDER                 PIC X         VALUE ' '.
*
   01   WRITE-CONTROL-CHARACTER      PIC X         VALUE 'H'.
*
```

Figure 8-8   Source listing for the transient data print program (part 1 of 3)

```
     PROCEDURE DIVISION.
*
 0000-PRINT-QUEUE-RECORDS SECTION.
*
     EXEC CICS
         HANDLE CONDITION QZERO(1100-QZERO)
     END-EXEC.
     MOVE LOW-VALUE TO BUFFER-AREA.
     SET BUFFER-INDEX TO 1.
     PERFORM 1000-PRINT-QUEUE-RECORD
         UNTIL PRINT-QUEUE-EOF.
     EXEC CICS
         RETURN
     END-EXEC.
*
 1000-PRINT-QUEUE-RECORD SECTION.
*
     PERFORM 1100-READ-QUEUE-RECORD.
     IF PRINT-QUEUE-EOF
         PERFORM 1240-SEND-BUFFER-DATA
     ELSE
         PERFORM 1200-FORMAT-BUFFER-DATA.
*
 1100-READ-QUEUE-RECORD SECTION.
*
     MOVE 133 TO PRINT-RECORD-LENGTH.
     EXEC CICS
         READQ TD QUEUE(EIBTRMID)
                  INTO(PRINT-QUEUE-RECORD)
                  LENGTH(PRINT-RECORD-LENGTH)
     END-EXEC.
     SET PRINT-INDEX TO 1.
     GO TO 1100-EXIT.
*
 1100-QZERO.
*
     MOVE 'Y' TO PRINT-QUEUE-EOF-SW.
*
 1100-EXIT.
*
     EXIT.
*
 1200-FORMAT-BUFFER-DATA SECTION.
*
     IF BUFFER-INDEX > 1916 - PRINT-RECORD-LENGTH
         PERFORM 1240-SEND-BUFFER-DATA
         MOVE LOW-VALUE TO BUFFER-AREA
         SET BUFFER-INDEX TO 1.
     PERFORM 1210-FORMAT-CONTROL-CHARACTERS.
     PERFORM 1230-MOVE-PRINT-CHARACTER
         VARYING PRINT-INDEX FROM 1 BY 1
             UNTIL PRINT-INDEX = PRINT-RECORD-LENGTH.
*
```

Figure 8-8 Source listing for the transient data print program (part 2 of 3)

```
    1210-FORMAT-CONTROL-CHARACTERS SECTION.
*
        IF NOT (    FORM-FEED
                OR SINGLE-SPACE
                OR DOUBLE-SPACE
                OR TRIPLE-SPACE)
            MOVE ' ' TO PRINT-CC.
        IF FORM-FEED
            MOVE CR-ORDER TO SET-CHAR
            PERFORM 1220-SET-BUFFER-CHARACTER
            MOVE FF-ORDER TO SET-CHAR
            PERFORM 1220-SET-BUFFER-CHARACTER
            MOVE CR-ORDER TO SET-CHAR
            PERFORM 1220-SET-BUFFER-CHARACTER
        ELSE
            IF SINGLE-SPACE
                MOVE 1 TO NL-COUNT
            ELSE IF DOUBLE-SPACE
                MOVE 2 TO NL-CCUNT
            ELSE IF TRIPLE-SPACE
                MOVE 3 TO NL-COUNT.
        IF NOT FORM-FEED
            IF BUFFER-INDEX = 1
                SUBTRACT 1 FROM NL-COUNT.
        IF NOT FORM-FEED
            MOVE NL-ORDER TO SET-CHAR
            PERFORM 1220-SET-BUFFER-CHARACTER
                NL-COUNT TIMES.
*
    1220-SET-BUFFER-CHARACTER SECTION.
*
        MOVE SET-CHAR TO BUFFER-CHAR(BUFFER-INDEX).
        SET BUFFER-INDEX UP BY 1.
*
    1230-MOVE-PRINT-CHARACTER SECTION.
*
        MOVE PRINT-CHAR(PRINT-INDEX) TO SET-CHAR.
        PERFORM 1220-SET-BUFFER-CHARACTER.
*
    1240-SEND-BUFFER-DATA SECTION.
*
        EXEC CICS
            SEND FROM(BUFFER-AREA)
                LENGTH(1920)
                CTLCHAR(WRITE-CONTROL-CHARACTER)
                ERASE
        END-EXEC.
```

Figure 8-8   Source listing for the transient data print program (part 3 of 3)

After the one-byte field used for the ASA control character (for clarity, I omitted the 88-level condition names subordinate to PRINT-CC), I define a table consisting of 132 occurrences of a one-byte field named PRINT-CHAR. That way, the program can process the print data one character at a time using PRINT-INDEX as an index. The definition for the 1920-byte buffer area is similar to the definition of the queue record. So the program can process the buffer area one character at a time using BUFFER-INDEX as an index.

The second thing I want you to notice in the Working-Storage Section is the 01-level item named PRINT-ORDERS. This group contains definitions of three printer orders. The NL-ORDER (hexadecimal 15) defines a new-line order (or just NL). That causes the printer to start printing on a new line. The FF-ORDER (hex 0C) defines a form-feed order (or FF); it causes the printer to advance to the top of the next page. And the CR-ORDER (hex 0D) defines a carriage-return order (or CR); it causes the printer to return the carriage to position 1 of the current line.

The transient data print program uses printer orders to implement the spacing indicated by the ASA control character in each print record. For example, if a print record contains a 0 in column 1, the program adds two new-line orders to the buffer area. That way, the printer skips two lines before printing. Since I described printer orders in more detail in topic 3 of chapter 6, you can review that unit if you need a refresher.

The third thing I want you to notice in the Working-Storage Section is the 01-level item named WRITE-CONTROL-CHARACTER. Whenever you issue a SEND command for a printer, you must supply a write control character in the CTLCHAR option to provide control information for the printer. Normally, the write control character's value should be the letter H. That causes the printer's printing mechanism to print the buffer data you send. Incidentally, the value 'H' has no special significance here. It just happens that the bit settings required to activate the printer correspond to that letter.

In the Procedure Division, module 0000 repeatedly invokes module 1000 to process transient data records. Module 1000, in turn, invokes module 1100 to read a queue record and module 1200 to format the record's print data into the buffer. Normally, module 1200 causes buffer data to be sent to the printer whenever necessary. When the end of the queue is reached, however, the buffer may contain data that hasn't yet been sent. In that case, module 1000 invokes module 1240 to send the buffer data.

Module 1200 begins with an IF statement:

```
IF BUFFER-INDEX > 1916 - PRINT-RECORD-LENGTH
    PERFORM 1240-SEND-BUFFER-DATA
    MOVE LOW-VALUE TO BUFFER-AREA
    SET BUFFER-INDEX TO 1.
```

Here, module 1240 is invoked to send data to the printer when the buffer area is full. BUFFER-INDEX always indicates the next available buffer position. So if it's greater than 1916 minus the length of the record just read (that value is stored in PRINT-RECORD-LENGTH as a result of the READQ TD command in module 1100), there's not enough room for the new record. (I use 1916 here rather than 1920 to allow for the maximum number of printer orders the record can require.) If the buffer is full, module 1200 invokes module 1240 to send the buffer data. Then, it clears the buffer area and resets the buffer index to 1.

Next, module 1200 invokes module 1210 to place the correct printer orders in the buffer area. Then, module 1230 is invoked repeatedly to move characters one at a time from the queue record to the buffer area.

Because modules 1210 and 1230 both use module 1220, I want to describe it first. It moves the character stored in SET-CHAR to the current buffer position indicated by BUFFER-INDEX. Then, it increases the value of BUFFER-INDEX by one.

Now look at module 1210. The first statement in this module checks to see if the space control character in the print record (PRINT-CC) is valid. If it's not, module 1210 moves a space to PRINT-CC so single spacing is assumed. Next, a series of statements formats the appropriate printer orders for each ASA control character. For a form feed ('1'), these statements are executed:

```
MOVE CR-ORDER TO SET-CHAR
PERFORM 1220-SET-BUFFER-CHARACTER
MOVE FF-ORDER TO SET-CHAR
PERFORM 1220-SET-BUFFER-CHARACTER
MOVE CR-ORDER TO SET-CHAR
PERFORM 1220-SET-BUFFER-CHARACTER
```

Here, module 1220 is invoked three times: first to move a CR order to the buffer, then to move an FF order to the buffer, and finally to move another CR order to the buffer. The resulting combination of printer orders (CR, FF, and CR) positions the printer to the first print position of the next page.

Here's why three orders are required to do a form-feed operation. First, a CR order is required to return the print carriage to the start of the line. That's because the next order, FF, must always appear at the beginning of a line. When the FF order is processed, the printer advances to the next page and prints a space in the first position of line 1, leaving the carriage at position 2. To reclaim the lost print position, another CR order returns the carriage to the start of line 1.

The rest of module 1210 handles formatting for single, double, or triple spacing. First, NL-COUNT is set to the number of lines to be skipped. Then, the next statement subtracts one from NL-COUNT if the current buffer position is one. That's because the printer automatically starts each buffer on a new line. And finally, these statements are executed:

```
MOVE NL-ORDER TO SET-CHAR
PERFORM 1220-SET-BUFFER-CHARACTER
        NL-COUNT TIMES.
```

Here, module 1220 is invoked up to three times, depending on the value of NL-COUNT, to move a new-line order to the buffer area.

Compared with module 1210, the operation of module 1230 is simple. It contains just two lines:

```
MOVE PRINT-CHAR(PRINT-INDEX) TO SET-CHAR.
PERFORM 1220-SET-BUFFER-CHARACTER.
```

If you look back to module 1200, you'll see that PRINT-INDEX is varied as module 1230 is invoked. As a result, each character in the print record is moved to the buffer area.

Module 1240 contains the SEND command that sends the buffer data to the printer. Although the command specifies that all 1920 bytes of BUFFER-AREA are to be sent to the printer, unused positions within BUFFER-AREA aren't transmitted because they contain LOW-VALUE. The CTLCHAR option specifies the write control character, required to start the printer. And the ERASE option causes the printer's buffer to be erased before data is transmitted. That way, there won't be any data left over from the previous SEND command in the printer's buffer.

DISCUSSION

I hope you now appreciate the complexity involved when you use terminal control facilities directly. The commands themselves present no difficulty—the problem is formatting and interpreting buffer data that contains control characters. For printer output, the processing requirements are complicated but manageable. For display terminal input and output, though, the processing requirements are unreasonably complex for all but the simplest applications. That's why you'll normally use BMS commands rather than terminal control commands for interactive programs.

Terminology

terminal control module
menu-driven application
command-driven application
menu program
order
write control character
WCC

Objective

Given a programming problem requiring the terminal control facilities presented in this chapter, code an acceptable solution.

Part 4

Other advanced
CICS features

The chapters in this part present a variety of CICS features you
might need to use on occasion. In chapter 9, you'll learn how to use
interval control commands. Then, in chapter 10, you'll learn about
three aspects of error processing under CICS: abend processing,
recovery processing, and journal control. And finally, in chapter
11, you'll learn how to use task control, program control, and
storage control commands.

Chapter 9

Interval control

The CICS *interval control program* provides a variety of time-related functions. You'll use interval control most to *schedule* a task for execution at some time in the future. In this chapter, you'll learn how to use three interval control commands: START, RETRIEVE, and CANCEL.

Tasks

To use interval control commands, you need to understand the difference between starting a task and using program control commands (LINK or XCTL) to invoke a program. Because CICS is a multi-tasking system, it processes more than one task at a time. As a result, a task initiated by a START command can execute simultaneously with the task that issued the START command. In other words, the *starting task* can run at the same time as the *started task*. In contrast, programs invoked by LINK and XCTL commands run one at a time as part of a single task.

For example, consider how you might use program control and interval control commands in a menu-driven application. When a user selects a data-entry program, the menu program issues an

XCTL command to transfer control directly to the data-entry program. In contrast, suppose the user selects a report-preparation function that doesn't require user interaction. If the menu program invoked the report-preparation program with an XCTL command, the terminal would be tied up while the report is prepared. If the report takes more than a few seconds to prepare, that could be an inconvenience for the user. But if the menu program uses interval control to schedule the report-preparation program, control returns directly to the menu program. As a result, the user can continue with other work while the report is prepared.

Automatic time-ordered transaction initiation

The interval control facility used to start a task is called *automatic time-ordered transaction initiation*, or *time-ordered ATI*. Although a task started with time-ordered ATI can begin processing immediately, it doesn't have to. When you code the START command, you can supply an optional *expiration time* that determines when the scheduled task should begin executing. For example, you can specify that a task should start in five minutes or at 12:30 p.m. If you don't supply an expiration time, your task starts immediately.

How a task is scheduled   Figure 9-1 shows how interval control schedules a task. As you can see, the START command is processed by a CICS module called *interval control services*. The services module creates a special data area called an *interval control element* (or *ICE*) that contains information about the task to be started, including its transaction-id, terminal-id, and expiration time. Then, if the START statement supplied any data to be passed to the started task, the services module invokes temporary storage control to store it. When these steps are complete, interval control services returns control to the starting task.

Although interval control uses temporary storage to store data passed between tasks, that's transparent to you. So don't worry if you haven't read about temporary storage in chapter 4. You don't need to know how temporary storage works to use interval control commands. And most of the time, you won't be passing data to a started task anyway.

How a scheduled task is started   Figure 9-2 shows how a time-ordered ATI task begins execution when its expiration time arrives.

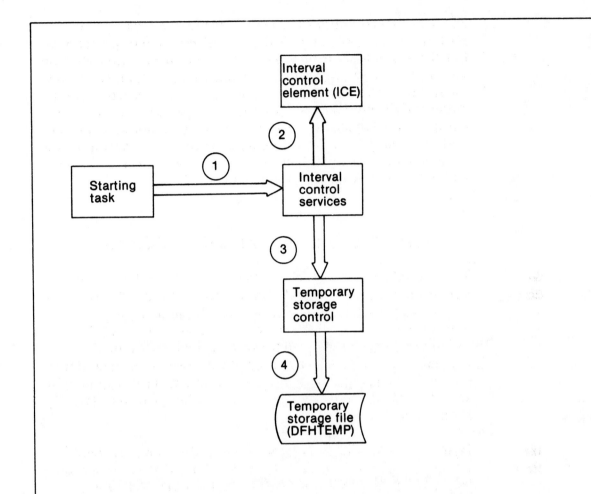

Explanation

1. A user task issues a START command that's processed by interval control services.

2. Interval control services creates an ICE that indicates the trans-id, expiration time, and terminal-id for the task to be started.

3. Interval control services invokes temporary storage control to save data that's passed to the started task.

4. Temporary storage control saves this data in the temporary storage file.

Figure 9-1 How a task is scheduled

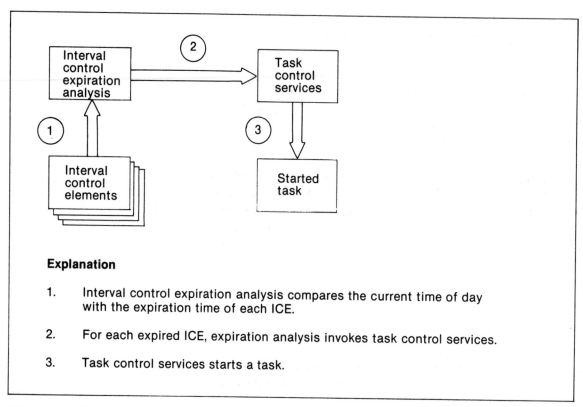

Explanation

1.   Interval control expiration analysis compares the current time of day with the expiration time of each ICE.

2.   For each expired ICE, expiration analysis invokes task control services.

3.   Task control services starts a task.

Figure 9-2   How a scheduled task is started

A CICS program called *interval control expiration analysis* periodically examines all interval control elements, comparing their expiration times with the system clock. When an ICE has expired, expiration analysis invokes the *task control services* module to start the new task, using the transaction-id and terminal-id saved in the ICE.

Note that the events in figure 9-2 are independent of those in figure 9-1. In other words, once a task issues a START command, it continues execution without regard for the status of the started task. Depending on the expiration time in the ICE, the started task may begin immediately or several hours later. Either way, the started task is independent of the starting task.

The START command

Figure 9-3 gives the format of the START command. Usually, you code it like this:

```
EXEC CICS
    START TRANSID('LST5')
END-EXEC
```

Here, a task identified by the transaction identifier LST5 is scheduled for immediate execution. Notice that you specify a transaction-id—*not* a program-name—in a START command. That's because CICS requires a trans-id to start a new task.

How to attach a started task to a terminal   In the previous example, LST5 will run without being attached to a terminal. As a result, it can't do terminal I/O directly. If you need to attach a task to a specific terminal, like a printer, you specify the TERMID option on the START command. For example, the command

```
EXEC CICS
    START TRANSID('LST4')
          TERMID('L86P')
END-EXEC
```

attaches transaction LST4 to the terminal L86P. In general, you should specify the TERMID option whenever the started task does terminal I/O.

How to specify an expiration time   If you don't want a started task to begin execution immediately, you can specify an expiration time with the TIME or INTERVAL option. For either option, you code a value in the format hhmmss where hh is hours, mm is minutes, and ss is seconds. With the TIME option, you specify a time of day using a 24-hour clock. As a result, 7:30 a.m. is 073000, and 2:00 p.m. is 140000. Midnight is 000000; one second before midnight is 235959. To illustrate, the command

```
EXEC CICS
    START TRANSID('LST4')
          TERMID('L86P')
          TIME(170000)
END-EXEC
```

causes transaction LST4 to start at 5:00 p.m. attached to terminal L86P.

One peculiarity of interval control is that you can't specify an expiration time that's more than 18 hours from the current time. If you do, interval control assumes that the time you specify has

The START command

```
EXEC CICS
    START TRANSID(data-name|literal)
        [{TIME(hhmmss)    }]
        [{INTERVAL(hhmmss)}]
        [TERMID(data-name|literal)
        [FROM(data-name)
         LENGTH(data-name|literal)]
        [RTERMID(data-name|literal)]
        [RTRANSID(data-name|literal)]
        [QUEUE(data-name|literal)]
        [REQID(data-name|literal)]
END-EXEC
```

Explanation

TRANSID	Specifies the transaction-identifier that will be used to start the task.
TIME	Specifies a time in the form hhmmss. If the time is more than 18 hours after the current time, it's considered to have expired already.
INTERVAL	Specifies an interval in the form hhmmss. CICS adds the interval to the current time to determine when the task will start.
TERMID	Specifies the name of a terminal at which the task will run. If omitted, the task will run without a terminal.
FROM	Specifies the name of a field that contains a value that's passed to the started task.
LENGTH	Specifies the length of the FROM field. If you code a data-name, it must be a binary half-word (PIC S9(4) COMP).
RTERMID	Specifies a four-byte value that's passed to the started task.
RTRANSID	Specifies a four-byte value that's passed to the started task.
QUEUE	Specifies an eight-byte value that's passed to the started task.
REQID	Specifies an eight-byte value that identifies this START command so the started task can be cancelled with a CANCEL command. If omitted, CICS generates a request-id and returns it in EIBREQID.

Figure 9-3   The START command

already expired, and the task is started immediately. For example, suppose you issue this command when the current time is 2:00 p.m. (140000):

```
EXEC CICS
    START TRANSID('LST5')
            TIME(104500)
END-EXEC
```

Although the intention of this command may be to start LST5 at 10:45 a.m. tomorrow, the effect of the command is that LST5 is started immediately. That's because 10:45 a.m. is more than 18 hours ahead of 2:00 p.m.

The second way to specify an expiration time is to use the INTERVAL option, like this:

```
EXEC CICS
    START TRANSID('LST5')
            INTERVAL(001500)
END-EXEC
```

Here, LST5 will be started in fifteen minutes. CICS adds the INTERVAL value you specify to the current time to determine the correct expiration time.

As you've already seen, you can omit the TIME and INTERVAL options altogether. In that case, the specified task is scheduled for immediate execution. Although some applications require that you specify an expiration time, you're most likely to use the START command without the TIME or INTERVAL options.

How to pass data to a started task   If you specify the FROM and LENGTH options on a START command, the data in the FROM area, whose length is indicated by the LENGTH value, is passed to the started task. For example, the command

```
EXEC CICS
    START TRANSID('LST6')
            FROM(ITEM-NUMBER)
            LENGTH(5)
END-EXEC
```

passes five bytes of data stored in the field ITEM-NUMBER to transaction LST6.

Besides the FROM option, the START command provides three other options that pass specific types of data to a started task: RTRANSID (for a transaction-id), RTERMID (for a terminal-id), and QUEUE (for a temporary storage queue name). These options work the same as the FROM option, except that you don't have to specify a length value for them. Both RTRANSID and RTERMID pass a four-byte data field; QUEUE passes an eight-byte data field. You probably won't use those options often.

The RETRIEVE command

To retrieve data passed to it by the starting task, the started task must issue a RETRIEVE command, illustrated in figure 9-4. Then, interval control services invokes temporary storage control, which retrieves the correct record from the temporary storage file and returns it to the started task. Interval control keeps track of where the data to be passed to various tasks is stored and insures that it's coordinated with the current interval control elements. As a result, a started task doesn't have to identify what temporary storage queue to retrieve its data from; interval control maintains that information.

For example, the command

```
EXEC CICS
    RETRIEVE INTO(ITEM-NUMBER)
                LENGTH(ITEM-NUMBER-LENGTH)
END-EXEC
```

obtains the passed data and places it in ITEM-NUMBER. The initial value of the LENGTH field should be the length of the INTO field. After the RETRIEVE command executes, the LENGTH field contains the actual length of the data retrieved.

Like the START command, the RETRIEVE command provides three options other than FROM for passing data: RTRANSID, RTERMID, and QUEUE. If the START command that initiated the task specified one or more of those options, you should specify them on the RETRIEVE command as well.

If a started program issues a RETRIEVE command, but no data was passed to it, the NOTFND condition is raised. In most cases, that's probably a serious error condition and you're just as well to let the task abend. However, when passing data to a started task is optional, you can use the NOTFND condition to determine whether or not data was passed.

```
The RETRIEVE command

EXEC CICS
     RETRIEVE INTO(data-name)
              LENGTH(data-name)
              [RTRANSID(data-name)]
              [RTERMID(data-name)]
              [QUEUE(data-name)]
END-EXEC


Explanation

INTO                    The area that will contain the data sent via the FROM option
                        of the START command.

LENGTH                  The length of the INTO area. Must be a binary half-word
                        (PIC S9(4) COMP).

RTRANSID                The area that will contain the data sent via the RTRANSID
                        option of the START command.

RTERMID                 The area that will contain the data sent via the RTERMID
                        option of the START command.

QUEUE                   The area that will contain the data sent via the QUEUE option
                        of the START command.
```

Figure 9-4   The RETRIEVE command

If the data that's retrieved is longer than your input area, the LENGERR condition is raised. If you handle this condition, as much of the data as will fit is placed in the INTO area, and your program can continue. If you don't handle the LENGERR condition, your program abends when it occurs.

How one task can fulfill several START requests   When a START command for the same transaction with the same expiration time is issued more than once, interval control creates an ICE for each START request. If data was passed, a separate temporary storage record is created for each START request. If your START commands specify a terminal, however, a single execution of the started task can fulfill all of the START requests by issuing RETRIEVE commands repeatedly. Each RETRIEVE command retrieves the data saved by one of the previous START commands, until there's no more data to be retrieved. And, each RETRIEVE command removes the ICE associated with the record that's retrieved, so once you retrieve a record, the START request is completely fulfilled.

CICS raises the ENDDATA condition when no more records are available for a RETRIEVE command. Because the default action for ENDDATA is to abend the task, you should handle the ENDDATA condition with a HANDLE CONDITION command if you issue more than one RETRIEVE command.

Bear in mind, however, that most START requests do *not* pass data to the started task. And of those that do, few require that multiple data records be passed to a single started task.

The CANCEL command

The CANCEL command, shown in figure 9-5, lets you cancel a task you've scheduled with a START command. In short, the CANCEL command removes the interval control element created by a START command. Once the task has started, though, you can't use a CANCEL command to cancel it.

On a CANCEL command, you must specify what START request to cancel by supplying a *request-id* in the REQID option. The request-id is an eight-character string that uniquely identifies a START command. For example, the command

```
EXEC CICS
    CANCEL REQID('TRANDEP1')
END-EXEC
```

deletes the ICE created by a START command identified as TRANDEP1.

How do you know the request-id of a particular START command? There are two ways. First, you can let CICS assign a request-id to your START command. Then, you can examine the EIBREQID field in the Execute Interface Block after the START command completes to find out what value CICS assigned.

To illustrate, suppose you code these commands:

```
EXEC CICS
    START TRANSID('LST5')
        INTERVAL(010000)
END-EXEC.
MOVE EIBREQID TO REQUEST-ID.
```

```
The CANCEL command

EXEC CICS
     CANCEL REQID(data-name|literal)
END-EXEC


Explanation

REQID                          An eight-byte value that identifies the START command to be
                               cancelled.
```

Figure 9-5   The CANCEL command

To cancel that START request, you can issue a CANCEL command like this:

```
EXEC CICS
     CANCEL REQID(REQUEST-ID)
END-EXEC
```

Note that you should move EIBREQID to a working-storage field before you issue another CICS command. That's because other CICS commands place request-ids in EIBREQID too.

The second way to determine a request-id is to assign it yourself using the REQID option of the START command. For example:

```
MOVE 'TRANELOG' TO REQUEST-ID.
EXEC CICS
     START TRANSID('LST5')
           INTERVAL(010000)
           REQID(REQUEST-ID)
END-EXEC.
```

Here, the value of REQUEST-ID (TRANELOG) is used as the request-id for the START command.

Quite frankly, it's uncommon to cancel a task once you've scheduled it. Most tasks are scheduled for immediate execution, so they can't be cancelled. As for a task that's scheduled for future execution, the only reason you might cancel it is if a serious error condition occurs in the starting task *after* it issues the START command.

Discussion

If you've read chapter 5, you should recall that transactions can also be initiated automatically based on the presence of data in a transient data queue. Now that you've seen how interval control task initiation works and how you use the START, RETRIEVE, and CANCEL commands, look at figure 9-6. Here, I compare the automatic transaction initiation features of transient data control and interval control. As you can see, the main difference is that transient data ATI is data-driven—that is, the ATI task is started based on the presence of data in a transient data queue—while the interval control ATI facility depends on time rather than data.

Although these two ATI facilities are similar, I've found that I use data-driven ATI more than time-ordered ATI. That's because data-driven ATI lends itself well to printing applications, as you saw in chapter 5.

Terminology

interval control program
schedule
starting task
started task
automatic time-ordered transaction initiation
time-ordered ATI
expiration time
interval control services
interval control element
ICE
interval control expiration analysis
task control services
request-id

Objective

Given a programming problem involving time-ordered automatic transaction initiation, code an acceptable program for its solution.

	Data-driven ATI	**Time-ordered ATI**
What causes the ATI task to begin execution?	The presence of data in a transient data queue.	The arrival of the specified expiration time.
How do you cause a task to be started immediately?	Specify a trigger level of 1.	Omit the expiration time from the START command.
Can the ATI task be attached to a terminal?	Yes.	Yes.
How is data passed to the started task?	Via a transient data queue: issue a WRITEQ TD command.	Via temporary storage: code the FROM option on the START command.
How does the started task retrieve data?	It issues a READQ TD command.	It issues a RETRIEVE command.
Can you cancel the ATI task before it begins?	No.	Yes.

Figure 9-6   A comparison of data-driven and time-ordered ATI features

Chapter 10

Error processing

In this chapter, you'll learn how CICS recovers from error
conditions that cause a task—or CICS itself—to terminate
abnormally. There are three topics in this chapter. In topic 1, you'll
learn how to supplement the standard processing CICS does when
an abend occurs. In topic 2, you'll learn about the recovery
facilities CICS provides. Finally, in topic 3, you'll learn how to use
CICS journal control features.

Topic 1   Abend processing

When a user task develops a problem that CICS, the host operating system (DOS or OS), or the hardware itself isn't designed to handle, a *transaction abend* occurs. When that happens, CICS produces a *transaction dump* that lists the contents of any main storage associated with the abending task. The transaction dump includes a *trace table* that shows the sequence of events that led to the abend. Using the transaction dump and trace table, you can determine the exact cause of the abend.

In this topic, you'll learn how you can supplement the standard processing CICS does when a task abends. First, you'll learn how to use an abend exit that gets control when an abend occurs. Then, you'll learn how to use the ABEND command to force your program to end abnormally.

Abend exits

An *abend exit* is a segment of code that supplements the standard abend processing CICS provides. Although it can be a paragraph or section within your program, an abend exit is usually a separate program. If an abend exit is active, it's automatically invoked whenever an abend occurs. To activate an abend exit, you issue a HANDLE ABEND command, as you'll see in a moment.

What does an abend exit do? In some cases, an abend exit tries to correct the problem that caused the abend. But that's unusual. More often, an abend exit just records information about the task that's abending. When it's finished, the abend exit ends by issuing an ABEND command, so CICS completes the abend processing and produces a transaction dump. You'll learn how to use the ABEND command later in this topic. Alternatively, an abend exit can issue CICS commands or macros to produce a dump and invoke dynamic transaction backout (which you'll learn about in the next topic). Then, the abend exit can display a standard error screen and return to the application.

Because they usually need to access information that's not available to command-level programs, abend exits are typically written as macro-level programs, often in assembler language.

The HANDLE ABEND command

```
EXEC CICS
                       (PROGRAM(data-name|literal))
      HANDLE ABEND     {LABEL(procedure-name)    }
                       |CANCEL                    |
                       (RESET                     )
END-EXEC
```

Explanation

PROGRAM   Specifies the one- to eight-character name of a program that should be invoked (via LINK) if the current program abends.

LABEL   Specifies the COBOL paragraph or section name of a routine within the current program that should be invoked (via GO TO) if the program abends.

CANCEL   Specifies that the effect of a previous HANDLE ABEND command should be cancelled.

RESET   Specifies that a previously cancelled abend exit should be reestablished.

Figure 10-1   The HANDLE ABEND command

Fortunately, most shops that use abend exits already have standard programs that are used throughout the system. So you probably won't be asked to write an abend exit yourself. In this topic, then, I'll just show you how to activate an abend exit so if your program abends, the abend exit will be invoked.

The HANDLE ABEND command

You use the HANDLE ABEND command, shown in figure 10-1, to control abend exits in your program. You'll code it most often like this:

```
EXEC CICS
    HANDLE ABEND PROGRAM('ABEND1')
END-EXEC
```

Here, the program named ABEND1 will be invoked automatically if an abend occurs. The program you specify in a HANDLE

ABEND command must be defined in the Processing Program Table, just like any other CICS program.

Usually, you'll code a HANDLE ABEND command at the start of your program. That way, an abend that occurs anywhere in your program causes the abend exit to be invoked. In any event, your shop probably has standards that govern when and how you code the HANDLE ABEND command. Find out what they are and follow them.

If you code the LABEL option rather than the PROGRAM option on a HANDLE ABEND command, the paragraph or section name you supply becomes the abend exit. When an abend occurs, CICS branches to that paragraph or section. The difference between the LABEL and PROGRAM options is that the LABEL option establishes an abend exit as a paragraph or section within the current program. In contrast, the PROGRAM option specifies a separate program as the abend exit. Because it's easier to provide standard abend processing in a separate program, I recommend you use the PROGRAM option rather than the LABEL option.

On rare occasions, you may need to deactivate an abend exit. That's what the CANCEL and RESET options are for. You deactivate an abend exit like this:

```
EXEC CICS
    HANDLE ABEND CANCEL
END-EXEC
```

Then, a subsequent abend does not invoke the abend exit. Later, you can reactivate the abend exit by issuing this command:

```
EXEC CICS
    HANDLE ABEND RESET
END-EXEC
```

This restores the abend exit that was active when you issued the HANDLE ABEND CANCEL command. Keep in mind that you probably won't use these forms of the HANDLE ABEND command often.

Abend exits and logical levels

Usually, the first program executed by a task issues a HANDLE ABEND command to establish an abend exit that's active for the entire task. However, it's possible to issue another HANDLE

ABEND command at any time to replace the current abend exit with a new one. If you issue HANDLE ABEND commands at various program levels within a task, you create a hierarchy of abend exits to be invoked depending on the program level at which the abend occurs. When an abend occurs, CICS uses the abend exit established by the last HANDLE ABEND command your task issued at the current program level or at a higher level.

To illustrate, figure 10-2 shows four application programs that run as part of a single task. Program-A begins by issuing a HANDLE ABEND command that makes ABEXIT1 the active abend exit. If an abend occurs in Program-A, ABEXIT1 is invoked. Next, Program-A invokes Program-B with a LINK command. Because Program-B doesn't issue a HANDLE ABEND command, ABEXIT1 is still the active abend exit. Program-B issues a LINK command to invoke Program-C, but Program-C *does* issue a HANDLE ABEND command, so ABEXIT2 becomes the current abend exit. Program-C invokes Program-D with an XCTL command; ABEXIT2 remains the active abend exit during the execution of Program-D. However, when Program-D returns control to Program-B, ABEXIT1 is restored as the active abend exit.

As I said, most tasks have just one abend exit. But if you use the LINK command to invoke programs, be aware that a HANDLE ABEND command you issue in the linked program won't be active in the program that issued the LINK command. That's because when you issue a RETURN command, CICS restores the abend exit that was active when you issued the LINK command.

The ABEND command

You use the ABEND command, whose format is given in figure 10-3, to force a task to end abnormally. You usually code the ABEND command like this:

```
EXEC CICS
    ABEND ABCODE('X100')
END-EXEC
```

The ABCODE option causes CICS to produce a transaction dump; the value you supply appears in the transaction dump and in the message that's written to the terminal operator. Because the transaction dump is the only way to determine what caused your

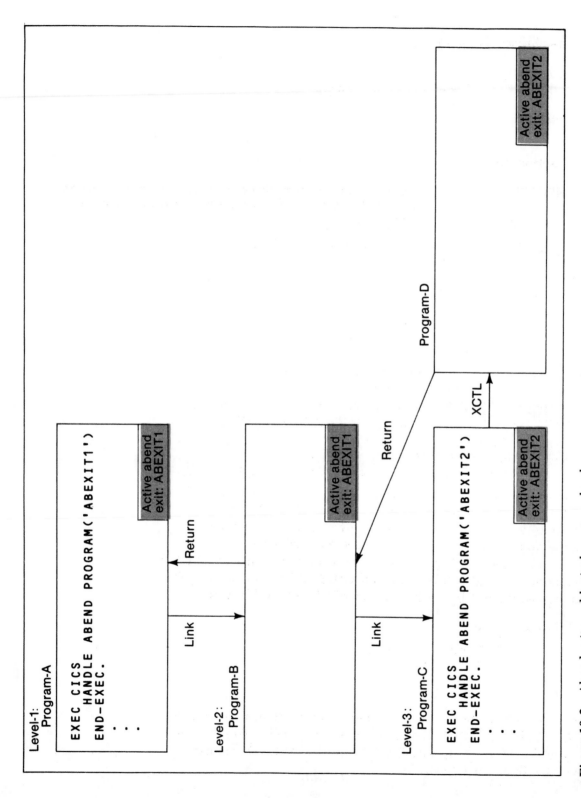

Figure 10-2 Abend exits and logical program levels

The ABEND command

```
EXEC CICS
     ABEND [ABCODE(data-name|literal)]
           [CANCEL]
END-EXEC
```

Explanation

ABCODE   Specifies that a transaction dump should be produced and the
                    one- to four-character value supplied should be used as the
                    abend code.

CANCEL   Specifies that the active abend exit should be ignored.

Figure 10-3   The ABEND command

program to abend, I recommend you always specify the ABCODE
option on your ABEND commands.

Why would you want to terminate a program using the
ABEND command rather than the RETURN command? There are
two reasons. First, the ABEND command gives you a transaction
dump. Second, the ABEND command invokes the CICS dynamic
transaction backout facility to reverse any changes your task made
to protected resources. (You'll learn about dynamic transaction
backout and protected resources in the next topic.) When your
program develops a serious error, you normally want both a
transaction dump and dynamic transaction backout.

If an abend exit is active when your program issues an ABEND
command, the exit is taken just as if CICS initiated the abend. You
can bypass the exit by coding the CANCEL option, like this:

```
EXEC CICS
     ABEND ABCODE('X100')
           CANCEL
END-EXEC
```

Here, the active abend exit is ignored. Bear in mind, however, that
CICS disables an active abend exit when it actually takes the exit.
So you don't have to specify CANCEL on an ABEND command
you code in an abend exit.

Terminology

transaction abend
transaction dump
trace table
abend exit

Objectives

1. Explain how to activate an abend exit.

2. Code an ABEND command to terminate a task abnormally,
    with or without a transaction dump.

Topic 2   Recovery processing

In this topic, you'll learn how CICS *recovery* facilities protect data sets and other important resources from a task or system abend. To understand CICS recovery facilities, you need to understand four things: logging, dynamic transaction backout, emergency restart, and logical units of work. After I describe these items, I'll show you how to use a CICS command that can make recovery more efficient when it's necessary: SYNCPOINT.

Logging

As a task executes, any changes it makes to protected resources are logged so the changes can be reversed if necessary. A *protected resource* is a file, destination, or temporary storage queue whose FCT, DCT, or TST entry provides for automatic recovery. Figure 10-4 shows how logging works for a protected file. As you can see, each time an application program invokes file control to update the file, file control in turn invokes the *journal control program* to log the change in the *system log*. Logging for protected destinations and temporary storage queues is similar.

The *dynamic log* maintains recovery data for a single task. While there's one system log for the entire CICS system, each CICS task has its own dynamic log. If a task ends abnormally, the data in the dynamic log is used to restore protected resources. If a task ends normally, its dynamic log is deleted.

Data in the dynamic log is placed initially in an area of main storage whose size is specified by a systems programmer. If the initial space is used up, temporary storage is used. As a result, the dynamic log can reside in a combination of main storage and temporary storage.

The recovery information that's stored in both the system log and the dynamic log consists of *before-images* of each file, destination, or temporary storage record that's added, changed, or deleted. In other words, journal control stores an exact image of each record as it existed before each update occurred. If an abend occurs, those updates can be reversed to restore the resource to its

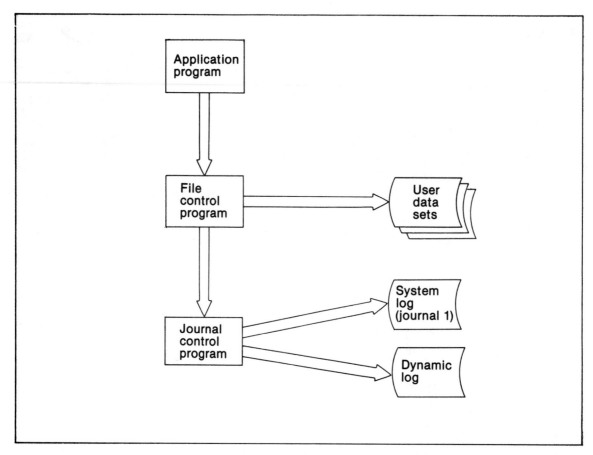

Figure 10-4 How file updates are logged to the system log and the dynamic log

previous condition. This type of recovery is often called *backward recovery*.

CICS also supports *forward recovery*. When forward recovery is used, CICS keeps *after-images* of records that are updated. Then, those after-images can be applied to a previous backup copy of a file to bring the file to a more current condition. Forward recovery is necessary only when the current version of a resource is so damaged that backward recovery isn't possible. Unfortunately, the forward recovery support provided by CICS is limited to saving forward recovery information: you have to code programs to restore resources using forward recovery information yourself.

Dynamic transaction backout

When a transaction terminates abnormally, CICS invokes the *dynamic backout program* to perform *dynamic transaction backout*

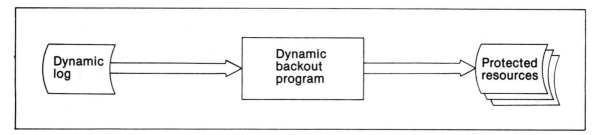

Figure 10-5   The dynamic backout program uses the dynamic log to restore protected resources after a transaction abend

(or *DTB*), as shown in figure 10-5. Dynamic transaction backout processes the before-images stored in the transaction's dynamic log to reverse any changes the transaction made to protected resources. When dynamic transaction backout completes, it's as if the transaction was never started.

Although it's an optional feature, dynamic transaction backout should be specified for all transactions. The dynamic log isn't allocated until a task issues a command that updates a protected resource. So there's no significant loss of performance when you specify DTB for a transaction that doesn't update protected resources.

Emergency restart

When CICS itself terminates abnormally, it must be restarted using a procedure called *emergency restart*. Figure 10-6 shows how CICS recovers protected resources during an emergency restart. First, the *recovery utility program* processes the system log, which contains a record of every update made during the previous CICS execution. The recovery utility program reads the system log backwards, determining which updates were made by *in-flight tasks*—that is, tasks that were active when the uncontrolled shutdown occurred. Each update that was made by an in-flight task is copied to the *restart data set*, which is then processed by the *transaction backout program* to restore the protected resources.

The transaction backout program is similar to the dynamic backout program. The difference is that the transaction backout program restores updates made by many tasks, while the dynamic backout program restores updates made by just one task. Because the transaction and system abend recovery facilities are similar, the programming considerations you'll learn in this topic apply equally to both.

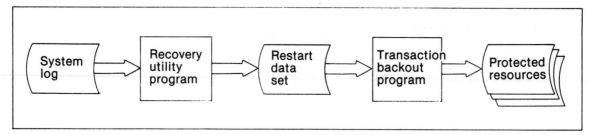

Figure 10-6   The recovery utility program and the transaction backout program work together during emergency restart to restore protected resources

Logical units of work

A *logical unit of work*, or *LUW*, is a collection of updating activity that's treated as a single unit during dynamic transaction backout or emergency restart. Normally, each LUW corresponds to a single task execution. In other words, when a task abends, all updates made by that task are reversed by dynamic transaction backout. And if CICS abends, all updates made by in-flight tasks are reversed during emergency restart.

Sometimes, it's not necessary to reverse all of the updates made by a task. For example, consider a program that reads invoice records stored in a sequential file (a VSAM ESDS) and updates corresponding master records in a customer file, an accounts receivable file, and an inventory file. If the program abends after processing 100 invoice records, DTB reverses the updates for all 100 records, even though that's probably not necessary: just the updates for the invoice that was being processed when the abend occurred need to be reversed. To limit the scope of an LUW, you issue a SYNCPOINT command.

The SYNCPOINT command

Figure 10-7 shows the format of the SYNCPOINT command. Normally, you'll code it like this:

```
EXEC CICS
     SYNCPOINT
END-EXEC
```

The SYNCPOINT command tells CICS that all of the updates made to protected resources so far are final: they shouldn't be backed out even if an abend occurs.

The SYNCPOINT command

```
EXEC CICS
      SYNCPOINT [ROLLBACK]
END-EXEC
```

Explanation

ROLLBACK   An infrequently used option. The SYNCPOINT command
                                  without the ROLLBACK option delimits a single LUW (logical
                                  unit of work). If you specify ROLLBACK, all updates logged
                                  since the last SYNCPOINT command (or the beginning of the
                                  task) are reversed.

Figure 10-7   The SYNCPOINT command

When you issue a SYNCPOINT command, three things
happen. First, CICS processes any *deferred work elements*, or
DWEs, associated with the task. A DWE is a record of activity that
should be performed when your task ends—or when you issue a
SYNCPOINT command. For example, when you issue a READ
UPDATE command for a file, CICS creates a DWE indicating that
the held record should eventually be released so other tasks can
process it. If you issue a SYNCPOINT command, then, any records
read with the UPDATE option are released.

Second, a SYNCPOINT command deletes any data stored in
the task's dynamic log. As a result, updates previously logged in the
dynamic log won't be reversed if the task abends.

Third, a SYNCPOINT command writes an *end-of-task record*
to the system log. That delimits records stored in the system log so
that updates previously logged there won't be reversed during an
emergency restart.

The ROLLBACK option on the SYNCPOINT command causes
any changes made since the previous SYNCPOINT (or the start of
the task) to be backed out, as if the task had abended. In other
words, the SYNCPOINT ROLLBACK command invokes dynamic
transaction backout without abending your task. As you might
guess, the SYNCPOINT ROLLBACK command is often used in an
abend exit.

Figure 10-8 shows a typical use of a SYNCPOINT command in
a program that reads a file of invoice transaction records and
updates related master file records. Module 0000 invokes module
1000 once for each record in the invoice file. After invoking module
1100 to read the invoice record, module 1000 invokes module 1200

```
*
  0000-POST-INVOICE-TRANSACTIONS SECTION.
*
        .
        .
        .
        PERFORM 1000-POST-INVOICE-TRANSACTION
            UNTIL INVOICE-EOF.
        .
        .
        .
*
  1000-POST-INVOICE-TRANSACTION SECTION.
*
        PERFORM 1100-READ-INVOICE-TRANSACTION.
        IF NOT INVOICE-EOF
            PERFORM 1200-UPDATE-MASTER-FILES
            EXEC CICS
                SYNCPOINT
            END-EXEC.
*
        .
        .
        .
```

Figure 10-8   Using the SYNCPOINT command in a program that posts invoice transactions accumulated in a sequential file

to update the master files. Then, it issues a SYNCPOINT command so all of the updates related to a single invoice record are considered to be a single logical unit of work.

Discussion

I suspect that you'll seldom need to use the SYNCPOINT command. It's appropriate only for programs that process previously accumulated batches of data—and that's *not* a typical CICS program.

Terminology

recovery
protected resource
journal control program
system log

dynamic log
before-image
backward recovery
forward recovery
after-image
dynamic backout program
dynamic transaction backout
DTB
emergency restart
recovery utility program
in-flight task
restart data set
transaction backout program
logical unit of work
LUW
deferred work element
DWE
end-of-task record

Objectives

1. Describe the recovery facilities provided by dynamic
    transaction backout and emergency restart.

2. Explain how to use the SYNCPOINT command to limit the
    scope of a logical unit of work.

Topic 3   Journal control

In the last topic, you learned how journal control automatically logs updates to protected resources in the system log. Actually, the system log is one of 99 *journal files* an installation can use. Journal files, which are simple sequential files on tape or disk, are numbered from 1 to 99. The first journal file—journal 1—is the system log; it's always required. Within a CICS system, every task that updates a protected resource causes recovery information to be logged in journal 1. As a result, the system log maintains complete recovery information for the entire CICS system.

The other journals—called *user journals*—can be used to supplement the standard logging provided by CICS; they're optional. Many installations use user journals for other purposes as well. For example, you might use a user journal to record audit information. Or, you might use a journal to record transactions that are to be processed later by a batch job.

It's important to realize from the start that as far as your application programs are concerned, journals are output-only files. There's no way a command-level CICS program can process a journal as an input file. Typically, records are written to a user journal during the day and processed by a batch program at night. In many cases, an application like that is better implemented using a simple sequential file (VSAM ESDS).

Before you can learn how to use journal control, you need to know how journal records are formatted and the difference between synchronous and asynchronous journal output. After I present that information, I'll show you how to use the JOURNAL command to write journal records. Then, I'll show you how to use the WAIT JOURNAL command when you use asynchronous journal output.

The format of journal records

Quite frankly, journal data is stored in a complicated format. It's so complicated, in fact, that the *System Programmer's Reference Manual* spends six pages just explaining the layout of journal

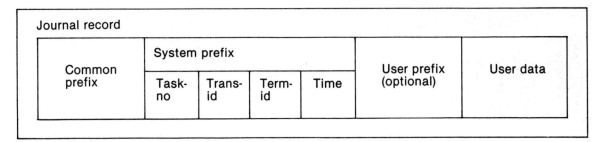

Figure 10-9 Simplified format of a journal record

records. Fortunately, you need to understand just the basic format
of journal records to create them. The details are important only
when you write a program that reads them. If you need to do that,
you'll have to refer to the *System Programmer's Reference Manual*
for more information.

Figure 10-9 shows how a journal record is organized. As you
can see, the record consists of four parts: a *common prefix*, a
system prefix, a *user prefix*, and user data. Bear in mind that the
record layout in figure 10-9 is simplified. I left out a number of
fields, including those that specify the length of each area; the
entire journal record and each of its components is variable length.

The common prefix contains information that identifies the
journal record type—whether it's a record written automatically by
CICS or a user-written record. The common prefix is created
automatically when you write a journal record. The system prefix,
also created automatically, contains the task-number, transaction-
identifier, and terminal-identifier for the task that wrote the
journal record. In addition, it includes the time of day when the
record was written. The user prefix is optional. You supply it if you
want to provide additional prefix information in a journal record.

Synchronous and asynchronous journal output

When you issue a JOURNAL command to write a journal record,
that record isn't immediately written to the journal file. To
understand why, look at figure 10-10. Here, an application
program running as part of a user's task issues a JOURNAL
command that invokes the journal control program. The journal
control program, in turn, places the user's output data in a storage
area called a *journal buffer*. The actual output operation is
performed by a separate system task called a *journal task*. Within a
CICS system, there's one journal task for each journal that's used.

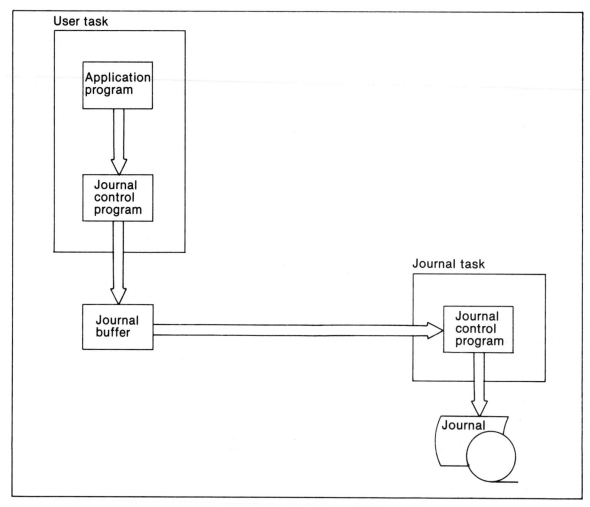

Figure 10-10   Journal output is actually written to journals by a separate task

The journal task writes the journal buffer to the journal file whenever the buffer becomes full. To help insure system integrity, the journal task also writes the journal buffer to the journal file at one-second intervals whether the buffer is full or not.

Synchronous journal output means that your program waits until the journal task has written the journal buffer before it continues. Because the journal task automatically writes the buffer at one-second intervals, your program won't have to wait more than one second. If other tasks write records to the journal buffer, the wait will be less.

If your program doesn't need to wait for the journal record to be written, *asynchronous journal output* is used. Here, your program continues execution without waiting for the journal task. The WAIT JOURNAL command lets an asynchronous task re-

synchronize itself with the journal task. Because asynchronous
journal output is more efficient than synchronous journal output,
you should use it whenever practical.

The JOURNAL command

You use the JOURNAL command, shown in figure 10-11, to write
a record to a journal. You typically code the JOURNAL command
like this:

```
EXEC CICS
    JOURNAL JFILEID(3)
            JTYPEID('A1')
            FROM(CUSTOMER-MASTER-RECORD)
            LENGTH(93)
            WAIT
    END-EXEC
```

Here, I write a 93-byte record named CUSTOMER-MASTER-
RECORD to journal number 3. The record type is A1, and WAIT
means that this is a synchronous output operation: the program
won't resume until the journal task actually writes the journal
record.

The JTYPEID option supplies a two-character field that
identifies the type of record written. The value you code here is
placed in the common prefix of the journal record. Because its
value depends on how your installation uses the journal file, you'll
have to find out how to code the JTYPEID option.

To use asynchronous journal output, omit the WAIT option.
Then, your program continues immediately without waiting for the
journal record to be written. When you use asynchronous journal
output, you may need to re-synchronize your task with the journal
task by issuing a WAIT JOURNAL command. To do that, you
need to code the REQID option on the JOURNAL command. In it,
you specify a field in which CICS will store a unique value that
identifies the journal record to be written. You'll use that value
later when you issue the WAIT JOURNAL command. The data-
name you supply in the REQID option must be a binary full-word
(PIC S9(8) COMP).

If you're writing a record to an infrequently used journal, you
might want to code the STARTIO option on the JOURNAL
command. That causes the journal task to immediately write out its
buffer, even if it isn't full. Use the STARTIO option with care:
although it improves your program's performance, it degrades the
performance of other tasks in the system.

The JOURNAL command

```
EXEC CICS
     JOURNAL JFILEID(data-name|literal)
             JTYPEID(data-name|literal)
             FROM(data-name)
             LENGTH(data-name|literal)
            [WAIT]
            [REQID(data-name)]
            [STARTIO]
            [PREFIX(data-name)
             PFXLENG(data-name|literal)]
END-EXEC
```

Explanation

JFILEID	Specifies a value from 1 to 99 that identifies the journal to which this record is written. If you use a data-name, it must be a binary half-word (PIC S9(4) COMP).
JTYPEID	Specifies a two-character code that's placed in the journal record to identify the record.
FROM	The field that contains the data to be written.
LENGTH	The length of the FROM area. If you use a data-name, it must be a binary half-word (PIC S9(4) COMP).
WAIT	Says that control should not return to the program until the record has actually been written to the journal file.
REQID	Specifies a data-name that will receive a unique identifier that can be used later in a WAIT JOURNAL command. The data name must be a binary full-word (PIC S9(8) COMP).
STARTIO	Says that the journal buffer should be written to the journal file immediately.
PREFIX	The field that contains the user prefix that's to be included in the journal record.
PFXLENG	The length of the PREFIX area. If you use a data-name, it must be a binary half-word (PIC S9(4) COMP).

Figure 10-11 The JOURNAL command

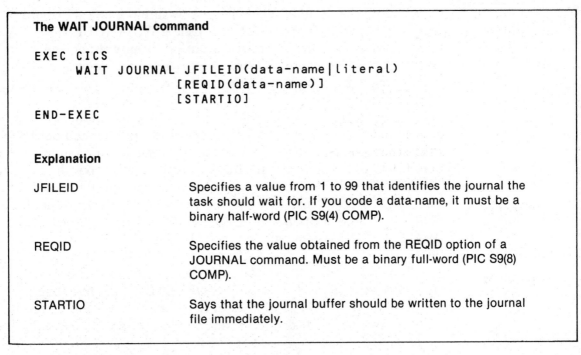

```
The WAIT JOURNAL command

EXEC CICS
     WAIT JOURNAL JFILEID(data-name|literal)
                  [REQID(data-name)]
                  [STARTIO]
END-EXEC


Explanation

JFILEID              Specifies a value from 1 to 99 that identifies the journal the
                     task should wait for. If you code a data-name, it must be a
                     binary half-word (PIC S9(4) COMP).

REQID                Specifies the value obtained from the REQID option of a
                     JOURNAL command. Must be a binary full-word (PIC S9(8)
                     COMP).

STARTIO              Says that the journal buffer should be written to the journal
                     file immediately.
```

Figure 10-12   The WAIT JOURNAL command

If your journal record requires a user prefix to supplement the information provided in the system prefix, you use the PREFIX option to provide that data. And the PFXLENG option provides the length of the field you specify in the PREFIX option. Your installation should have a standard format for the user-prefix area of each user journal.

The WAIT JOURNAL command

The WAIT JOURNAL command, whose format is given in figure 10-12, suspends your task until the journal record you identify with the REQID option is written to the journal file. Then, your task continues. If you specify STARTIO, the journal buffer is immediately written to disk. If you omit it, your task waits until the journal buffer is filled or one second has elapsed, when the journal task automatically writes the buffer.

The WAIT JOURNAL command can sometimes help you improve your program's efficiency by reducing the amount of time your program would have to wait if you used synchronous journal output. The idea here is to issue a JOURNAL command *without* the WAIT option, then continue with other work until your program reaches a point where it must be sure the journal record has been written. At that point, you issue a WAIT JOURNAL command. If the journal record has already been written, the WAIT JOURNAL command simply returns to your program. If not, your program waits until the journal record is written before it continues.

To illustrate, figure 10-13 shows two versions of a routine that writes an image of a customer record to a user journal and deletes the record from a customer master file. In version 1, synchronous journal output is used: the JOURNAL command specifies the WAIT option. In version 2, asynchronous journal output is used: the JOURNAL command doesn't specify WAIT. To ensure that the journal record is written before the program continues, I coded a WAIT JOURNAL command after the DELETE command in version 2.

In figure 10-13, version 2 executes more efficiently than version 1. That's because version 2 issues its DELETE command while the journal task writes the journal record. In contrast, version 1 must wait for the journal task to complete before it issues the DELETE command.

Discussion

Quite frankly, you probably won't use the CICS commands this topic presents often. Most installations don't use journal control other than for the standard recovery facility provided by the system log.

Terminology

journal file
user journal
common prefix
system prefix
user prefix
journal buffer
journal task
synchronous journal output
asynchronous journal output

Objective

Explain how you use journal control commands for both synchronous and asynchronous journal output.

```
Version 1

     •
     •
     •
EXEC CICS
     JOURNAL JFILEID(7)
             JTYPEID('CD')
             FROM(CUSTOMER-MASTER-RECORD)
             LENGTH(97)
             WAIT
END-EXEC.
EXEC CICS
     DELETE FILE('CUSTMAS')
            RIDFLD(CM-CUSTOMER-NUMBER)
END-EXEC.
     •
     •
     •




Version 2

     •
     •
     •
EXEC CICS
     JOURNAL JFILEID(7)
             JTYPEID('CD')
             FROM(CUSTOMER-MASTER-RECORD)
             LENGTH(97)
             REQID(WS-REQID)
END-EXEC.
EXEC CICS
     DELETE FILE('CUSTMAS')
            RIDFLD(CM-CUSTOMER-NUMBER)
END-EXEC.
EXEC CICS
     WAIT JOURNAL JFILEID(7)
                  REQID(WS-REQID)
END-EXEC.
     •
     •
     •
```

Figure 10-13   Using synchronous and asynchronous journal output

Chapter 11

Task control, program control, and storage control

In this chapter, you'll learn about CICS commands related to the task control, program control, and storage control facilities of CICS. Frankly, most CICS programs don't require these commands. But because some programs do, it's good to know about them. Just keep in mind that this chapter is extra: you've already learned the most important elements of CICS.

TASK CONTROL FEATURES

As you know, the *task control module* handles the execution of tasks within a CICS system. One of task control's major functions is *task selection*—that is, determining which of several waiting tasks should be allowed to execute. Task selection is done by a program called the *dispatcher*. Although task selection is mostly an automatic function, task control provides two facilities that let an application program influence task selection: (1) the SUSPEND command and (2) the ENQ and DEQ commands.

297

The SUSPEND command

```
EXEC CICS
     SUSPEND
END-EXEC
```

Explanation

The SUSPEND command has no options.

Figure 11-1 The SUSPEND command

The SUSPEND command

Normally, an application program gives up control whenever it issues a CICS command. For example, when your program issues a READ command, it gives up control while CICS fulfills the read request. In the meantime, CICS gives control to another task. In this way, many tasks can be operating at once. Only one of them is actually executing, though; the rest are either waiting for an I/O operation to complete, or just waiting for their turn to execute.

An important point to note about multitasking is that whenever your program gains control, it continues to execute until it issues a CICS command. For most applications, that's not a long time. But some unusual applications may require a long stretch of CPU processing without an intervening CICS command. An application like that can cause two problems. First, it degrades the performance of other tasks in the system because it monopolizes CPU time. And second, it might exceed the CICS limit for how long a task can run without returning control to CICS. To avoid both problems, you use the SUSPEND command.

The SUSPEND command, shown in figure 11-1, doesn't do anything except temporarily return control to CICS. Because the SUSPEND command has no options, you always code it like this:

```
EXEC CICS
     SUSPEND
END-EXEC
```

When you issue a SUSPEND command, control returns to the dispatcher. Then, the dispatcher scans the list of tasks waiting to execute. If the dispatcher finds a task that's ready to execute whose

---

The ENQ command

```
EXEC CICS
     ENQ RESOURCE(data-name)
         LENGTH(data-name|literal)
END-EXEC
```

The DEQ command

```
EXEC CICS
     DEQ RESOURCE(data-name)
         LENGTH(data-name|literal)
END-EXEC
```

Explanation

RESOURCE   A 1- to 255-character field that identifies the resource to be enqueued or dequeued.

LENGTH   The length of the RESOURCE field. If you use a data-name, it must be a binary half-word (PIC S9(4) COMP).

Figure 11-2 The ENQ and DEQ commands

priority is equal to or greater than your task's priority, control is given to that task. Otherwise, control returns to your task.

The ENQ and DEQ commands

The ENQ and DEQ commands, shown in figure 11-2, provide a general queuing facility that's similar to the UPDATE option of the READ command: they let you ensure that two or more tasks don't access a non-sharable resource (like a printer terminal) at the same time. That's called *single-threading* because only one task at a time can access the resource. Any other tasks that try to access that resource must wait their turn.

You use the ENQ command to single-thread a resource, or *enqueue* it. Once you enqueue a resource, any other tasks that try to enqueue the same resource are suspended until you issue a DEQ command to release, or *dequeue*, the resource, or your task ends. Don't confuse the terms enqueue and dequeue with a transient data or temporary storage queue. There's no relationship at all.

To understand the ENQ and DEQ commands, you must understand what a *resource* is. In short, a resource is any CICS facility you want to single-thread. Typically, it's a printer terminal, a transient data destination, a temporary storage queue, or an area of main storage like a table. To identify a resource, you give it a *resource name* that's 1 to 255 characters long. You don't define resource names in a CICS table. Instead, each task that needs to enqueue a resource identifies it with the resource name. Then, CICS checks to see if any other tasks have enqueued the same name. If so, the task must wait.

There's no internal mechanism that relates a resource name to an actual CICS facility. As far as CICS is concerned, resource names are just character strings. When you issue an ENQ command, all CICS does is check to see if another task has already issued an ENQ command using the same name. As a result, the ENQ and DEQ commands provide a general facility: a resource can be anything you want it to be. Unfortunately, this flexibility puts the burden on you to make sure the ENQ and DEQ commands work. That's because a task that processes a resource without first enqueuing it will continue, even if another task has enqueued that resource. Every program that processes the resource must enqueue it, or the ENQ/DEQ facility won't work.

Figure 11-3 shows a typical use of the ENQ and DEQ commands. If you've read chapter 5, you'll recognize that figure 11-3 is a portion of the inventory-listing program presented in that chapter. The program produces a report by writing records to a transient data destination. To prevent output lines from being mixed, each task that writes records to this destination enqueues it first. That's what the ENQ command at the start of module 0000 does. After the program is finished processing the destination, it issues a DEQ command to release it. Then, other tasks that enqueue the destination can continue. Incidentally, CICS automatically dequeues any resources you've enqueued when your task ends. Because its slightly more efficient to let CICS dequeue resources automatically, then, I recommend you don't use the DEQ command unless your program's logic requires it.

In the ENQ and DEQ commands, the RESOURCE option specifies the name of a field that contains the resource name. In this case, DESTINATION-ID is a four-character field whose value is 'L86P'. The actual character string you use as a resource name doesn't really matter, as long as every program in your system uses the same name for that resource. Remember, resource names are *not* defined in a CICS table. So it's important that you follow shop standards for creating and using resource names.

```
               •
               •
               •
     ✿
       01   DESTINATION-ID            PIC X(4)           VALUE 'L86P'.
     ✿
        PROCEDURE DIVISION.
     ✿
        0000-PRODUCE-INVENTORY-LISTING SECTION.
     ✿
               •
               •
               •
          EXEC CICS
              ENQ RESOURCE(DESTINATION-ID)
                  LENGTH(4)
          END-EXEC.
          PERFORM 2000-PRODUCE-INVENTORY-LINE
              UNTIL INVMAST-EOF.
          PERFORM 3000-PRINT-TOTAL-LINE.
          EXEC CICS
              DEQ RESOURCE(DESTINATION-ID)
                  LENGTH(4)
          END-EXEC.
            •
            •
            •
          EXEC CICS
              RETURN
          END-EXEC.
     ✿
            •
            •
            •
```

Figure 11-3   A portion of a program that enqueues a transient data destination

PROGRAM CONTROL FEATURES

In *Part 1: An introductory course*, you learned about three program
control commands: RETURN, XCTL, and LINK. You use those
commands to manage the execution of programs within a task.
Now, you'll learn about a fourth program control command:
LOAD.

The LOAD command

The LOAD command, illustrated in figure 11-4, retrieves an object
program from disk and loads it into main storage. The program

```
The LOAD command

EXEC CICS
     LOAD PROGRAM(data-name|literal)
          SET(pointer)
          [HOLD]
END-EXEC


Explanation

PROGRAM                 The one- to eight-character name of the program to be loaded.
                        This name must appear in the Processing Program Table.

SET                     A pointer variable (BLL cell) that's set to the address of the
                        loaded program.

HOLD                    Specifies that the program should remain in storage after the
                        task that issues the LOAD command ends.
```

Figure 11-4   The LOAD command

isn't executed; it's just loaded into storage. Why would you load a
program but not execute it? Normally, you wouldn't. The one case
where you're likely to use the LOAD command is when you're
using a *constant table*. A constant table is an area of main storage
that contains values for a commonly used table that's not likely to
change. For example, a list of the codes for the 50 states (plus
Puerto Rico and the District of Columbia) is a good candidate for a
constant table because its entries aren't likely to change.

Rather than code the constant table in the Working-Storage
Section of each program that needs it, you can code the table as an
assembler-language program, like the one in figure 11-5. Then, you
assemble and catalog the program. The listing in figure 11-5 isn't a
program in the normal sense, because it doesn't have any
executable instructions. Still, CICS treats it as a program, so you
must define it in the Processing Program Table.

To access a constant table, you define it in your program's
Linkage Section. Like any other area in the Linkage Section, you
must use a BLL cell to establish addressability to it. (I explained
how BLL cells work in chapter 3 of this book and in chapter 8 of
Part 1. If you don't understand BLL cells, refer to one of those
chapters.) Once you've made the correct Linkage Section entries,
you issue a LOAD command to bring the table into storage and
establish addressability to it.

```
STATABL   START  O
*******************************************************************************
*                                                                             *
*           THIS CONSTANT TABLE CONTAINS 52 TWO-BYTE ENTRIES                   *
*           CORRESPONDING TO THE FIFTY STATES PLUS PUERTO RICO                 *
*           AND THE DISTRICT OF COLUMBIA                                       *
*                                                                             *
*******************************************************************************
          DC     CL10'AKALARAZCA'
          DC     CL10'COCTDCDEFL'
          DC     CL10'GAHIIAIDIL'
          DC     CL10'INKSKYLAMA'
          DC     CL10'MDMEMIMNMO'
          DC     CL10'MSMTNCNDNE'
          DC     CL10'NHNJNMNVNY'
          DC     CL10'OHOKORPAPR'
          DC     CL10'RISCSDTNTX'
          DC     CL10'UTVAVTWAWV'
          DC     CL4'WIWY'
          END
```

Figure 11-5   An assembler-language constant table

Figure 11-6 shows a section of a program that defines the state table in the Linkage Section and issues a LOAD command to establish addressability to it. Here, BLL-STATE-TABLE is the BLL cell for the state table. The SET option in the LOAD command specifies that the address of the state table (named STATABL) is placed in BLL-STATE-TABLE. As a result, when the LOAD command completes, the state table has been loaded into storage and the BLL-cell addressing convention has been established so the table can be addressed.

The HOLD option means that the loaded program should stay in storage even after your task ends. If you use the HOLD option, a commonly used table can be loaded into storage once and used repeatedly throughout the day. Since the table is already in main storage, LOAD commands executed by subsequent programs don't reload it from disk. Instead, they just establish addressability to the existing table by returning its address in the specified BLL field.

STORAGE CONTROL FEATURES

As you know, there are several ways you can acquire and use main storage. The simplest is through the Working-Storage Section of your program; CICS automatically manages that storage for you. Any other storage your program requires exists outside your program, so you define it in the Linkage Section and use the BLL

```
            •
            •
            •
     ✿
       LINKAGE  SECTION.
     ✿
       01   BLL-CELLS.
     ✿
            05   FILLER              PIC  S9(8)      COMP.
            05   BLL-STATE-TABLE     PIC  S9(8)      COMP.
     ✿
       01   STATE-TABLE.
     ✿
            05   STATE-CODE          OCCURS  52      PIC XX.
     ✿
       PROCEDURE  DIVISION.
     ✿
       0000-ACCEPT-CUSTOMER-ORDERS SECTION.
     ✿
            EXEC  CICS
                LOAD  PROGRAM('STATABL')
                      SET(BLL-STATE-TABLE)
                      HOLD
            END-EXEC.
            •
            •
            •
```

Figure 11-6   A portion of a program that uses a constant table

addressing convention to address it. (If you don't know how the BLL addressing convention works, refer to chapter 3 of this book or chapter 8 of *Part 1.*) You already know several ways to acquire storage outside your program: the communication area, the Common Work Area (CWA) and other system areas, DL/I areas like the UIB and PCB, and areas acquired by the LOAD command. Now, you'll learn how to use *storage control* facilities directly to obtain and release main storage.

Frankly, you usually don't need to use storage control commands. One case where you might is when you use *locate-mode I/O* rather than move-mode I/O. When you use locate-mode I/O, your program processes data while it's still in a CICS buffer. Because move-mode I/O is both safer and easier to use, I recommend you use it instead of locate-mode I/O. However, if you find yourself maintaining a locate-mode I/O program, or if your shop has a standard requiring locate-mode I/O, you'll have to use storage control commands to acquire main storage for I/O areas.

The GETMAIN command

```
EXEC CICS
    GETMAIN SET(pointer)
            LENGTH(data-name|literal)
            [INITIMG(data-name)]
END-EXEC
```

Explanation

SET	The BLL cell that points to the Linkage Section entry for the acquired storage area.
LENGTH	The number of bytes of main storage to acquire. If you use a data-name, it must be a binary full-word (PIC S9(8) COMP).
INITIMG	A one-byte field whose value is used to initialize the storage acquired. If omitted, the storage is *not* initialized.

Figure 11-7   The GETMAIN command

The GETMAIN command

The GETMAIN command, shown in figure 11-7, acquires a specified amount of main storage and returns the address of that storage. For example, suppose you code this command:

```
EXEC CICS
    GETMAIN SET(BLL-INVENTORY-RECORD)
            LENGTH(32)
END-EXEC
```

Here, CICS acquires a 32-byte storage area and places its address in BLL-INVENTORY-RECORD. Assuming BLL-INVENTORY-RECORD is a BLL cell for a Linkage Section field named INVENTORY-RECORD, this command not only acquires storage but establishes addressability to it through the BLL cell.

You can initialize the storage area to any one-byte value by coding the INITIMG option. First, set up a one-byte field like this:

```
01 HEX-00    PIC X  VALUE LOW-VALUE.
```

Then, issue a GETMAIN command like this:

```
EXEC CICS
    GETMAIN SET(BLL-INVENTORY-RECORD)
            LENGTH(32)
            INITIMG(HEX-00)
END-EXEC
```

Here, a 32-byte area is acquired and initialized to LOW-VALUE.

The FREEMAIN command

The FREEMAIN command, shown in figure 11-8, releases an area of storage acquired by a GETMAIN command. In the DATA parameter, you code the name of the Linkage Section field that overlays the area—not the name of the BLL cell that addresses it. For example, the command

```
EXEC CICS
    FREEMAIN DATA(INVENTORY-RECORD)
END-EXEC
```

releases the storage allocated by the GETMAIN command I just showed you.

Normally, any storage acquired for your task—whether by a GETMAIN command or any other means—is released automatically when your task ends. So the only time you need to use the FREEMAIN command is when you want to release an area of storage before your task ends for efficiency reasons.

DISCUSSION

In this chapter, I've presented a variety of unrelated CICS commands. I frankly doubt that you'll use many of them often. So don't spend much time now mastering the commands in this chapter. Instead, just remember the general functions they provide. Then, if you need one of them, you can return here to refresh your memory on how they're used.

```
The FREEMAIN command

EXEC CICS
     FREEMAIN DATA(data-name)
END-EXEC


Explanation

DATA                      The Linkage Section field for the storage to be released.
```

Figure 11-8   The FREEMAIN command

Terminology

task control module
task selection
dispatcher
single-threading
enqueue
dequeue
resource
resource name
constant table
storage control
locate-mode I/O

Objective

Describe the function of each of these commands:

      a. SUSPEND
      b. ENQ
      c. DEQ
      d. LOAD
      e. GETMAIN
      f. FREEMAIN

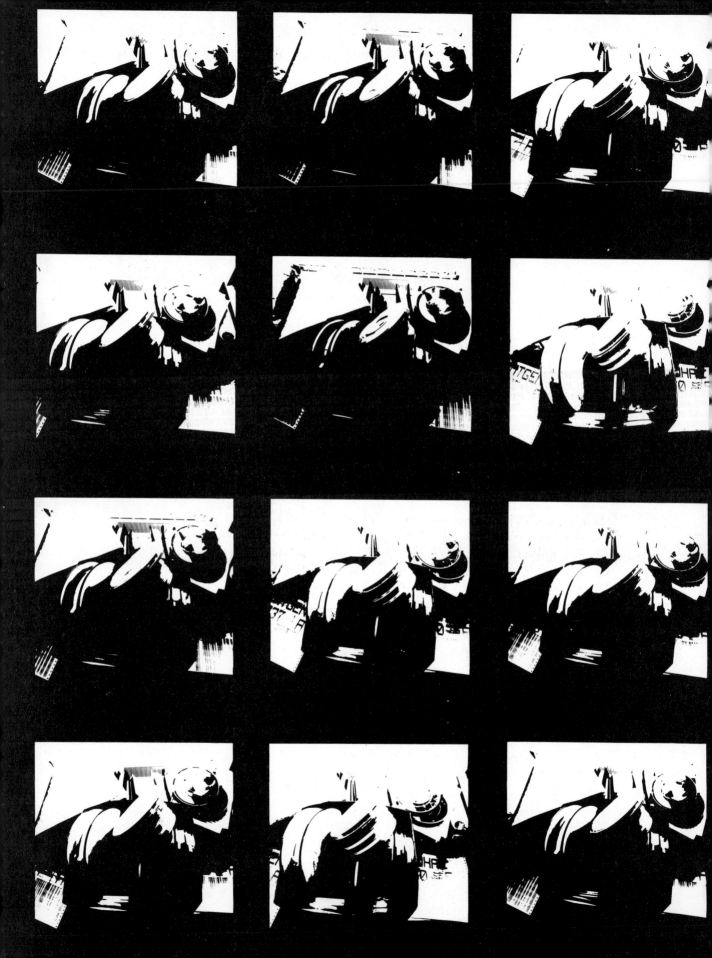

Appendix

CICS command summary

This appendix summarizes the CICS commands presented in this book. For each command, you'll find a complete format as well as a chapter reference that will help you find more detailed information for the command. You can use this summary as a quick refresher on how to code a particular command or option.

The ABEND command

Chapter 3 Topic 1
Chapter 10 Topic 1

```
EXEC CICS
     ABEND [ABCODE(data-name|literal)]
           [CANCEL]
END-EXEC
```

The CANCEL command

Chapter 9

```
EXEC CICS
     CANCEL REQID(data-name|literal)
END-EXEC
```

The DELETEQ TD command

Chapter 5

```
EXEC CICS
     DELETEQ TD QUEUE(data-name|literal)
END-EXEC
```

The DELETEQ TS command

Chapter 4

```
EXEC CICS
     DELETEQ TS QUEUE(data-name|literal)
END-EXEC
```

The DEQ command

Chapter 5
Chapter 11

```
EXEC CICS
     DEQ RESOURCE(data-name)
         LENGTH(data-name|literal)
END-EXEC
```

The ENDBR command   Chapter 1

```
EXEC CICS
     ENDBR DATASET(data-name|literal)
END-EXEC
```

The ENQ command   Chapter 5
                                            Chapter 11

```
EXEC CICS
     ENQ RESOURCE(data-name)
         LENGTH(data-name|literal)
END-EXEC
```

The FREEMAIN command   Chapter 11

```
EXEC CICS
     FREEMAIN DATA(data-name)
END-EXEC
```

The GETMAIN command   Chapter 11

```
EXEC CICS
     GETMAIN SET(pointer)
             LENGTH(data-name|literal)
             [INITIMG(data-name)]
END-EXEC
```

The HANDLE ABEND command   Chapter 10 Topic 1

```
EXEC CICS

                    ⎧PROGRAM(data-name|literal)⎫
                    ⎪LABEL(procedure-name)     ⎪
     HANDLE ABEND   ⎨CANCEL                    ⎬
                    ⎩RESET                     ⎭

END-EXEC
```

The JOURNAL command   Chapter 10 Topic 3

```
EXEC CICS
     JOURNAL JFILEID(data-name|literal)
             JTYPEID(data-name|literal)
             FROM(data-name)
             LENGTH(data-name|literal)
             [WAIT]
             [REQID(data-name)]
             [STARTIO]
             [PREFIX(data-name)
              PFXLENG(data-name|literal)]
END-EXEC
```

The LOAD command   Chapter 11

```
EXEC CICS
     LOAD PROGRAM(data-name|literal)
          SET(pointer)
          [HOLD]
END-EXEC
```

The READNEXT command   Chapter 1

```
EXEC CICS
     READNEXT DATASET(data-name|literal)
              INTO(data-name)
              RIDFLD(data-name)
             [RRN|RBA]
END-EXEC
```

The READPREV command   Chapter 1

```
EXEC CICS
     READPREV DATASET(data-name|literal)
              INTO(data-name)
              RIDFLD(data-name)
             [RRN|RBA]
END-EXEC
```

The READQ TD command   Chapter 5

```
EXEC CICS
     READQ TD QUEUE(data-name|literal)
              INTO(data-name)
              LENGTH(data-name)
END-EXEC
```

The READQ TS command   Chapter 4

```
EXEC CICS
     READQ TS QUEUE(data-name|literal)
              INTO(data-name)
              LENGTH(data-name)
             (ITEM(data-name|literal))
             (NEXT                    )
END-EXEC
```

The RECEIVE command   Chapter 8

```
EXEC CICS
     RECEIVE INTO(data-name)
             LENGTH(data-name)
END-EXEC
```

The RESETBR command   Chapter 1

```
EXEC CICS
     RESETBR DATASET(data-name|literal)
             RIDFLD(data-name)
            [RRN|RBA]
            [GTEQ|EQUAL]
END-EXEC
```

The RETRIEVE command   Chapter 9

```
EXEC CICS
     RETRIEVE INTO(data-name)
              LENGTH(data-name)
              [RTRANSID(data-name)]
              [RTERMID(data-name)]
              [QUEUE(data-name)]
END-EXEC
```

The ROUTE command   Chapter 6 Topic 3

```
EXEC CICS
     ROUTE LIST(data-name)
           [{INTERVAL(hhmmss)}]
           [{TIME(hhmmss)    }]
           [NLEOM]
END-EXEC
```

The SEND command   Chapter 8

```
EXEC CICS
     SEND FROM(data-name)
          LENGTH(data-name|literal)
          [CTLCHAR(data-name)]
          [ERASE]
END-EXEC
```

The SEND MAP command   Chapter 6 Topics 2 and 3

```
EXEC CICS
     SEND MAP(data-name|literal)
          MAPSET(data-name|literal)
          [FROM(data-name)]
          [MAPONLY|DATAONLY]
          [ACCUM]
          [PAGING]
          [ERASE]
          [PRINT]
          [NLEOM]
END-EXEC
```

The SEND PAGE command Chapter 6 Topics 2 and 3

```
EXEC CICS
    SEND PAGE
        [OPERPURGE]
END-EXEC
```

The SEND TEXT command Chapter 6 Topics 2 and 3

```
EXEC CICS
    SEND TEXT FROM(data-name)
            LENGTH(data-name|literal)
        [ACCUM]
        [PAGING]
        [ERASE]
        [HEADER(data-name)]
        [TRAILER(data-name)]
        [PRINT]
        [NLEOM]
END-EXEC
```

The START command Chapter 9

```
EXEC CICS
    START TRANSID(data-name|literal)
        [{TIME(hhmmss)    }]
        [{INTERVAL(hhmmss)}]
        [TERMID(data-name|literal)]
        [FROM(data-name)
         LENGTH(data-name|literal)]
        [RTERMID(data-name|literal)]
        [RTRANSID(data-name|literal)]
        [QUEUE(data-name|literal)]
        [REQID(data-name|literal)]
END-EXEC
```

The STARTBR command Chapter 1

```
EXEC CICS
    STARTBR DATASET(data-name|literal)
            RIDFLD(data-name)
        [RRN|RBA]
        [GTEQ|EQUAL]
END-EXEC
```

The SUSPEND command   Chapter 11

```
EXEC CICS
     SUSPEND
END-EXEC
```

The SYNCPOINT command   Chapter 10 Topic 2

```
EXEC CICS
     SYNCPOINT [ROLLBACK]
END-EXEC
```

The WAIT JOURNAL command   Chapter 10 Topic 2

```
EXEC CICS
     WAIT JOURNAL JFILEID(data-name|literal)
               [REQID(data-name)]
               [STARTIO]
END-EXEC
```

The WRITEQ TD command   Chapter 5

```
EXEC CICS
     WRITEQ TD QUEUE(data-name|literal)
               FROM(data-name)
               LENGTH(data-name|literal)
END-EXEC
```

The WRITEQ TS command   Chapter 4

```
EXEC CICS
     WRITEQ TS QUEUE(data-name|literal)
               FROM(data-name)
               LENGTH(data-name|literal)
               [ITEM(data-name)
                REWRITE]
               (MAIN     )
               (AUXILIARY)
END-EXEC
```

Index

198X COBOL compiler, 87
3270 terminals
    advanced display features, 221-223
    printers, 202-205
ABEND command, 88-89, 277-279
abend exit, 274-277
ACCUM option
    SEND MAP, 193-194
    SEND TEXT, 182, 208-209
addressability
    constant table, 302-303
    DL/I areas, 79-87
    GETMAIN, 303-306
after-image, 282
alternate index, 39-61
    base cluster, 40
    browsing, 46-60
    DUPKEY condition, 58-60
    duplicate keys, 41
    path, 41-42
    primary key, 40
    upgrade set, 42-44
alternate key, 40-41
application data structure, 69

ASA control characters, 152, 247
asynchronous journal output, 290-291
ATI, see automatic transaction
    initiation
automatic time-ordered transaction
    initiation, 260-262, 270
automatic transaction initiation
    transient data, 144-145, 270
    interval control, 260-262, 270
autopage status, 167-168
AUXILIARY option (WRITEQ TS),
    119

backward recovery, 282
base cluster, 40
base color terminal, 222
base key, 40
base locator for linkage
    constant table, 302-303
    DL/I areas, 79-87
    GETMAIN, 303-306
before-image, 281
blinking, 223
BLL cell, see base locator for linkage

browse commands, 7-31
  for alternate index, 46-60
buffer
  journal, 289-291
  printer, 202-205

CALL interface (DL/I), 70-73
CANCEL command, 268-269
carriage return order, 204
CBLTDLI, 70
child segment, 67
CICS command
  ABEND, 88-89, 277-279
  CANCEL, 268-269
  DELETEQ TD, 149
  DELETEQ TS, 122
  DEQ, 150, 299-300
  ENDBR, 16
  ENQ, 150, 299-300
  FREEMAIN, 306
  GETMAIN, 305-306
  HANDLE ABEND, 275-277
  HANDLE AID, 244-245
  JOURNAL, 291-293
  LOAD, 301-303
  READNEXT, 12-14
  READPREV, 14-16
  READQ TD, 148-149
  READQ TS, 120-122
  RECEIVE, 240-245
  RESETBR, 16-17
  RETRIEVE, 266-268
  ROUTE, 214-216
  SEND, 245-247
  SEND MAP, 192-200, 205-206
  SEND PAGE, 185, 209
  SEND TEXT, 175-185, 205-206
  START, 205, 262-266
  STARTBR, 8-11, 46-51
  SUSPEND, 298-299
  SYNCPOINT, 284-286
  WAIT JOURNAL, 293-294
  WRITEQ TD, 147-148
  WRITEQ TS, 118-120
color display, 222-223
COLOR parameter (DFHMDF),
  226-227

COLUMN parameter (DFHMDI),
  190-191
command, see CICS command
command-driven application, 238
common prefix (journal record), 289
condition, see exceptional condition
constant table, 302-303
CR order, 204
CTLCHAR option (SEND), 246-247
customer inquiry program
  alternate index version, 44-60
  browse version, 25-37
  terminal control version, 238-247
customer maintenance program,
  122-139

data base, 66
data base record, 67
Data Language/I, 64-111
  CALL interface, 70-73
  functions, 70-71
  PCB 70, 76-87
  PCB, status code, 88
  PSB, 69-70, 76
  scheduling call, 76-87
  segment search argument, 73
  UIB, 76-77, 80-88
  UIBDLCTR, 87-88
  UIBRCTR, 87-88
  UIBPCBAL, 77-87
  UIBRCODE, 77, 87-88
data-driven transaction, 144-145, 270
data-id (temporary storage), 116
DCT, 142, 145-146
deferred work element, 285
DELETEQ TD command, 149
DELETEQ TS command, 122
DEQ command, 150, 299-300
dequeue, 150, 299-300
destination, 142
Destination Control Table, 142,
  145-146
destination-id, 142
DFHBMPNL, 179-181
DFHBMSCA, 179-181, 231
DFHMDF macro, 224-227
DFHMDI macro, 186-192

DFHMSD macro, 224
DFHNTRA, 143
DFHTEMP, 117
dispatcher, 297
disposition (message), 165-166
DL/I, see Data Language/I
DL/I DOS/VS, 64
DL/I function, 70-71
DTB, 282-283
DUPKEY condition, 58-60
duplicate key, 41
DWE, 285
dynamic backout program, 282-283
dynamic log, 281-283
dynamic transaction backout, 282-283

EIBAID, 244
EM order, 205
emergency restart, 283
ENDBR command, 16
ENDDATA condition (RETRIEVE),
    267-268
ENDFILE condition
  READNEXT, 12
  READPREV, 14
end-of-message order, 205
end-of-task record, 285
ENQ command, 150, 299-300
enqueue, 150, 299-300
error processing
  ABEND command, 88-89, 277-279
  abend exit, 274-277
  DL/I, 87-89
  recovery, 281-286
exceptional condition
  DUPKEY, 58-60
  ENDDATA, 267-268
  ENDFILE, 12, 14
  LENGERR, 120, 149, 244, 266
  NOTFND, 8, 14, 266
  OVERFLOW, 191-192, 194-200
  QIDERR, 119-120, 122
  QZERO, 149
expiration time, 215-216, 263-265
EXTATT parameter (DFHMSD), 224
extended attribute byte, 223, 230-234
extended color terminal, 222-223

extended highlighting, 223
extrapartition transient data queue,
    142-143

FF order, 204
form-feed order, 204
forward recovery, 282
FREEMAIN command, 306

GETMAIN command, 305-306
GTEQ option (STARTBR), 8

HANDLE ABEND command, 275-277
HANDLE AID command, 244-245
header, 173
HEADER option (SEND TEXT),
    182-184
HILIGHT parameter (DFHMDF),
    227

ICE, 260-262
IMS/VS, 64
indirect destination, 145-146
in-flight task, 283
Information Management
    System/Virtual Storage, 64
inquiry program, see customer inquiry
    program
interval control, 259-271
interval control element, 260-262
interval control expiration analysis,
    262
interval control program, 259
interval control services, 260
INTERVAL option
  ROUTE, 215-216
  START, 263-265
intrapartition transient data queue,
    142-143
inventory listing program
  ROUTE version, 216-218
  SEND MAP version, 186-200
  SEND TEXT version, 173-185
  SEND TEXT (printer) version,
    206-213
  transient data version, 152-159
item number, 116-117

item, 115-117

journal buffer, 289-291
JOURNAL command, 291-293
journal file, 288
journal task, 289-291
JUSTIFY parameter (DFHMDI),
    190-191

LENGERR condition
    READQ TD, 149
    READQ TS, 120
    RECEIVE, 244
    RETRIEVE, 266
LINE parameter (DFHMDI), 190-191
LOAD command, 301-303
locate-mode I/O, 304
logical message, 164
logical message building, 164-169
logical unit of work, 284-286
LUW, 284-286

MAIN option (WRITEQ TS), 119
maintenance program, 122-139
mask, 71-72
menu program, 238
menu-driven application, 238
message building, 164-169
message building program, 164-165
message delivery, 165-169
message retrieval command, 167,
    169-171
message routing, 166, 169, 213-218

new-line character, 179-182
new-line order, 204
NL order, 204
NLEOM option (SEND MAP and
    SEND TEXT), 206
nonunique key, 41
NOTFND condition
    READPREV, 14
    RETRIEVE, 266
    STARTBR, 8

OPERPURGE option (SEND PAGE),
    184

order, 245
order entry program (DL/I), 90-111
order summary program, 19-25
OVERFLOW condition, 191-192,
    194-200
overflow processing
    SEND MAP, 191-192, 194-200,
      202-203
    SEND TEXT, 182-185
overflow routine, 191-192, 199-200

P/ command, 170-171
page (message), 165
page and text build program, 165
page buffer, 165
page building, 164
page retrieval program, 167
paging disposition, 165-166
PAGING option
    SEND MAP, 193-194
    SEND TEXT, 182
paging status, 166-167
parent segment, 67
parentage, 67
path, 41-42
PCB, see program communication
    block
PCB mask, 71-72
PCB status code, 88
PF keys
    detecting with RECEIVE, 244-245
    for SKR, 171
primary key, 40
PRINT option (SEND MAP and
    SEND TEXT), 206
print program (transient data),
    247-254
printer order, 181-182, 203-205,
    252-254
printer output
    message building, 202-218
    terminal control, 247-254
    transient data, 141
program communication block, 70,
    76-87
    mask, 71-72
    status code, 88

program specification block, 69-70, 76
protected resource, 281
PSB, 69-70, 76
QIDERR condition
    DELETEQ TS, 122
    WRITEQ TS, 119-120
qualified SSA, 73
queue name, 116
QZERO condition (READQ TD), 149

RBA option
    READNEXT, 13
    STARTBR, 8
READNEXT command, 12-14
READPREV command, 14-16
READQ TD command, 148-149
READQ TS command, 120-122
RECEIVE command, 240-245
recovery, 281-286
recovery utility program, 283
request-id (interval control), 268-269
RESETBR command, 16-17
resource, 150, 300
resource name, 150, 300
restart data set, 283
RETRIEVE command, 266-268
reverse video, 223
REWRITE option (WRITEQ TS),
    119-120
RIDFLD option
    STARTBR, 8
    READNEXT, 13
ROLLBACK option (SYNCPOINT),
    285
root segment, 67
ROUTE command, 214-216
route list, 214-215

schedule (a task), 259-260
scheduling call (DL/I), 76-87
scratchpad, 115
segment, 67
segment dependence, 67
segment I/O area, 72
segment occurrence, 67
segment search argument, 73
segment type, 67

SEND command, 245-247
SEND MAP command
    message building, 192-200
    printer options, 205-206
SEND PAGE command, 185, 209
SEND TEXT command
    message building, 175-185
    printer options, 205-206
sensitive field, 70
sensitive segment, 70
single keystroke retrieval, 171
single-threading, 299-300
SIZE parameter (DFHMDI), 189-190
SKR, 171
SSA, 73
START command, 205, 262-266
START statement, 8
STARTBR command, 8-11
    for alternate index, 46-51
started task, 259
starting task, 259
status code (PCB), 88
storage control, 303-306
SUSPEND command, 298-299
synchronous journal output, 290
SYNCPOINT command, 284-286
system log, 281
system prefix (journal record), 289

T/ command, 171
task, 259-260
task control, 262, 297
task selection, 297
TD queue, 142
temporary storage control, 115-139
temporary storage file, 117
temporary storage queue, 115-117
Temporary Storage Table, 116
terminal control module, 237-255
terminal disposition, 165-166, 168
terminal page processor, 165
terminal paging, 164
terminal status, 166-168
TIME option
    ROUTE, 215-216
    START, 263-265
time-ordered ATI, 260-262

trace table, 274
trailer, 173
TRAILER option (SEND TEXT),
    182-184
TRAILER parameter (DFHMDI),
    191-192
transaction abend, 274
transaction backout program, 283
transaction dump, 274
transient data control, 141-161, 247
transient data print program, 247-254
transient data queue, 142
trigger level, 144
TS queue, 115-117
TST, 116

UIB, 76-77, 80-88
UIBDLTR, 87-88
UIBFCTR, 87-88
UIBPCBAL, 77-87
UIBRCODE, 77, 87-88
underlining, 223
unique key, 41
unqualified SSA, 73
upgradable index, 42-44
upgrade set, 42-44
upgrading, 42-44
User Interface Block, 76-77, 80-88
user journal, 288
user prefix (journal record), 289

view, 69
VS COBOL II, 87
VSAM
    alternate index, 39-61
    browsing, 7-8

WAIT JOURNAL command, 293-294
WCC, 246-247
write control character, 246-247
WRITEQ TD command, 147-148
WRITEQ TS command, 118-120

Comment Form

Your opinions count

Your opinions today will affect our future products and policies. So if you have questions, criticisms, or suggestions, I'm eager to get them. You can expect a response within a week of the time we receive your comments.

   Also, if you discover any errors in this book, typographical or otherwise, please point them out. We'll correct them when the book is reprinted.

   Thanks for your help!

Mike Murach, President
Mike Murach and Associates, Inc.

Book title: CICS for the COBOL Programmer, Part 2

Dear Mike: _____

_____

_____

_____

_____

_____

_____

_____

_____

_____

_____

_____

_____

_____

_____

Name and Title _____

Company (if any) _____

Address _____

City, State, Zip _____

Fold where indicated and staple.
No postage necessary if mailed in the U.S.

fold

fold

fold

fold

fold

NO POSTAGE
NECESSARY
IF MAILED
IN THE
UNITED STATES

BUSINESS REPLY MAIL

First Class   Permit No. 3063   Fresno, CA

POSTAGE WILL BE PAID BY ADDRESSEE

Mike Murach & Associates, Inc.

4697 West Jacquelyn Avenue
Fresno, CA 93722-9960

fold

fold

fold

Order Form

Our Unlimited Guarantee

To our customers who order directly from us: You must be satisfied. Our books must work for you, or you can send them back for a full refund . . . no matter how many you buy, no matter how long you've had them.

Name & Title _____

Company (if company address) _____

Address_____

City, State, Zip _____

Phone number (including area code) _____

Qty	Product code and title	*Price
CICS		
_____ CIC1	CICS for the COBOL Programmer: Part 1	$27.50
_____ CIC2	CICS for the COBOL Programmer: Part 2	27.50
_____ CCIG	CICS Instructor's Guide	100.00
_____ CREF	The CICS Programmer's Desk Reference	35.00
VSAM		
_____ VSMX	VSAM: Access Method Services and Application Programming	$25.00
_____ VSMR	VSAM for the COBOL Programmer	17.50
COBOL Language Elements		
_____ SC1R	Structured ANS COBOL: Part 1	$27.50
_____ SC2R	Structured ANS COBOL: Part 2	27.50
_____ RW	Report Writer	13.50
_____ VSC2	VS COBOL II	25.00
COBOL Program Development		
_____ DDCP	How to Design and Develop COBOL Programs	$30.00
_____ CPHB	The COBOL Programmer's Handbook	20.00

Qty	Product code and title	*Price
VM Subjects		
_____ VMCC	VM/CMS: Commands and Concepts	$25.00
_____ VMXE	VM/CMS: XEDIT	25.00
OS/MVS Subjects		
_____ MJCL	MVS JCL	$32.50
_____ TSO	MVS TSO	27.50
_____ MBAL	MVS Assembler Language	32.50
_____ OSUT	OS Utilities	15.00
DOS/VSE Subjects		
_____ VJLR	DOS/VSE JCL	$32.50
_____ ICCF	DOS/VSE ICCF	27.50
_____ VBAL	DOS/VSE Assembler Language	32.50
Data Base Processing		
_____ IMS1	IMS for the COBOL Programmer Part 1: DL/I Data Base Processing	$30.00
_____ IMS2	IMS for the COBOL Programmer Part 2: Data Communications and MFS	32.50

☐ Bill me the appropriate price plus UPS shipping and handling (and sales tax in California) for each book ordered.

☐ Bill the appropriate book prices plus UPS shipping and handling (and sales tax in California) to my
_____VISA _____MasterCard:
Card number_____
Valid thru (month/year)_____
Cardowner's signature_____
_____(not valid without signature)

☐ I want to **save** UPS shipping and handling charges. Here's my check or money order for $_____. California residents, please add 6% sales tax to your total. (Offer valid in the U.S. only.)

***Prices are subject to change.
Please call for current prices.**

To order more quickly,

 Call **toll-free** 1-800-221-5528

(Weekdays, 9 to 4 Pacific Std. Time)

In California, call 1-800-221-5527

4697 West Jacquelyn Avenue
Fresno, California 93722
(209) 275-3335
Fax: (209) 275-9035

fold

NO POSTAGE
NECESSARY
IF MAILED
IN THE
UNITED STATES

fold

BUSINESS REPLY MAIL

First Class   Permit No. 3063   Fresno, CA

POSTAGE WILL BE PAID BY ADDRESSEE

Mike Murach & Associates, Inc.

4697 West Jacquelyn Avenue
Fresno, CA 93722-9960

fold

fold